THE
WESTERN
FELLS

WAL ERS EDITIONS

Published 2015		First published	First revision
Book One:	The Eastern Fells	1955	2005
Book Two:	The Far Eastern Fells	1957	2005

Published 2016		First published	First revision
Book Three:	The Central Fells	1958	2006

Published 2017		First published	First revision
Book Four:	The Southern Fells	1960	2007

Published 2018		First published	First revision
Book Five:	The Northern Fells	1962	2008

Published 2019		First published	First revision
Book Six:	The North-Western Fells	1964	2008

Published 2020		First published	First revision
Book Seven:	The Western Fells	1966	2009

PUBLISHER'S NOTE

Fellwalking can be dangerous, especially
in wet, windy, foggy or icy conditions.
Please be sure to take sensible precautions
when out on the fells. As A. Wainwright himself
frequently wrote: use your common sense
and watch where you are putting your feet.

A PICTORIAL GUIDE
TO THE
LAKELAND FELLS

WALKERS EDITION
REVISED BY CLIVE HUTCHBY

being an illustrated account
of a study and exploration
of the mountains in the
English Lake District
by

AWainwright

BOOK SEVEN
THE WESTERN FELLS

Originally published by Westmorland Gazette, entmere, 1966
First published by Frances Lincoln 2003
Second (revised) edition published by Frances Lincoln, 2009

Walkers Edition published in 2020 by Frances Lincoln,
an imprint of The Quarto Group
The Old Brewery, 6 Blundell Street
London N7 9BH, United ingdom

Printed and bound in the U
by CPI Group (U) Ltd, Croydon, CR0 4YY

A CIP catalogue for this book
is available from the British Library

ISBN 978 0 7112 3660 8

9 8 7 6 5 4 3 2 1

THIS REVISED AND UPDATED EDITION
FOR WAL ERS PUBLISHED BY
FRANCES LINCOLN, LONDON

THE WESTERN FELLS

Natural Boundaries

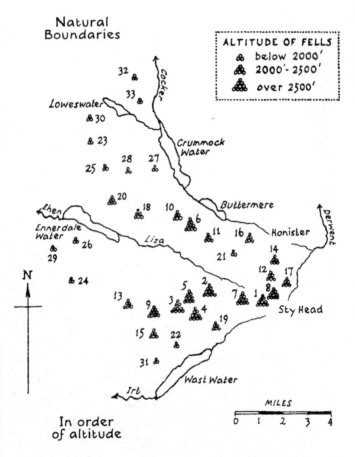

ALTITUDE OF FELLS
- below 2000'
- 2000'– 2500'
- over 2500'

Loweswater

Cocker

Crummock Water

Buttermere

Ehen

Enderdale Water

Liza

Honister

Derwent

N

Sty Head

Irt

Wast Water

MILES
0 1 2 3 4

In order of altitude

1 GREAT GABLE
2 PILLAR
3 SCOAT FELL
4 RED PI E
  Wasdale
5 STEEPLE
6 HIGH STILE
7 IR FELL
8 GREEN GABLE
9 HAYCOC
10 RED PI E
  Buttermere

11 HIGH CRAG
12 BRANDRETH
13 CAW FELL
14 GREY NOTTS
15 SEATALLAN
16 FLEETWITH PI E
17 BASE BROWN
18 STARLING DODD
19 YEWBARROW
20 GREAT BORNE
21 HAYSTAC S
22 MIDDLE FELL

23 BLA E FELL
24 LAN RIGG
25 GAVEL FELL
26 CRAG FELL
27 MELLBREA
28 HEN COMB
29 GRI E
30 BURNBAN FELL
31 BUC BARROW
32 FELLBARROW
33 LOW FELL

THE WESTERN FELLS

Each fell is the subject of a separate chapter

INTRODUCTION
TO THE
WAL ERS EDITION
BY CLIVE HUTCHBY

When I finished work on *The Wainwright Companion* in April 2012 I never expected that, less than two years later, I would be following literally in the footsteps of AW on his beloved Lakeland fells. And those of Chris Jesty as well, whose Second Edition revision of the guidebooks spurred me, at the end of 2010, to purchase the complete set for the umpteenth time — oh, how must the publishers have loved me down the years.

The full extent of Chris Jesty's revisions might surprise many people, but to revise books that were half a century old really was a monumental task. Typical changes in that period have been stiles being replaced by gates, new footbridges, paths being repaired — and even re-aligned — by Fix the Fells, the construction of fences, planting and felling of trees, as well as all the usual things that happen when thousands of people tramp the fells and fellrunners take the line of least resistance: some paths fall out of fashion, others spring up from nowhere.

I have largely succeeded in checking all the recommended routes with and without paths in the Western Fells, but once again tree felling operations, this time in Ennerdale, caused problems; by then, of course, I was getting used to it (from earlier revisions Wythburn—Swirls, Dodd Wood and Whinlatter still give me nightmares!).

Many readers may be unaware that some ascents described by AW in his original Book Seven (now available in the 'Readers Edition' series) were dropped for the second edition because of access issues raised by landowners. This meant a number of illustrations were omitted from the Second Edition; I'm happy to report that they are all back in this edition, plus there are new ascent diagrams in the following chapters: Burnbank Fell (from Fangs Brow), Fellbarrow (from Waterend), Great Borne (*via* Rake Beck), Low Fell (from Loweswater), and Starling Dodd (from Buttermere and also from Ennerdale). In the Pillar chapter, too, there are significant changes on page 7 (map) and page 12 (ascent diagram), both showing the new approach to High Beck from Irish Bridge. Look out, too, for Yewbarrow 3, where I have added further detail to explain the confusing topography of the south ridge in the vicinity of Great Door. There are also new paths and routes too numerous to mention here. In fact, I think this revision has been the most challenging in this respect, and I certainly could not have managed all this without Maggie Allan, who has been helping me revise these guides since Book Two and whose fellwalking knowledge is second to none, particularly in the Western Fells where it doesn't seem there is a path, a cairn, a stile, a gate, a pool or anything of which she is not aware. Thank you, Maggie.

While revising Books One to Six in the series it was hard to look at the Western Fells and to think 'It will be *x* more years before I'll be climbing those', and I have to report that on several occasions I gave in to temptation and took a 'day off' to visit them. It is not easy to resist the lure of the High Stile Range, the Mosedale Horseshoe, Green and Great Gable, Haystacks, Fleetwith Pike, Mellbreak and, a personal favourite, Yewbarrow.

These are great fells that everyone knows, but there is something else about the fells out west that has made their exploration very welcome — they remind me of the Far Eastern Fells, for which I have a particular fondness. There are places to the east of irkstone and Patterdale where you can be truly alone on the fells, which I didn't think I would experience anywhere else; the back o' Skiddaw is lonely, true, but not in that 'Far Eastern' way (only Far Eastern fans will know what I mean).

However, rather unexpectedly, I have found many such locations among the Western Fells, with the pride of place going to the Blackbeck notts and nott Ends ridge south-east of Red Pike (Wasdale); needless to say, Maggie tipped me off about that. Honorary mentions must go to: Scoat Tarn; Gavel Fell from High Nook Farm; Grey notts direct from Seatoller; Tewit How; Floutern Tarn on a sunny day; the 'woman's face' boulder on Haystacks — which takes some finding; and the delectable summit of Bowness nott. And what can I say about Low Fell? It is a modest-looking fell between Loweswater and the Vale of Lorton, but one with the most sublime late-afternoon and early-evening views over Crummock Water along the Buttermere valley towards Haystacks and beyond. All this *and* a solitary pine tree that simply has to be visited.

AW said that he hoped people would use his guidebooks as a basis for their own notes, and he was certainly right about that. I now have in my possession Books One to Seven of the Chris Jesty edition with many of the pages littered with comments, sketches, diagrams and the like. My big regret is that I didn't start colour-coding with a multi-coloured ballpoint until the very last of these. It would have made deciphering all my notes so much easier.

Finally, I would like to thank the following for their help and support in revising Book Seven: Maggie Allan (mentioned earlier), Michell Thurmond, Sean McMahon and Derek Cockell, plus Jane ing and Annie Sellar (from the Wainwright Estate) and Michael Brunström (from publishers Frances Lincoln).

Clive Hutchby
February 2020

Wasdale Head

INTRODUCTION
BY
A Wainwright

INTRODUCTION

Surely there is no other place in this whole wonderful world quite like Lakeland ... no other so exquisitely lovely, no other so charming, no other that calls so insistently across a gulf of distance. All who truly love Lakeland are exiles when away from it.

Here, in small space, is the wonderland of childhood's dreams, lingering far beyond childhood through the span of a man's life: its enchantment grows with passing years and quiet eventide is enriched by the haunting sweetness of dear memories, memories that remain evergreen through the flight of time, that refresh and sustain in the darker days. How many, these memories .... *the moment of wakening, and the sudden joyful realisation that this is to be another day of freedom on the hills ...... the dawn chorus of bird song ...... the delicate lacework of birches against the sky .... morning sun drawing aside the veils of mist; black-stockinged lambs, in springtime, amongst the daffodils .... silver cascades dancing and leaping down bracken steeps ..... autumn colours .... a red fox running over snow .... the silence of lonely hills ...... storm and tempest in the high places, and the unexpected glimpses of valleys dappled in sunlight far beneath the swirling clouds .... rain, and the intimate shelter of lichened walls .... fierce winds on the heights and soft breezes that are no more than gentle caresses .... a sheepdog watching its master ...... the snow and ice and freezing stillnesses of*

midwinter: a white world, rosy-pink as the sun goes down ...... the supreme moment when the top cairn comes into sight at last, only minutes away, after the long climb .... the small ragged sheep that brave the blizzards ...... the symphonies of murmuring streams, unending, with never a discord .... curling smoke from the chimneys of the farm down below amongst the trees, where the day shall end ...... oil lamps in flagged kitchens, huge fires in huge fireplaces, huge suppers .... glittering moonlight on placid waters ...... stars above dark peaks ..... the tranquillity that comes before sleep, when thoughts are of the day that is gone and the day that is to come .... All these memories, and so many more, breathing anew the rare quality and magical atmosphere of Lakeland .... memories that belong to Lakeland, and could not belong in the same way to any other place .... memories that enslave the mind forever.

Many are they who have fallen under the spell of Lakeland, and many are they who have been moved to tell of their affection, in story and verse and picture and song.

This book is one man's way of expressing his devotion to Lakeland's friendly hills. It was conceived, and is born, after many years of inarticulate worshipping at their shrines.

It is, in very truth, a love letter.

Classification and Definition

Any division of the Lakeland fells into geographical districts must necessarily be arbitrary, just as the location of the outer boundaries of Lakeland must always be a matter of opinion. Any attempt to define internal or external boundaries is certain to invite criticism, and he who takes it upon himself to say where Lakeland starts and finishes, or, for example, where the Central Fells merge into the Southern Fells and which fells are the Central Fells and which the Southern and why they need be so classified, must not expect his pronouncements to be generally accepted.

Yet for present purposes some plan of classification and definition must be used. County and parochial boundaries are no help, nor is the recently defined area of the Lakeland National Park, for this book is concerned only with the high ground.

First, the external boundaries. Straight lines linking the extremities of the outlying lakes enclose all the higher fells very conveniently. There are a few fells of lesser height to the north and east, however, that are typically Lakeland in character and cannot properly be omitted: these are brought in, somewhat untidily, by extending the lines in those areas. Thus:

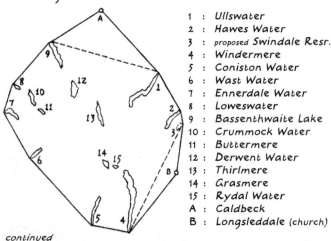

1 : *Ullswater*
2 : *Hawes Water*
3 : proposed *Swindale Resr.*
4 : *Windermere*
5 : *Coniston Water*
6 : *Wast Water*
7 : *Ennerdale Water*
8 : *Loweswater*
9 : *Bassenthwaite Lake*
10 : *Crummock Water*
11 : *Buttermere*
12 : *Derwent Water*
13 : *Thirlmere*
14 : *Grasmere*
15 : *Rydal Water*
A : *Caldbeck*
B : *Longsleddale* (church)

continued

Classification and Definition

continued   The complete Guide includes all
the fells in the area enclosed by the straight lines of the
diagram. This is an undertaking quite beyond the
compass of a single volume, and it is necessary, therefore,
to divide the area into convenient sections, making
the fullest use of natural boundaries (lakes, valleys
and low passes) so that each district is, as far as possible,
self-contained and independent of the rest.

This division gives seven areas,
each with a well defined group
of fells, and each area is the
subject of a separate volume

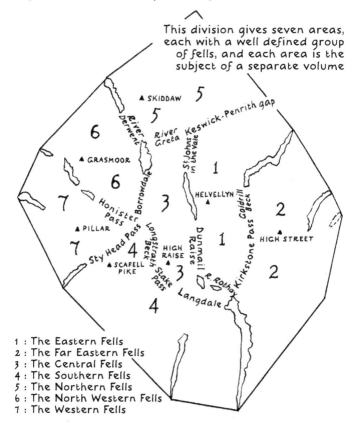

1 : The Eastern Fells
2 : The Far Eastern Fells
3 : The Central Fells
4 : The Southern Fells
5 : The Northern Fells
6 : The North Western Fells
7 : The Western Fells

INTRODUCTION

Notes on the Illustrations

THE MAPS .... Many excellent books have been written about
Lakeland, but the best literature of all for the walker is that
published by the Director General of Ordnance Survey, the 1"
map for companionship and guidance on expeditions, the 2½"
map for exploration both on the fells and by the fireside. These
admirable maps are remarkably accurate topographically but
there is a crying need for a revision of the paths on the hills:
several walkers' tracks that have come into use during the past
few decades, some of them now broad highways, are not shown
at all; other paths still shown on the maps have fallen into
neglect and can no longer be traced on the ground.

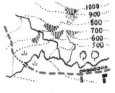

The popular Bartholomew 1" map is a
beautiful picture, fit for a frame, but this
too is unreliable for paths; indeed here
the defect is much more serious, for
routes are indicated where no paths
ever existed, nor ever could — the
cartographer has preferred to take
precipices in his stride rather than
deflect his graceful curves over easy
ground.

Hence the justification for the maps in this book: they have
the one merit (of importance to walkers) of being dependable as
regards delineation of paths. They are intended as supplements
to the Ordnance Survey maps, certainly not as substitutes.

THE VIEWS .... Various devices have
been used to illustrate the views from
the summits of the fells. The full
panorama in the form of an outline
drawing is most satisfactory generally,
and this method has been adopted for
the main viewpoints.

THE DIAGRAMS OF ASCENT .... The routes of ascent of the
higher fells are depicted by diagrams that do not pretend to
strict accuracy: they are neither plans
nor elevations; in fact there is deliberate
distortion in order to show detail clearly:
usually they are represented as viewed
from imaginary 'space stations'. But it is
hoped they will be useful and interesting.

THE DRAWINGS .... The drawings at least are honest attempts
to reproduce what the eye sees: they illustrate features of
interest and also serve the dual purpose of breaking up the
text and balancing the layout of the pages, and of filling up
awkward blank spaces, like this:

THE
WESTERN
FELLS

If Lakeland can be thought of as being circular in plan, the Western Fells may be described as being contained within a wide sector, the apex driving deep into the heart of the district at Sty Head and the boundaries running therefrom north-west along the valley of the Cocker, jewelled by the lovely lakes of Buttermere and Crummock Water, and south-west along Wasdale towards the sea.

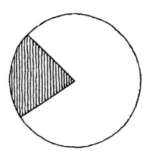

If Lakeland can be thought of as a wheel, the Western Fells may be likened, simply yet appropriately, to two spokes (the Pillar and High Stile ranges) radiating from a central hub (Great Gable), with Ennerdale between the spokes and the two valleys of the Cocker and Wasdale bordering them.

In this area is a wide diversity of scenery. The section nearest to and including the hub is entirely mountainous, crowded with fine peaks although none quite attain 3000 feet. Here is the hoary old favourite, Great Gable, and the magnificent Pillar, the fascinating Haystacks and the exhilarating spine of the High Stile ridge: a rugged territory of volcanic rock and syenite. Further west the slopes are smooth and rounded, characteristic of the underlying slate; towards the arc of the circle they decline into low grassy foothills and rolling sheep pastures, a splendid walking country but comparatively unexciting and unfrequented.

The Western Boundary

Valley and lake scenery is of the very best vintage, excepting Ennerdale, where natural beauty has been sacrificed to material gain, an irretrievable mistake. There is water extraction from some of the lakes, a process carried out by the responsible authorities unobtrusively and with due regard to amenities.

There are no centres of population within the area, and only hamlets and small villages around the perimeter; most of them cater for visitors but accommodation is necessarily restricted. Buttermere and Wasdale Head in particular are popular resorts.

The western boundary of the area described in this book is fairly well defined by the fells themselves, although lesser hills continue into the industrial belt of West Cumbria. This arbitrary boundary coincides, in places, with that of the Lake District National Park but is generally within it.

Base Brown

2120'

OS grid ref: NY225115

Seatoller ●
Seathwaite ●
BASE ▲ BROWN

▲ GREAT GABLE
// StyHead Pass

MILES
0   1   2   3

from the Borrowdale Yews

NATURAL FEATURES

Base Brown marks the end of roads and farmsteads, of woods and green pastures, as one proceeds into the upper recesses of Borrowdale. It marks the beginning of wildness and desolation. It is the first of the rough and rugged heights extending to and around Wasdale, and introduces its hinterland excellently, being itself of striking appearance, gaunt, steep-sided, a pyramid of tumbled boulders and scree, a desert abandoned to nature. It is a cornerstone, walkers' paths to Sty Head curving around its base below sixteen hundred feet of chaotic fellside scarred by gully and crag and strewn with the natural debris of ages; a stark declivity. The opposite slope, although also rimmed and pitted with rocks, is much shorter, being halted by the hanging glacial valley of Gillercomb. Only along the narrow crest of the fell are walkers likely to venture, and but rarely even here, for the ridge rising from Borrowdale is defended by bristly crags; the continuation beyond the summit, however, to a grassy neck of land linking with Green Gable and overlooking Sty Head on one side and Gillercomb on the other, is much easier, and a very popular path (Seathwaite direct to Great Gable) comes into the scene at this point. Base Brown belongs to Borrowdale exclusively, and its streams, attractively broken by the waterfalls and cascades of Taylorgill Force and Sourmilk Gill, feed the youthful Derwent only.

Taylorgill Force

Sourmilk Gill

The attention of intrepid and
well insured explorers is drawn
to the remarkable cleft vertically
splitting the crag. It is not listed
as a rock climb, either because
it is too easy or too impossible.
It is certain to be dangerous.
The author, still unnerved after
his climb of Jack's Rake in 1957,
has no information to impart.

*The East Face
above Taylor Gill*

Hanging Stone

The Hanging Stone is repeatedly featured conspicuously in successive editions of the Ordnance Survey maps, where its name is given as much prominence as that of the fell itself, although its precise location is never pinpointed. The Stone occupies a startling position balanced on the rim of a crag, apparently half its bulk being unsupported and overhanging the void, but it is smaller than one is led to expect (a few tons only) and the special distinction given to it on the O.S. maps is not really merited.

looking steeply upwards

People with bad coughs should keep out of the line of fall

Sixty yards further up the ridge a large rounded boulder has come to rest on a number of small ones.

Fallen Stone

Immediately below the crag is a tremendous mass of rock that must at some time have fallen from it, although silting now gives it the appearance of a natural outcrop. It has been badly fractured in the fall, and identifiable fragments from it can be found lower down the slope.

Near the top end of the rock several large boulders have tumbled together, forming caves and foxholes.

MAP

Seathwaite is provided with a telephone box (useful, because getting a mobile signal is rare), public toilets (very useful) and a camp site. With 130" of rain a year, this is reputed to be the rainiest inhabited place in England.

continuation GREY KNOTTS 3

continuation BRANDRETH 3

SEATOLLER 1

roadside parking

Seathwaite

Borrowdale

old fold

Fawn Crag

BASE BROWN 2120'

Stockley Bridge

Mitchell Gill

STY HEAD

ESK HAUSE

N

ONE MILE

The suggested route (dotted line) from the depression to the south-west of the summit is a quick and very easy line of descent, on grass that leads to the Sty Head—Stockley Bridge path; in fact, this is an excellent route down to Borrowdale.

On its way to join the Derwent, Styhead Gill falls steeply down a wooded and stony ravine. Here is a fine cataract, Taylorgill Force.

But why *Taylorgill*? Clearly the ravine must be named Taylor Gill, yet both above and below it the beck is Styhead Gill. Why not *Styheadgill Force*? This change of name for a small intermediate section of a watercourse is unusual.

Walkers are again reminded that the spectacular (but rough) track through Taylor Gill is a far better way to Sty Head than that in common use via Stockley Bridge. There are some slightly exposed sections which are easy with care — avoid this route if such walking is worrisome.

The top waterfall, Sourmilk Gill

ASCENT FROM SEATHWAITE
1750 feet of ascent : 1½ miles

BASE BROWN

When the direct route comes fully into view its appearance is hostile. Those walkers who do not like the look of it may still reach the summit without trouble by continuing along the Green Gable path through Gillercomb to the *col* at 2000 feet, an easy stroll on grass then leading to the top.

looking south-west

1800 ... *depression*

Gillercomb

1700

1600

perched boulder

— *Hanging Stone*

× *fold*

Direct Route:
Leave the Green Gable path where it becomes quite level and turn left uphill on grass, picking your way through rocks to reach the big boulder on its right-hand side. From here a thin but good path leads to the base of the crag directly below the Hanging Stone. It continues round the corner to the left, where the top of the crag may be gained without difficulty as the path climbs up a grass slope to the ridge above.

1500

caves

big boulder

1300

1200

1100

GREEN GABLE

Sourmilk Gill

gate

1000

Short rocky section of scrambling

900

800

700

600 *unusual stile; more like a double ramp*

500

400

Seathwaite Slabs —
a training ground for novice rockclimbers, conveniently sited five minutes from Seathwaite.

R. Derwent

roadside parking

lane

STOCKLEY BRIDGE ¾

SEATOLLER 1¼

Seathwaite

Start under the arch of the farm buildings. The footbridge over the Derwent was provided as a war memorial by the Ramblers' Association. The path between 500′ and 950′ has been paved, although not particularly well; rounded stones make this a bad route for descent in rain or ice. The scrambling section requires some agility.

An adventurous route that was once pathless but now has the benefit of a track through the key section. For those who like exploration, this is highly recommended.

THE SUMMIT

The summit is out of character, being a broad grassy expanse with no suggestion of the rough craggy slopes that support it. A sprinkling of boulders and some low outcrops do their best to relieve the monotony.

DESCENTS: The eastern slope is excessively steep in all parts, and above Taylor Gill, positively dangerous. The north-west side overlooking Gillercomb is precipitous.

For Borrowdale the best way off in mist is to proceed down the gentle slope south-west, there joining the Green Gable-Seathwaite path as it turns to descend into Gillercomb; in clear weather the pathless route left from the depression to Sty Head Gill is easier on the legs and better underfoot. The direct route of ascent may be reversed in clear weather, but it is advisable NOT to persist in following the ridge to its extremity, which is a 40-foot vertical cliff; instead, follow the ridge path down to the right — it becomes sketchy but a distinct horizontal path is soon reached. Go along this path, left, to the area of boulders below the 40-foot crag, where a way may be made downhill to the Green Gable-Seathwaite path clearly seen 200 yards below.

If Wasdale is the objective, get Styhead Tarn in view and make a beeline for it, crossing Mitchell Gill; an easy stroll.

RIDGE ROUTE

To GREEN GABLE, 2628': 1 mile: SW
Depression at 1990': 620 feet of ascent

Interest quickens as the walk proceeds.

Soon after leaving the summit south-west the distinct path coming up from Gillercomb is seen in the depression ahead; this is joined and followed up the opposite slope, which becomes stony, to the main watershed and the broad path from Honister 300 yards short of the top of Green Gable.

In snow, the path from the depression and that from Honister is easy to follow with numerous cairns marking the route.

THE VIEW

Higher fells on three sides restrict the open view to the section between north and east, where the village of Rosthwaite and much of Borrowdale are also seen. South is the mountain wall of the Scafells in close detail. West, Pillar and Scoat Fell make an unexpected appearance over Gillercomb Head.

Principal Fells

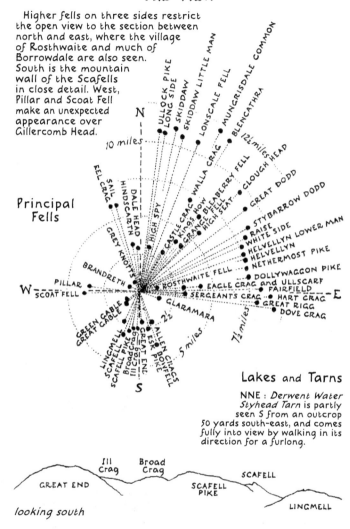

Lakes and Tarns

NNE: *Derwent Water*
Styhead Tarn is partly seen S from an outcrop 50 yards south-east, and comes fully into view by walking in its direction for a furlong.

looking south

In good lighting conditions this view south to the Scafells calls for a photograph, but before releasing the shutter walk towards the scene until Styhead Tarn appears fully in the middle distance and gives relief to the sombre background. Then do it.

Blake Fell

1878'

OS grid ref: NY110197

Lamplugh   Loweswater
●   ▲   ●
    BURNBANK FELL
        ▲ BLAKE FELL

        ▲ GAVEL FELL
● Croasdale
        MILES
0   1   2   3

from Cogra Moss

NATURAL FEATURES

Blake Fell (locally known simply as Blake) is the highest of the Loweswater uplands, overtopping the others considerably and asserting this superiority by a distinctive final upthrust that makes it prominent in views of the group. A long high shoulder, Carling nott, extends towards Loweswater, hiding the main summit from that valley, but on the opposite western flank, facing industrial Cumbria, a scree-covered declivity drops immediately from the summit cairn to the hollow of Cogra Moss and encircling arms comprise many subsidiary tops, of which the chief is the shapely peak of nock Murton. This side of the fell has for long been commissioned to the service of man: here, up to a century ago, were extensive iron-ore mines and a railway to serve them; Cogra Moss has been dammed to make a reservoir, and in the 1960s the Forestry Commission moved in and planted the first trees in a project that has altered the landscape completely. The fell, by reason of its fringe situation, gives the feeling of belonging more to West Cumbria than to the Lake District; more to Lamplugh, where everybody knows it, than to Loweswater, where Mellbreak is favourite. Its waters mainly feed the Derwent.

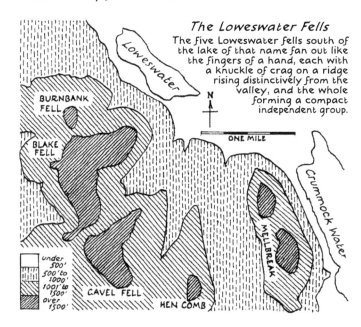

The Loweswater Fells

The five Loweswater fells south of the lake of that name fan out like the fingers of a hand, each with a knuckle of crag on a ridge rising distinctively from the valley, and the whole forming a compact independent group.

Loweswater

N

ONE MILE

BURNBANK FELL

BLAKE FELL

Crummock Water

MELLBREAK

CAVEL FELL

HEN COMB

under 500'
500' to 1000'
1001' to 1500'
over 1500'

Blake Fell 3

MAP

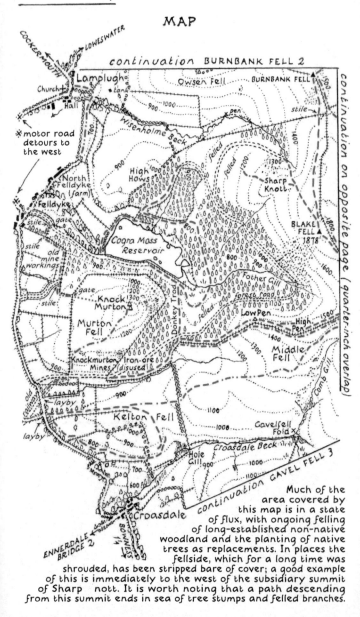

continuation BURNBANK FELL 2

continuation on opposite page (quarter-inch overlap)

COCKERMOUTH

LOWESWATER

Lamplugh

Church

Hall

tarn

* motor road
detours to
the west

Owsen Fell

BURNBANK FELL

pen

stile

Wisenholme Beck

felled

North
Felldyke
(farm)

Felldyke

stile

gate

stile

old
mine
workings

High
Hows

felled

felled

Sharp
Knott

BLAKE
FELL
1878

gate

stile

Cogra Moss
Reservoir

Knock
Murton

Murton
Fell

Donkey Trod

Fother Gill

forest road

felled

Low Pen

High
Pen

Middle
Fell

Knockmurton Iron-ore
Mines (disused)

old
railway

layby

Redwood

layby

Kelton Fell

Comb Gill

Gavelfell
Fold X

Croasdale Beck

Hole
Gill

continuation GAVEL FELL 3

Croasdale

ENNERDALE
BRIDGE 2

BOWNESS 1¼

Much of the
area covered by
this map is in a state
of flux, with ongoing felling
of long-established non-native
woodland and the planting of native
trees as replacements. In places the
fellside, which for a long time was
shrouded, has been stripped bare of cover; a good example
of this is immediately to the west of the subsidiary summit
of Sharp Knott. It is worth noting that a path descending
from this summit ends in sea of tree stumps and felled branches.

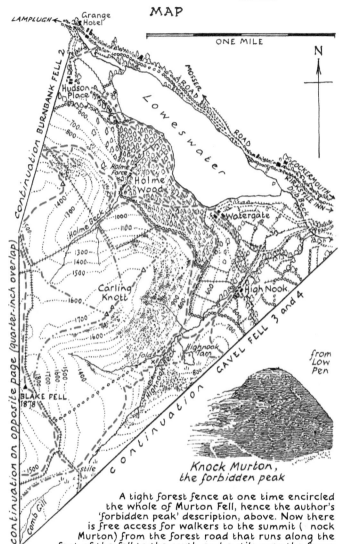

MAP

ONE MILE

N

LAMPLUGH←

Grange Hotel

continuation BURNBANK FELL 2

Hudson Place

Loweswater

MOSSER ROAD

ROAD

COCKERMOUTH

KIRKSTILE INN

Dub Beck

Holme Force

Holme Wood

Watergate

Holme Beck

continuation on opposite page (quarter-inch overlap)

Carling Knott

High Nook

Highnook Tarn

folds

Highnook Beck

continuation GAVEL FELL 3 and 4

from Low Pen

BLAKE FELL 1878

stile

Comb Gill

Knock Murton, the forbidden peak

A tight forest fence at one time encircled the whole of Murton Fell, hence the author's 'forbidden peak' description, above. Now there is free access for walkers to the summit (nock Murton) from the forest road that runs along the foot of the fell to the south and a stile over the fence to the north-west, from near a stone memorial bench; a series of green arrows indicate the way to the open fell. On the summit is a well made wind shelter with seats inside. The main cairn is twenty yards north-east, and there are two smaller cairns in the vicinity.

ASCENT FROM LOWESWATER
1550 feet of ascent : 3 miles (from Kirkstile Inn)

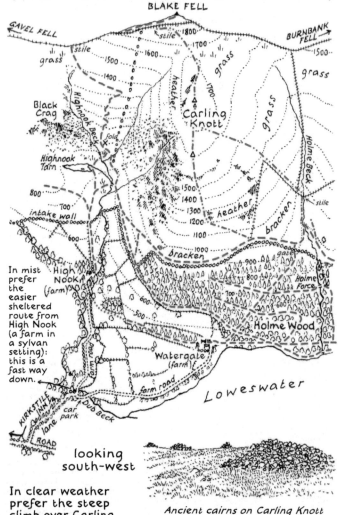

BLAKE FELL

GAVEL FELL

BURNBANK FELL

stile 1800
1700
1600
grass
grass
stile
grass
1500
1400
1500
heather
1700
Carling Knott
Black Crag
Highnook Beck
fold
Highnook Tarn
800
1500
1400
1300
1200
1100
1000
heather
bracken
Holme Beck
stile
grass
700
intake wall
600
bracken
900
800
gate
In mist prefer the easier sheltered route from High Nook (a farm in a sylvan setting): this is a fast way down.
High Nook (farm)
700
Holme Force
600
500
Holme Wood
Watergate (farm)
farm road
Loweswater
KIRKSTILE INN
car park
lane
Dub Beck
ROAD

looking south-west

Ancient cairns on Carling Knott

In clear weather prefer the steep climb over Carling Knott from Watergate *via* Holme Wood a route of interesting detail and lovely views. The approach from Holme Beck has little to recommend it.

ASCENT FROM LAMPLUGH
1400 feet of ascent : 3¼ miles

BLAKE FELL

1800
1700
1600
1500

High Pen

GAVEL FELL

looking east-
south-east

Blakefell
Screes

1400

1300

Middle Fell

1500

1200

Low Pen

1100

Knock
Murton

forest road

forest road

1200

1100

col

felled area

1000

Fother Gill

Donkey Trod

900

old fence

800

Cogra
Moss
Reservoir

felled

900

1000

At the col
the route
crosses the
forest road
coming up from
the disused mine
on the south side
of nock Murton. At
present, this is the only
access for vehicles into
the new forest. It
is not available to
private cars.

From the west
the approach
by Cogra Moss
has always been
the best. The
reservoir is
used by the
Cockermouth
Angling Association.

dam

gate

At the
head of the
reservoir turn
up Donkey
Trod to the col;
then follow
the fence
along the
ridge around
the hollow
to the
summit.

The reservoir is not a natural
lake, having been formed by damming
the outflow from Cogra Moss, once a
marsh. There are two small islands in
the lake, namely Blake Island, nock
Island and an unnamed islet.

Rakegill Beck

800

gate

At Lamplugh there is room to park
opposite the church when it is not
in use, but it is difficult to cross the
stream and better to start
at Felldyke.

100

North
Felldyke

gate

Felldyke

ROAD

car
park

stile
and SP

A

church

Note the well preserved 16th-century
gateway of the former Lamplugh Hall.

Lamplugh

B

A : road to
    LOWESWATER
B : road to
    COCKERMOUTH

It will be seen from the map on page 3
that there are two alternative routes
from the west. One crosses the reservoir
dam and approaches the summit from
Sharp nott. The other utilises the
forest road to the south of nock
Murton. They are better used in descent.

Blake Fell 7

THE SUMMIT

HIGH RAISE — GLARAMARA — HIGH STILE — PILLAR — SCAFELL — Black Crag — SCOAT FELL

The summit is well defined by rising ground on all sides, and the large cairn merely emphasises the obvious. It is a fine airy place, overtopping everything around: the highest point of the Loweswater fells. As on nock Murton, the cairn has been fashioned into an exceptionally well constructed wind shelter. A short path heads south-west to a viewpoint from which the Cogra Moss Reservoir is well seen.

A hundred yards east of the summit is a wire mesh fence erected in the 1960s to mark the boundary of the land acquired by the Forestry Commission. It was put up without a stile, so denying to fellwalkers their inherited right to visit the cairn. Two stiles were later provided, one to link with Gavel Fell, the other with Carling nott. The former has since completely collapsed and the latter looks as though it is about to do so. In 2008, it must have been decided that the fence no longer served a purpose, for gaps were created at both these places. Between the two gaps, in an old sheepfold, is another wind shelter.

DESCENTS: For Lamplugh or Felldyke follow the ridge over High Pen and Low Pen and cut down to Cogra Moss Reservoir. If this route has already been used for ascent then follow the route past Sharp nott to the reservoir dam (but not the path west from the summit of Sharp nott which ends in a horrible felled area). For Loweswater, cross the fence 200 yards south of the summit; then follow the ridge over Carling nott in clear weather, or, *in mist*, use the good path on the easy tongue on the west side of Highnook Beck.

Summit cairns on Knock Murton

THE VIEW

The view inland, comprising a splendid array of mountains, is excellent; seawards, it extends uninterrupted far across West Cumbria to the Scottish hills.

Principal Fells

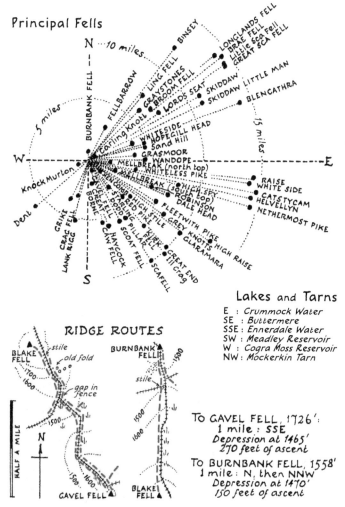

Lakes and Tarns

E : Crummock Water
SE : Buttermere
SSE : Ennerdale Water
SW : Meadley Reservoir
W : Cogra Moss Reservoir
NW : Mockerkin Tarn

RIDGE ROUTES

TO GAVEL FELL, 1726':
1 mile : SSE
Depression at 1465'
270 feet of ascent

TO BURNBANK FELL, 1558':
1 mile : N, then NNW
Depression at 1470'
150 feet of ascent

Both routes are easy, on grass throughout, with no problems following clear paths. The depression before Gavel Fell is damp.

Brandreth

2344'

OS grid ref: NY215119

Gatesgarth

Honister
Pass

Black Sail
Y.H.
BRANDRETH ▲

▲ GREY KNOTTS

Seathwaite

▲ GREEN GABLE
▲ GREAT GABLE

MILES

0   1   2   3

from Base Brown

NATURAL FEATURES

Brandreth is an intermediate height on the broad tilted ridge, almost a tableland, rising gently from the back of Honister Crag and culminating in Great Gable. Its summit is little higher than the general level of the plateau and has nothing of particular interest; indeed, the path along the ridge takes a wide sweep to avoid it, preferring to maintain an easy contour rather than go up and down over the top.

Brandreth's one claim to distinction is based on its superb view of the High Stile range flanked by the valleys of Ennerdale and Buttermere, a magnificent prospect; but this is a view as well seen from the west slope, around which the path curves, as from the top. This western slope is broad and sprawling, part of it declining to Ennerdale and part re-shaping into the undulating summit of Haystacks; in sharp contrast, the eastern is abruptly cut away in cliffs falling into the great upland basin of Gillercomb. On this side any attempt to determine the boundaries separating this and the adjoining fells of Grey notts and Green Gable must be purely arbitrary, the long craggy wall of Gillercomb Head extending the length of all three, but without any dividing watercourses; an unusual arrangement.

Of the fells on this watershed between Windy Gap and Honister, Brandreth is geographically the most important, being the only one to feed three distinct river systems — Derwent, Liza and Cocker.

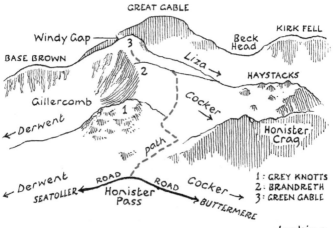

The Honister—Windy Gap watershed

looking south

1: GREY KNOTTS
2: BRANDRETH
3: GREEN GABLE

MAP

The map is extended to the north to include
the old quarry tramway, by which the
approach from Honister Pass or
Gatesgarth is usually made.

N

The
three
paths on
the sprawling
western flank of
Brandreth are of
special interest to
walkers. Starting as one
from the Drum House, each
has a distinct objective: one
aims for Great Gable via Green Gable, another for Wasdale,
and the third for Ennerdale. The first is a popular and well
trodden way; the second, less known, is Moses' Trod, a very
quiet route of great charm; and the third — the route of the
author's *A Coast to Coast Walk* — is mainly used by hostellers
passing between the Honister and Black Sail Youth Hostels. The
point of divergence of the first and third occurs at an angle in
the path, a rocky corner with a good view.

Moses' Trod used to have no obvious start at its north end,
but now there is a clear path leaving the Great Gable track
at the lower of two stiles crossing the Brandreth fence. This
old pony track is of unique interest and it is given a page to
itself in the Great Gable chapter, page 7.

ASCENT FROM HONISTER PASS
1150 feet of ascent : 2 miles

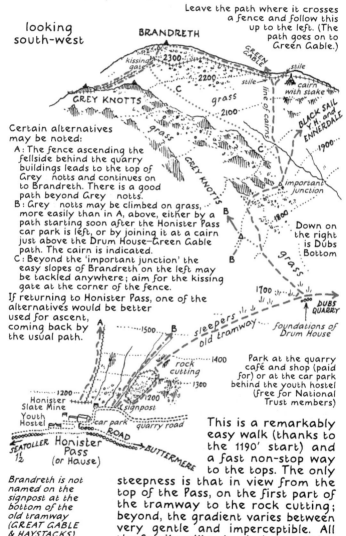

looking
south-west

Leave the path where it crosses
a fence and follow this
up to the left. (The
path goes on to
Green Gable.)

BRANDRETH

2300

kissing
gate

GREEN GABLE

stile

2200

C

stile

cairn
with stake

grass

GREY KNOTTS

2100

line of cairns

BLACK SAIL
Y.H. and
ENNERDALE

grass

1900

GREY KNOTTS

C

important
junction

Certain alternatives
may be noted:
A: The fence ascending the
   fellside behind the quarry
   buildings leads to the top of
   Grey Knotts and continues on
   to Brandreth. There is a good
   path beyond Grey Knotts.
B: Grey Knotts may be climbed on grass,
   more easily than in A, above, either by a
   path starting soon after the Honister Pass
   car park is left, or by joining it at a cairn
   just above the Drum House–Green Gable
   path. The cairn is indicated.
C: Beyond the 'important junction' the
   easy slopes of Brandreth on the left may
   be tackled anywhere; aim for the kissing
   gate at the corner of the fence.

If returning to Honister Pass, one of the
alternatives would be better
used for ascent,
coming back by
the usual path.

B

A

B

1800

Down on
the right
is Dubs
Bottom

grass

1700

DUBS
QUARRY

sleepers old tramway

foundations of
Drum House

A   1500   B

rock
cutting

1400

Park at the quarry
café and shop (paid
for) or at the car park
behind the youth hostel
(free for National
Trust members)

1300

1200

Honister
Slate Mine

1200

signpost

Youth
Hostel

car park   quarry road

SEATOLLER
1½

Honister   ROAD   BUTTERMERE

Pass
(or Hause)

This is a remarkably
easy walk (thanks to
the 1190' start) and
a fast non-stop way
to the tops. The only
steepness is that in view from the
top of the Pass, on the first part of
the tramway to the rock cutting;
beyond, the gradient varies between
very gentle and imperceptible. All
the family will enjoy it, irrespective
of age.

Brandreth is not
named on the
signpost at the
bottom of the
old tramway
(GREAT GABLE
& HAYSTACKS).
This is the route,
nevertheless.

ASCENT FROM GATESGARTH
2,000 feet of ascent : 3 miles

BRANDRETH

Gillercomb Head

GREEN GABLE

On the final section, alongside the fence, three important paths are crossed. The first is the Honister–Ennerdale track; the second, less distinct, is 'Moses' Trod', heading for Wasdale; and the third is the well blazed Honister–Great Gable 'highway'.

WASDALE

ENNERDALE

Great Round How

fine cliffs of good clean rock

Hereabouts are many iron posts embedded in rock and marking the Lonsdale Estate boundary.

A : Dubs Hut (bothy)
B : Warnscale Bothy

HONISTER

Little Round How

HAYSTACKS

Dubs Quarry (disused)

Green Crag

Black Beck

Cross Warnscale Beck by the footbridge where Black Beck joins in, and use the old path on the far bank, an interesting route on a clear path over rough ground. Alternatively the beck may be crossed by the stepping stones below Dubs Hut. In addition there is a third crossing point between the two, but this is more difficult. The three routes unite below Little Round How.
Elsewhere, Warnscale Beck runs deep in an impassable and dangerous ravine.

falls

Warnscale Bottom

ruin

bracken

looking south-east

easy level walking

Great Round How

ROAD

Gatesgarth

HONISTER PASS
SEATOLLER 3½

car park

Gatesgarthdale Beck

Unlike most mountain climbs, the interest and excitement of this walk occur in the first thousand feet of ascent. For dramatic scenery, the zig-zag path to the right (west) of Warnscale Beck is to be preferred.

ASCENT FROM ENNERDALE
(BLACK SAIL YOUTH HOSTEL)
1400 feet of ascent : 1¾ miles

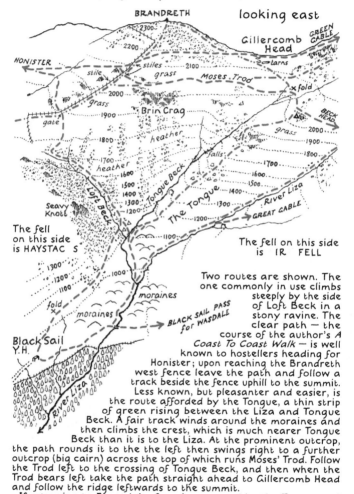

looking east

BRANDRETH

Gillercomb Head

GREEN GABLE

HONISTER

stiles grass Moses Trod
stile tarns
fold

grass 2100
2000
gate 1900
Brin Crag

BECK HEAD
grass 2000

heather
1800
1700
heather 1600
1500
1400
1300 Tongue Beck
1200

The Tongue

falls 1700
1600
1500
1400

River Liza
1300

Seavy Knott

1100

GREAT GABLE

The fell
on this side
is HAYSTACKS

The fell on this side
is KIRK FELL

1300
1200
1100
fold
moraines
1000
moraines

Black Sail
Y.H.

BLACK SAIL PASS
for WASDALE

River Liza

Two routes are shown. The
one commonly in use climbs
steeply by the side
of Loft Beck in a
stony ravine. The
clear path — the
course of the author's *A
Coast To Coast Walk* — is well
known to hostellers heading for
Honister; upon reaching the Brandreth
west fence leave the path and follow a
track beside the fence uphill to the summit.
Less known, but pleasanter and easier, is
the route afforded by the Tongue, a thin strip
of green rising between the Liza and Tongue
Beck. A fair track winds around the moraines and
then climbs the crest, which is much nearer Tongue
Beck than it is to the Liza. At the prominent outcrop,
the path rounds it to the the left then swings right to a further
outcrop (big cairn) across the top of which runs Moses' Trod.
Follow the Trod left to the crossing of Tongue Beck, and then when the
Trod bears left take the path straight ahead to Gillercomb Head
and follow the ridge leftwards to the summit.

If returning to Ennerdale: for *views*, ascend by the Tongue and
come down by Loft Beck, the best views being in front all the way;
for *ease of descent*, go up by Loft Beck and down by the Tongue.

This is the easiest mountain ascent
available from the head of Ennerdale.

ASCENT FROM SEATHWAITE
2000 feet of ascent : 2 miles

The hollow of Gillercomb Head contains three small tarns. The regular path from Honister to Great Gable crosses the depression, rounding the tarns in a sharp curve.

GREEN GABLE

BRANDRETH

Gillercomb Head

2300

2200

2100

2100

2000

1900

1800

1700

1600

1500

GREEN GABLE

looking west-south-west

Brandreth does not lend itself to a direct frontal attack from the floor of Gillercomb, its defences being crags and rough scree, but there is one line of weakness — a simple grass rake — not apparent until one is looking straight along it from a point on the Green Gable path soon after passing the last rocks of Base Brown. Here cross the stream where five little tributaries join, and further another meeting place of streams, the right branch of which sets the direction for reaching the ridge at Gillercomb Head. Take the thin path to the right.

The fell on this side is GREY NOTTS

The big cliff over here is Raven Crag (also known as Gillercomb Buttress)

Gillercomb

Sourmilk Gill

On this side is BASE BROWN

This section is an unavoidable scramble that requires the use of hands and some basic agility.

1100

gate

1000

900

800

700

600

500

Seathwaite Slabs

This is unlikely ever to become a popular climb; from Seathwaite there are several far more desirable objectives. It may be noted, however, for future reference, that Gillercomb Head, reached as shown here, offers the fastest passage over the tops to Ennerdale.

R. Derwent

lane

awkward stile

ROAD

Seathwaite ↑

roadside parking

The steep section from the stile to the gate has been heavily pitched, but the rounded stones are not easy to negotiate in descent.

Gillercomb Head

THE SUMMIT

*Looking to Green Gable
and Great Gable*

The summit is a bare and
cheerless place, a desert
of stones. The main
cairn incorporates
three iron posts.
Most of the fence
posts in the
illustration
have gone.

DESCENTS: For HONISTER PASS direct, the fence heading north-east across Grey notts is a perfect guide; keep on north-east at a junction of fences. If an easier path is preferred, go down by the western fence for a quarter-mile to join a broad cairned path and turn to the right along it for Honister *via* the Drum House. For BUTTERMERE *via* Warnscale, use this route but turn left at the Drum House. For ENNERDALE, continue along the western fence beyond the first path for another quarter-mile (ignoring a thin track crossing midway) and turn left downhill along a fair path with cairns. For BORROWDALE, head south until the Honister—Gable 'highway' is met and go left along it to the nearby depression of Gillercomb Head, where there are three tarns. Leave the ridge here to go left down a grass slope into Gillercomb and cross the beck to join the Sourmilk Gill path for Seathwaite; this needs care on the final steep section, and some scrambling is required.

To GREY KNOTTS, 2287': ½ mile: NE
Depression at 2250': 50 feet of ascent

Follow the fence north-east and arrival on Grey notts is inevitable. There are paths either side: left is recommended, switching sides at the stile.

BRANDRETH

To GREEN GABLE, 2628': 1 mile: S
*Depression (Gillercomb Head)
at 2160': 450 feet of ascent*

Head in a southerly direction to join the Honister—Great Gable path, which is distinct and well cairned on the long climb to the top of Green Gable.

GREY KNOTTS

tarns

kissing gate

stile

ONE MILE

BRANDRETH

GREEN GABLE

THE VIEW

Brandreth's position on the Derwent—Cocker—Liza watershed is sufficient guarantee of a commanding view, and this is extensive in all directions except south, where the two Gables form a near and lofty horizon. Best of all the objects in view are the Grasmoor fells in the north-west, soaring in splendid array from deeply inurned Crummock Water. Pillar and High Stile are also well displayed. Scafell Pike is hidden behind Green Gable. The conspicuous pyramid on Glaramara, left of the summit, is Combe Head.

For photographic purposes note that the beautiful view north-west is seen to greater advantage from the western slope below the summit. In fine weather, a stroll down by the west fence might well produce the most magnificent picture of the year. Contrast and composition are excellent.

Principal Fells

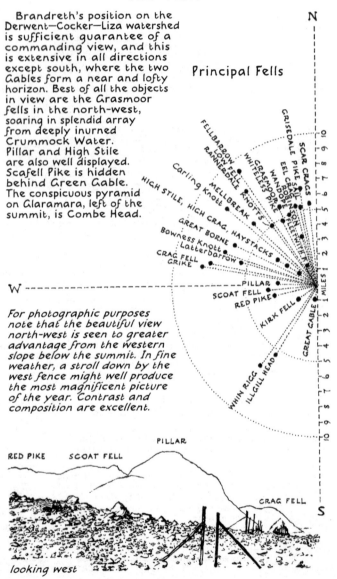

looking west

THE VIEW

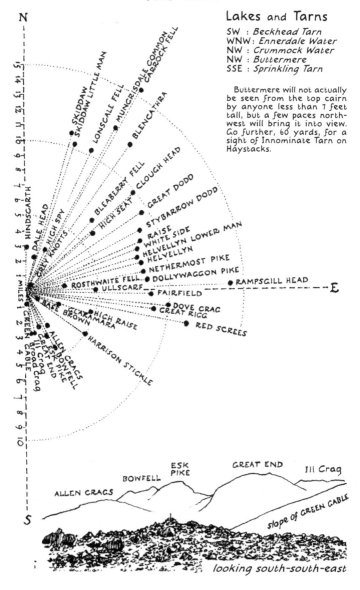

Lakes and Tarns

SW : *Beckhead Tarn*
WNW: *Ennerdale Water*
NW : *Crummock Water*
NW : *Buttermere*
SSE : *Sprinkling Tarn*

Buttermere will not actually be seen from the top cairn by anyone less than 7 feet tall, but a few paces north-west will bring it into view. Go further, 60 yards, for a sight of Innominate Tarn on Haystacks.

looking south-south-east

Buckbarrow

1410'
approx

OS grid ref: NY136061

from Harrow Head

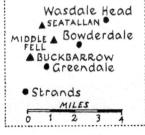

Wasdale Head
▲ SEATALLAN ●
MIDDLE ▲ Bowderdale ●
FELL ▲
▲ BUCKBARROW
● Greendale

● Strands

MILES
0   1   2   3   4

Buckbarrow faces the famous Screes across Wast Water and being itself a steep and stony declivity bears some resemblance, if only in miniature. From the road along its base, Buckbarrow seems to be a separate fell, but the name has reference merely to the half-mile rock escarpment, beyond which a grassy plateau is succeeded by a featureless slope rising easily to the top of Buckbarrow's parent fell, Seatallan.

MAP

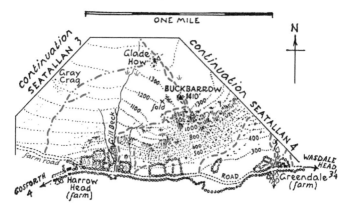

ASCENT FROM WASDALE
(HARROW HEAD)
1100 feet of ascent: 1 mile

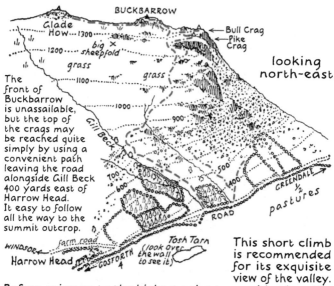

looking north-east

The front of Buckbarrow is unassailable, but the top of the crags may be reached quite simply by using a convenient path leaving the road alongside Gill Beck 400 yards east of Harrow Head. It easy to follow all the way to the summit outcrop.

This short climb is recommended for its exquisite view of the valley.

Before going on to the highest point turn aside along the top of either (or both) of the craggy spurs prominent in the later stages of the climb (for the best views).

THE SUMMIT

Sellafield complex ⟶ ᴨᴨ ⸺⸺ ᴨᴨ·ɪɪ⸺⸺

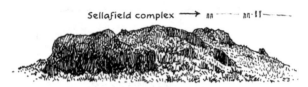

The highest point in the vicinity of the escarpment is a rocky mound behind the edge of the crags, overlooking the grassy basin below Seatallan. It is undistinguished as a viewpoint in comparison with several less elevated places along the cliff tops. A quarter of a mile west of north is the prominent cairn on Glade How. (The four cooling towers at Sellafield, shown above, were demolished in 2007.)

DESCENTS: The route recommended for ascent is also the best way down, but if a alternatives are wanted they may be found (in clear weather): a) by skirting the head of Tongues Gills at 1250' to join the path from Greendale Tarn down to the road. Aim for Joss Naylor's cairn (see map on *Seatallan 4*); or b) by continuing to Glade How and then finding the sketchy track, later becoming a decent path, which leads down to the farm road above Harrow Head.

The cairn on Glade How

SCAFELL PIKE

A perched and split boulder (obviously split after perching, probably by frost or lightning)

Buckbarrow from Greendale

THE VIEW

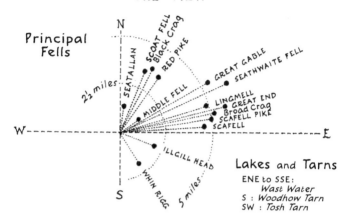

Principal Fells

Lakes and Tarns

ENE to SSE:
Wast Water
S : Woodhow Tarn
SW : Tosh Tarn

It happens frequently that a view from a point below the top of a fell is more attractive than that from the summit, but only rarely that it is more extensive. On Buckbarrow, the best view is obtained from the end of the rocky spur prominently seen in the ascent (Pike Crag), this being much finer than that from the summit and actually covering a wider range. Nothing more can be seen from the summit, and a good deal less. The diagrams on this page are based on the end of the spur overlooking Wasdale. The Screes are directly opposite, Wast Water is seen full length and the head of the valley is magnificently closed in by the Scafells.

Due south, the horizon is occupied by the massive outline of Black Combe.

Great Gable cannot be seen from the actual summit of the fell.

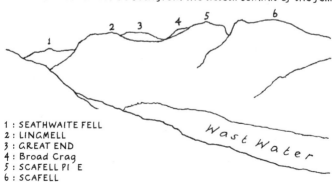

1 : SEATHWAITE FELL
2 : LINGMELL
3 : GREAT END
4 : Broad Crag
5 : SCAFELL PIKE
6 : SCAFELL

The Scafells, from Buckbarrow

Burnbank Fell 1558'

OS grid ref: NY110209

from Waterend

West of Loweswater the high ground of Lakeland gives place to the undulating rural countryside of the quiet Marron valley, and the last height of all is the grassy dome of Burnbank Fell, a cornerstone, a beginning and an end. This is a dull hill, with little to suggest the grandeur of the mountain masses piled inland from it and nothing to divert the attention of a passing traveller. Helped by Holme Wood the northern slope makes a colourful background to Loweswater and has a fine terrace path (not well enough known) contouring high above the lake with charming views, but the sprawling west flank going down to Lamplugh over a lesser height, Owsen Fell, is a moorland lacking interest.

• Mockerkin

Lamplugh Loweswater
▲ •
BURNBANK FELL
▲ BLAKE FELL

MILES
0 1 2 3 4

MAP

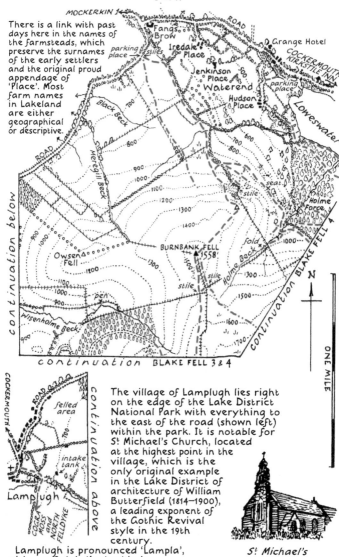

There is a link with past days here in the names of the farmsteads, which preserve the surnames of the early settlers and the original proud appendage of 'Place'. Most farm names in Lakeland are either geographical or descriptive.

The village of Lamplugh lies right on the edge of the Lake District National Park with everything to the east of the road (shown left) within the park. It is notable for St Michael's Church, located at the highest point in the village, which is the only original example in the Lake District of architecture of William Butterfield (1814–1900), a leading exponent of the Gothic Revival style in the 19th century.

Lamplugh is pronounced 'Lampla', with a soft 'a'; Mockerkin is pronounced 'Mocker-kin'.

St Michael's Church, Lamplugh

ASCENT FROM WATEREND
1250 feet of ascent : 2¾ miles

Note that no stile is provided
on the summit of Burnbank Fell.

The path
from the cairn
to the summit is
at such a gentle
gradient that
the walk seems
almost effortless.

This is the
route from
Fangs Brow;
see facing
page

Note that it
is possible (and
preferable) to avoid
the first half
of the road
to Hudson
Place. A way
may be made
through the fields
from the layby to
Dub Beck, where
the marshy ground
is crossed by
a wooden
causeway.

There is a
camping barn at
Waterend Farm

There is extensive parking
at the layby, between the
telephone box and the gate.

looking south

This is a dull climb if done straight up the slope, but it
can be made interesting and attractive by including
in the itinerary a visit to the delightful Holme Force,
which is set in extensive woodland, and a stroll along
the terrace path. The route recommended is arrowed
on the diagram. If views only are the object of the
walk there is no point in going on beyond the cairn.

ASCENT FROM FANGS BROW
900 feet of ascent : 1½ miles

looking south

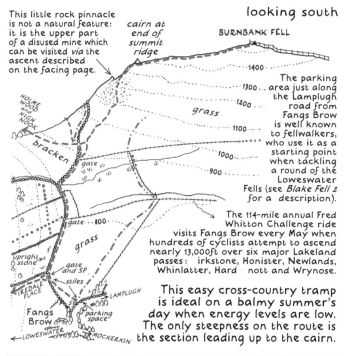

This little rock pinnacle is not a natural feature: it is the upper part of a disused mine which can be visited *via* the ascent described on the facing page.

cairn at end of summit ridge

BURNBANK FELL

HOLME WOOD and HIGH NOOK

bracken

gate

grass

1400
1300
1200
1100
1000
900
gate — 800
grass

upright stone

gate and SP

stiles

IREDALE PLACE

LAMPLUGH

Fangs Brow

parking space

←LOWESWATER — MOCKERKIN

The parking area just along the Lamplugh road from Fangs Brow is well known to fellwalkers, who use it as a starting point when tackling a round of the Loweswater Fells (see *Blake Fell 2* for a description).

The 114-mile annual Fred Whitton Challenge ride visits Fangs Brow every May when hundreds of cyclists attempt to ascend nearly 13,000ft over six major Lakeland passes: irkstone, Honister, Newlands, Whinlatter, Hard nott and Wrynose.

This easy cross-country tramp is ideal on a balmy summer's day when energy levels are low. The only steepness on the route is the section leading up to the cairn.

Holme Wood and Holme Force

Holme Wood is the property of the National Trust and is traversed by a pleasant path near the lakeside amongst mature and beautiful trees (the higher parts of the wood have been afforested).

The gem of the place is Holme Force, a series of lovely waterfalls in a sylvan setting, reached by a detour along a side path and easily viewed from a bridge that straddles the gill just below the falls. In spate it is a particularly impressive sight, when the roar of water can be heard from quite a distance.

The natural woods are a mixture of alder, oak, lime, chestnut, ash, rowan and sycamore, and provide a home for red squirrels.

Holme Force

THE SUMMIT

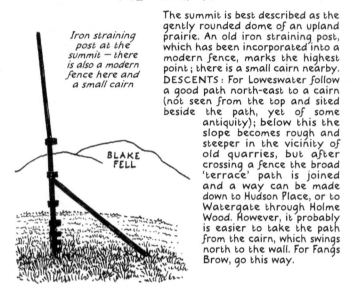

Iron straining post at the summit — there is also a modern fence here and a small cairn

BLAKE FELL

The summit is best described as the gently rounded dome of an upland prairie. An old iron straining post, which has been incorporated into a modern fence, marks the highest point; there is a small cairn nearby.

DESCENTS: For Loweswater follow a good path north-east to a cairn (not seen from the top and sited beside the path, yet of some antiquity); below this the slope becomes rough and steeper in the vicinity of old quarries, but after crossing a fence the broad 'terrace' path is joined and a way can be made down to Hudson Place, or to Watergate through Holme Wood. However, it probably is easier to take the path from the cairn, which swings north to the wall. For Fangs Brow, go this way.

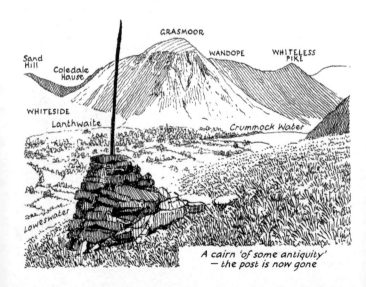

Sand Hill · Coledale Hause · GRASMOOR · WANDOPE · WHITELESS PIKE

WHITESIDE · Lanthwaite · Crummock Water

Loweswater

A cairn 'of some antiquity' — the post is now gone

THE VIEW

Landward, the distant view is greatly restricted by the nearby Carling nott and Blake Fell, which hide all that lies beyond, but seaward there is an uninterrupted panorama from the Isle of Man (see over S! Bees Head) round to Criffel in Scotland, and nearer the West Cumbrian coastal area is revealed in detail.

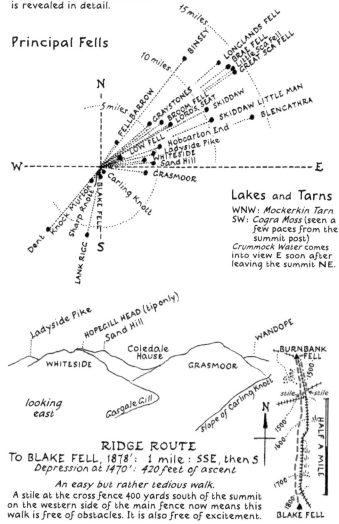

Principal Fells

Lakes and Tarns

WNW: *Mockerkin Tarn*
SW: *Cogra Moss* (seen a few paces from the summit post)
Crummock Water comes into view E soon after leaving the summit NE.

An easy but rather tedious walk.

RIDGE ROUTE

TO BLAKE FELL, 1878': 1 mile : SSE, then S
Depression at 1470': 420 feet of ascent

An easy but rather tedious walk.

A stile at the cross fence 400 yards south of the summit on the western side of the main fence now means this walk is free of obstacles. It is also free of excitement.

Caw Fell

2288'

OS grid ref: NY132110

Caw Fell, like many of us who lack a good shape and attractive features, objects to having his picture taken and is not at all co-operative as a subject for illustration. From no point of view does the fell look like anything other than a broadly buttressed sprawling uncorseted graceless lump with a vast flattened summit similarly devoid of a single distinguishing landmark.

In the drawing above, of Caw Fell as seen from Lank Rigg, the great scoop in the western ridge shows prominently. The highest point of the fell occurs above the dark shadow, top left, here seen overtopped by Haycock.

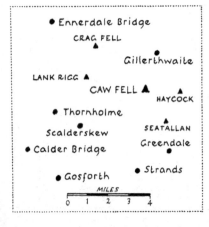

• Ennerdale Bridge
CRAG FELL ▲

Gillerthwaite •

LANK RIGG ▲
CAW FELL ▲   ▲ HAYCOCK

• Thornholme

Scalderskew •   ▲ SEATALLAN
                       Greendale
• Calder Bridge

                  • Strands
• Gosforth

MILES
0   1   2   3   4

NATURAL FEATURES

The magnificent group of mountains between Wasdale and Ennerdale, topped by Pillar and including several other redoubtable peaks, is as rugged and craggy as any in the district, exhibiting steep and precipitous slopes to north and east, where they overlook deep valleys. To south and west, however, this upland area is of entirely different character, declining much more gradually, in easy stages. Mountain gives way to moorland, and the rocky nature of the terrain smooths into wide pastures, slow in descent from the tops and therefore more amiable in gradient; the streams follow long and gentler courses but thread their way through gathering grounds so vast that they quickly assume the proportions of rivers. These are the sheepwalks of Copeland Forest, of Stockdale Moor and of innside Common, rolling grasslands linking the untamed heights with the cultivated valleys — a region uninhabited and unfrequented in this day and age, yet at one time, from evidences that still remain to be seen, the home of primitive man.

Caw Fell occupies much of this territory. It has many unnamed summits, many ridges and many streams. Its ten square miles contain much geographical detail of interest rather than importance, for all its waters ultimately mingle in the Irish Sea off the Seascale coast although to get there they flow in all directions of the compass.

There is not much here to attract walkers whose liking is for rough ground and airy ridges; there is little to excite the senses, nothing of beautiful or dramatic effect. Yet here one can stride out for hour after hour in undisturbed solitude and enjoy invigorating exercise amongst scenery that has not changed since the world began. Only when the lower ground is reached does one become mindful again of the 20th century: here, spreading like a dark cloak from the valleys are plantations of conifers alongside the ancient settlements of the first Britons.

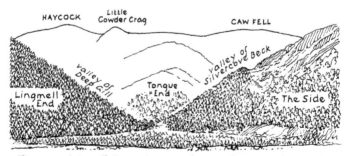

The top of Caw Fell can be seen from a short section only of the walk up Ennerdale, near the first footbridge, where, across the valley, Deep Gill has carved a great opening in the fellside.

MAP

Caw Fell is a rolling upland of modest height, predominantly grass-covered, and of mainly easy gradients. *But this is a fell that should not be underestimated.* It is remote from shelter or habitation; in these four pages of maps there is one dwelling only: the isolated farmstead known as Scalderskew. A fair march is needed even to get a foothold on the fell, from any direction, and a long climb follows before the summit is reached. Good advice to those who plan its ascent is to divide the time available by two, and if the top is not gained by half-time *turn back.* An exhausted walker on Caw Fell is in bad trouble. The miles to safety are long and lonely, and the surrounding rivers run wide and fast, unbridged. Before setting out, study the map carefully, noting the many watercourses and ridges that leave the mile-long top, and where they lead in relation to the nearest road, and plan the route in terms of hours. If it is necessary to cross any streams, do so near the source, not lower down. Time spent on a study of the geography on a map, in advance, means time saved on the walk.

Ennerdale Water

continuation CRAG FELL 3

Red Beck

ENNERDALE BRIDGE 4

disused mines

felled area

Boathow Crag

stile

gate

continuation on opposite page

continuation LANK RIGG 4

Whoap

pool

Short Grain

Red Gill

fold

Long Grain

Worm Gill

Bleaberry Gill

old sheepfold

water intake works (disused)

continuation on page 5

Water intake works, Worm Gill (long-since disused)

MAP

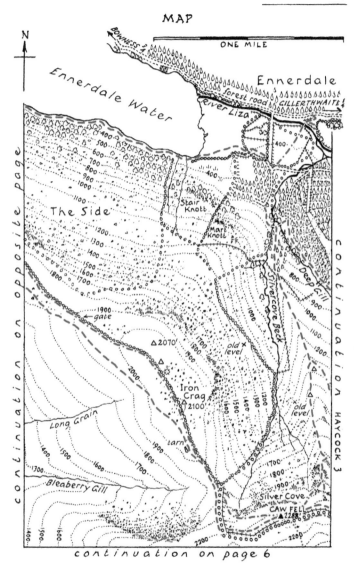

Iron Crag is regarded by some writers as a separate fell.
Remains of a Royal Canadian Air Force Sabre jet, which crashed
near the summit in June 1959, can be found over a wide area.

Caw Fell 5

MAP

continuation on page 3

The mountain pinfold near Worm Gill is unique, being the only Lakeland sheepfold so named by the Ordnance Survey on their maps. The distinction lies in the purpose of the structure, this one being to confine stray fell sheep for collection by their owners.

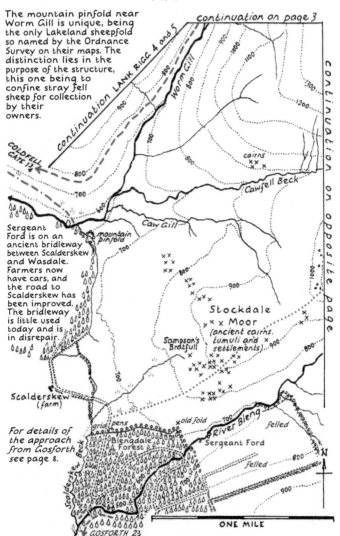

continuation LANK RIGG 4 and 5

continuation on opposite page

Worm Gill

COLDFELL GATE 13

cairns

Cawfell Beck

Caw Gill

Sergeant Ford is on an ancient bridleway between Scalderskew and Wasdale. Farmers now have cars, and the road to Scalderskew has been improved. The bridleway is little used today and is in disrepair.

mountain pinfold

Stockdale Moor (ancient cairns, tumuli and settlements)

Sampson's Bratfull

Scalderskew (farm)

For details of the approach from Gosforth see page 8.

grid pens

Blengdale Forest

old fold

River Bleng

Scalderskew Beck

Sergeant Ford

felled

felled

GOSFORTH 23

ONE MILE

The continuation of the path shown at the foot of this page (to the south of Sergeant's Ford) can be found on *Seatallan 2* and thence on to *Seatallan 3*.

MAP

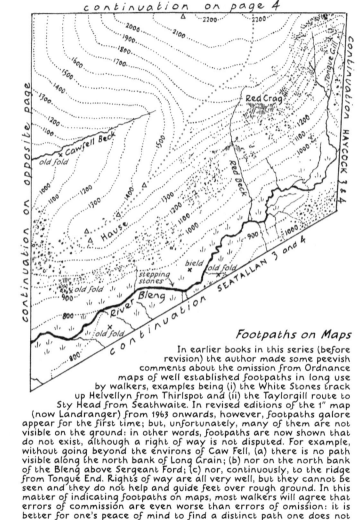

continuation on page 4

Footpaths on Maps

In earlier books in this series (before revision) the author made some peevish comments about the omission from Ordnance maps of well established footpaths in long use by walkers, examples being (i) the White Stones track up Helvellyn from Thirlspot and (ii) the Taylorgill route to Sty Head from Seathwaite. In revised editions of the 1" map (now Landranger) from 1963 onwards, however, footpaths galore appear for the first time; but, unfortunately, many of them are not visible on the ground: in other words, footpaths are now shown that do not exist, although a right of way is not disputed. For example, without going beyond the environs of Caw Fell, (a) there is no path visible along the north bank of Long Grain; (b) nor on the north bank of the Bleng above Sergeant Ford; (c) nor, continuously, to the ridge from Tongue End. Rights of way are all very well, but they cannot be seen and they do not help and guide feet over rough ground. In this matter of indicating footpaths on maps, most walkers will agree that errors of commission are even worse than errors of omission: it is better for one's peace of mind to find a distinct path one does not expect than to fail to find a path one is told to expect.

A prime example of this from the Ordnance's Explorer series are the dashed bright green lines denoting public rights of way, which a walker might assume to show the line of a path but which do not necessarily indicate that one can be found on the ground.

A tumulus

The Antiquities of Stockdale Moor

In the uncultivated areas of the Lake District, many evidences remain of the former existence of primitive habitations and settlements, and these are usually, to be found on open moorlands around the 900'–1200' contours at the upper fringe of the early forests, lying between the swampy valleys, as they would then be, and the inhospitable mountains. These evidences are very profuse in the area of Stockdale Moor and on the nearby slopes of Town Bank (Lank Rigg) and Seatallan. Here are to be seen the walled enclosures, hut circles, cairns, clearance heaps, barrows and tumuli of a prehistoric community, with traces of cultivation terraces. This is a great field of exploration for the archaeologist, and much work has been done and recorded, notably in the Transactions of the local Cumberland and Westmorland Antiquarian and Archaeological Society.

Walkers should not visit the area, however, expecting to see a pageant of the past unfold before their eyes. Knowledge and imagination are necessary to recognise and understand the remains. A person both uninformed and unobservant may tramp across Stockdale Moor and notice nothing to distinguish his surroundings from those of any other boulder-strewn upland. Indeed, except for the purposes of a study of the subject, a special visit to the area cannot really be recommended: the scenery is drab and desolate, there is no quick run-off for water on the flattish ground and consequently most of it is marsh; on a wet day the moor is downright depressing.

A cairn

A name that arouses interest on the map of Stockdale Moor is *Sampson's Bratfull*, a concentration of stones dropped from the apron of a giant as he strode across the moor. So legend has it, but learned sources prefer the opinion that this is the site of a tumulus or barrow (a burial place), giving its measurements

An enclosure

as 35 yards long and 12 yards wide tapering to the west end.

ASCENT FROM BLENGDALE LODGE
2100 feet of ascent : 5½ miles (7½ from Gosforth)

This is a long walk, tedious in the later part, but it can be halted on Stockdale Moor and further activity restricted to a search for the antiquities there but it is no longer possible to return *via* Sergeant Ford because the stepping stones have gone.

Blengdale is well hidden from the eyes of passing tourists, but is quickly reached from Gosforth by following the Wasdale road for a mile to Wellington Bridge, where take a narrow lane upstream on the west side of the Bleng. The lane is not signposted.

looking north-east

CAW FELL

2200
2100
2000
ruins of aeroplane

Haze

Cawfell Beck

900

old fold

grass

1000

Stockdale Moor
(many ancient remains)

River Bleng

900

800

Scalderskew (farm)

700

grass

700

cattle grid   old fold

700   felled

Sergeant Ford

Sergeant Ford

The quickest and best way through the forest from Bleng Bridge is *via* the footbridge (which is not visible from the path) to the cattle grid at the top of the plantation.

Blengdale Forest

fall

footbridge

Blengdale Lodge   Bleng Bridge

cattle grid

500

400   300   200

GOSFORTH 1½

The Forestry Commission suffer much criticism on amenity grounds in connection with their schemes of afforestation, and it is pleasant to record their pronounced success in Blengdale, where the older sections of the forest alongside the river are now transformed into a lovely woodland with magnificent trees and charming glades, made easily accessible by forest roads. The scenery is not characteristic of Lakeland, being more reminiscent of a Scottish glen, but does not offend on that account and is a very good example of landscape gardening on a big scale. The Commission have created beauty here, and nobody should object if they want to tackle the further three-mile wilderness of marshy ground up to the head of the valley, which at present is no good either to man or beast, but, if irrigated and planted discreetly, could make Blengdale attractive throughout its length.

ASCENT FROM KINNISIDE STONE CIRCLE
1850 feet of ascent : 6 miles

Walkers of only average ability must bear in mind that if it is six miles to Caw Fell it is also six miles back. Think of the walk as one of twelve miles, because there is no short way off whichever route is used to get down.

Strong walkers may make a magnificent day of it by continuing from Caw Fell to Haycock and Scoat Fell, or even Pillar, thence descending to Wasdale Head or Ennerdale.

Note that Grike, Crag Fell and Lank Rigg can all be alternative ascents.

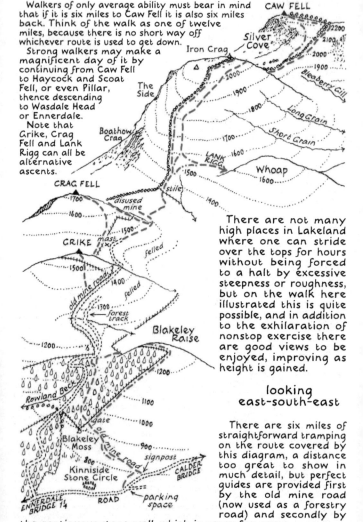

CAW FELL
Silver Cove
Iron Crag
The Side
Boathow Crag
CRAG FELL
disused mine
GRIKE
mast
felled
felled
old mine road
forest track
Blakeley Raise
Rowland Beck
gate
old mine road
Blakeley Moss
signpost
Kinniside Stone Circle
CALDER BRIDGE
parking space
ENNERDALE BRIDGE 14
ROAD

Bleaberry Gill
Long Grain
Short Grain
LANK RIGG
Whoap
stile

2200 2100 2000 1900 1800 1700 1600 1500 1400 1300 1200 1100 1000 900 800 1600 1700 1600 1500

There are not many high places in Lakeland where one can stride over the tops for hours without being forced to a halt by excessive steepness or roughness, but on the walk here illustrated this is quite possible, and in addition to the exhilaration of nonstop exercise there are good views to be enjoyed, improving as height is gained.

looking east-south-east

There are six miles of straightforward tramping on the route covered by this diagram, a distance too great to show in much detail, but perfect guides are provided first by the old mine road (now used as a forestry road) and secondly by the continuous stone wall, which is never far away.

On this route of ascent there are no crossings of streams to worry about. In fact, the whole way is remarkably dry underfoot.

ASCENT FROM ENNERDALE
(LOW GILLERTHWAITE)
1950 feet of ascent : 2¾ miles

Little Gowder Crag

← HAYCOCK stile stile CAW FELL

2200

Great Cove

Silver Cove

2100
2000
1900
1800
1700
1500

× old level

1500
1400
1300
1200
1100
1000
900

Heather

Heather

Deep Gill

Silvercove Beck

Tongue End

falls

Woundell Beck

forest road

SOUTH SHORE OF ENNERDALE WATER

looking south

GILLERTHWAITE (and ENNERDALE Y.H.)

valley road

Char Dub (River Liza)

→ BOWNESS POINT 2

This is not only the shortest way from valley level to the summit of Caw Fell, but the best. The river and woodland and gorge scenery in the vicinity of the confluence of Deep Gill and Silvercove Beck is charming, the more so because the spot is known to very few and rarely visited; indeed, the side opening in which it is situated, being across the valley from the Ennerdale highway, may escape the notice altogether of travellers thereon. The footbridge over the Liza is useful for those coming down the valley from the east or when Irish Bridge is under water. The public path leading onto Tongue End from the confluence of Deep Gill and Silvercove Beck is in danger of becoming lost in a jungle of young trees. A stile is provided in the forest fence, but unless the path is kept in use it may be lost.

This route is especially worth noting as a different approach to the main ridge, for the Pillar group.

This plantation has been felled, but natural regeneration has resulted in small trees growing too close to the path.

Here the path encounters a sudden drop that can be difficult to negotiate.

Irish Bridge (a very low bridge without parapets which serves as a ford when the river is high).

Permitted ways out of the floor of Ennerdale are few and far between since afforestation: this is the easiest route for gradients and certainly the most beautiful.

THE SUMMIT

The highest of the several tops in the territory of Caw Fell is immediately above Silver Cove, at 2288', on an unattractive stony plateau bisected by the crumbling wall (part of the 'Ennerdale fence') that runs for miles hereabouts along the south Ennerdale watershed and is a depressing ornament in fair weather but a reliable friend in foul. Sharp eyes will discern fragments of an aeroplane a quarter of a mile south of the wall; otherwise there are no items of interest and very little to warrant a prolonged halt.

DESCENTS: For the head of Ennerdale Water, reverse the route of ascent over Tongue End in preference to a more direct course alongside Silvercove Beck; for the foot of the lake follow the north-west ridge to Crag Fell and descend through the plantation; avoid an intermediate line down The Side, which is very rough. For Gosforth use the south-west ridge (the Hause) to reach Blengdale Lodge, but if, in mist, this route cannot be located, it is reassuring to know that all ways off down the western slopes are free from hazard.

RIDGE ROUTES

To HAYCOCK, 2618': 1 mile: E, then SE
450 feet of ascent: Depression at 2210'

An interesting move to rougher country.

There is no danger of going astray, however bad the weather, the wall leading directly to the top of Haycock over ground at first grassy but becoming very stony. Little Gowder Crag is an interesting feature *en route*; it can be bypassed by an easy path to the south.

*The boundary
wall is interrupted
by the low crags of
Little Gowder Crag*

ONE MILE

To CRAG FELL, 1716': 3½ miles: W, then NNW, NW and NNW
550 feet of ascent: Depressions at 1900' and 1325'

Too far unless heading thereafter for Ennerdale Bridge.

This is a long walk over easy ground, as shown on the maps on *Crag Fell 5* and *6*. For much of its length the path runs parallel with the wall along the north-west ridge, of which Crag Fell is really a continuation. The path to Crag Fell from the old mine road can be missed: look out for a cairn at its beginning.

THE VIEW

Caw Fell is sufficiently removed from the dominant heights of the Pillar group to permit a fairly good all-round view; it is not, however, particularly attractive in any direction.
The wall across the top obstructs the panorama and those fells named in the diagram south of Scafell can only be seen by looking over it, all the others being visible from the cairn.

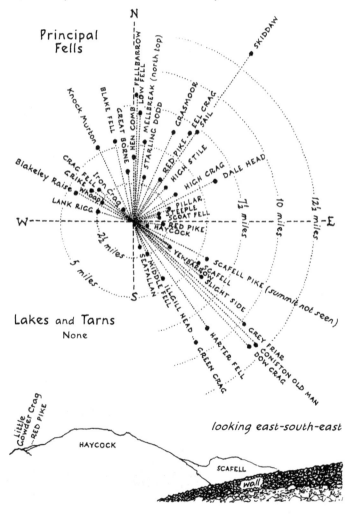

Principal Fells

Lakes and Tarns
None

looking east-south-east

Crag Fell

1716'

OS grid ref: NY097144

from Bowness Point

● Ennerdale
Bridge

GRIKE ▲   ▲ CRAG
            FELL

▲
LANK RIGG

MILES

0   1   2

from
Ennerdale
Bridge

NATURAL FEATURES

Crag Fell is a fine, abrupt height, prominently in view on the approach to Ennerdale, from the west, its configuration being such that it may easily be, and often is, mistaken for Pillar by those who have not studied their maps sufficiently, the illusion being strengthened by the conspicuous excrescence of rock on its north slope, which, seen in profile, might, at a glance, be thought to be the famous Pillar Rock. This comparison is a compliment to Crag Fell because Pillar is in fact a greater mountain by far and its Rock much more impressive than anything Crag Fell can show. Yet the north face of Crag Fell, falling sheer into Ennerdale Water, is an arresting sight; it is the dull hinterland of of smooth grassy slopes around the source of the River Calder that detracts from all round merit. In the rocky headland of Anglers' Crag, jutting into the lake; in the curious pinnacles of Revelin Crag, above; and not least in the tremendous ravine of Ben Gill, are centered the attractions of Crag Fell, and all face north. Elsewhere is moorland with nothing of interest but the few decayed remains of the former Cragfell Iron Ore Mines.

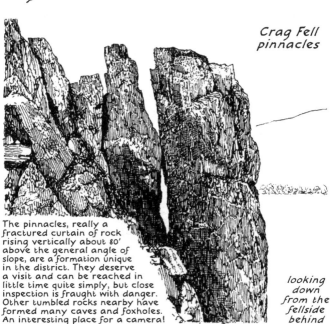

Crag Fell pinnacles

The pinnacles, really a fractured curtain of rock rising vertically about 80' above the general angle of slope, are a formation unique in the district. They deserve a visit and can be reached in little time quite simply, but close inspection is fraught with danger. Other tumbled rocks nearby have formed many caves and foxholes. An interesting place for a camera!

looking down from the fellside behind

MAP

Ennerdale Water is a reservoir
owned and operated by United
Utilities to supply the towns of
West Cumbria. A third of a mile
below the outlet are the water
treatment works, which
have been designed to
resemble a farm.

Angler's Crag

*(also known as
Angling Crag)*

The lakeside path
below Anglers' Crag
was formerly regarded
as dangerous, and walkers
were recommended to take
the longer route over the top. The
passage of many boots, however,
has smoothed out the difficulties,
and today it is no more than as
simple, rather rough, walk.

ASCENT FROM ENNERDALE BRIDGE
1350 feet of ascent : 2½ miles

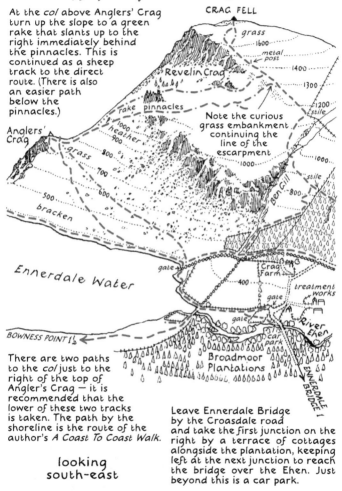

At the *col* above Anglers' Crag turn up the slope to a green rake that slants up to the right immediately behind the pinnacles. This is continued as a sheep track to the direct route. (There is also an easier path below the pinnacles.)

CRAG FELL

grass
1600
metal post
1400
1300
1200 stile

Revelin Crag

rake pinnacles

Note the curious grass embankment continuing the line of the escarpment

Anglers' Crag

grass

1000
heather
900
800
700
600
500

bracken

1000

1000

stile
800

Ben Gill

stile

Ennerdale Water

gate
400
Crag Farm

treatment works

gate
gate
car park

River Ehen

BOWNESS POINT 1½ ←

Broadmoor Plantations

ENNERDALE BRIDGE 1

There are two paths to the *col* just to the right of the top of Anglers' Crag — it is recommended that the lower of these two tracks is taken. The path by the shoreline is the route of the author's *A Coast To Coast Walk*.

looking south-east

Leave Ennerdale Bridge by the Croasdale road and take the first junction on the right by a terrace of cottages alongside the plantation, keeping left at the next junction to reach the bridge over the Ehen. Just beyond this is a car park.

Shown here are two routes: an adventurous way up visiting the pinnacles below Revelin Crag, and an easier approach from Crag Farm (even easier from here is the path through the plantation on the right edge of the diagram — see diagram on *Grike 5*).

RIDGE ROUTES

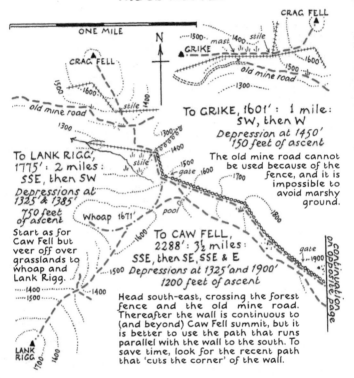

ONE MILE

N

CRAG FELL

GRIKE

mast

stile

old mine road

TO GRIKE, 1601' : 1 mile: SW, then W
Depression at 1450'
150 feet of ascent

The old mine road cannot be used because of the fence, and it is impossible to avoid marshy ground.

TO LANK RIGG', 1775' : 2 miles: SSE, then SW
Depressions at 1325' & 1385'
750 feet of ascent

Start as for Caw Fell but veer off over grasslands to Whoap and Lank Rigg.

Whoap 1671'

pool

stile

gate

TO CAW FELL, 2288' : 3½ miles: SSE, then SE, SSE & E
Depressions at 1325' and 1900'
1200 feet of ascent

Head south-east, crossing the forest fence and the old mine road. Thereafter the wall is continuous to (and beyond) Caw Fell summit, but it is better to use the path that runs parallel with the wall to the south. To save time, look for the recent path that 'cuts the corner' of the wall.

gate

continuation on opposite page

LANK RIGG

THE SUMMIT

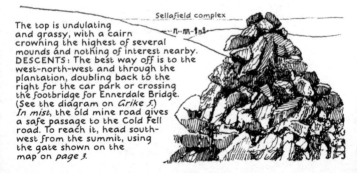

Sellafield complex

The top is undulating and grassy, with a cairn crowning the highest of several mounds and nothing of interest nearby. DESCENTS: The best way off is to the west-north-west and through the plantation, doubling back to the right for the car park or crossing the footbridge for Ennerdale Bridge. (See the diagram on *Grike 5*.) *In mist*, the old mine road gives a safe passage to the Cold Fell road. To reach it, head south-west from the summit, using the gate shown on the map on *page 3*.

THE VIEW

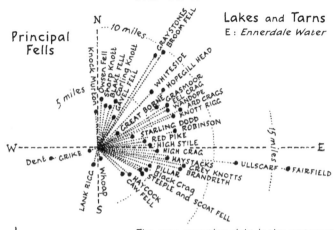

Principal Fells

Lakes and Tarns
E : Ennerdale Water

N
10 miles
GRAYSTONES
BROOM FELL
Knock Murton
SHEEP FELL
BLAKE FELL
GAVEL FELL
BURNBANK KNOTT
WHITESIDE
HOPEGILL HEAD
GREAT BORNE
GRASMOOR
FEL CRAG
WANDOPE
ARD CRAGS
KNOTT RIGG
STARLING DODD
ROBINSON
RED PIKE
HIGH STILE
HIGH CRAG
HAYSTACKS
GREY KNOTTS
BRANDRETH
PILLAR
Black Crag
STEEPLE and SCOAT FELL
HAYCOCK
CAW FELL
5 miles
W
Dent • GRIKE
LANK RIGG
WHOAP
S
15 miles
E
ULLSCARF • FAIRFIELD

RIDGE ROUTE
continued

continuation on opposite page

Iron Crag

2000
2000
2000
tarn
1900

This walk to Caw Fell is easy, but distance and time should be considered carefully in advance.
Caw Fell is in the heart of lonely and inhospitable fells, and a long way from shelter and accommodation. It is extensive, and in mist, if sight of the wall is lost, there may be difficulty in taking bearings on the indefinite top. Before setting out for Caw Fell there should be a well thought out plan for getting off it.

2000
stile
CAW FELL ▲ 2200
2200
2000

The most arresting sight is the grotesque collection of towers and minarets of the Sellafield plant, strangely tormenting the land horizon south-west; it is seen along the valley of the Calder, with the sea beyond, in a frame of serene fells. The contrast is striking: a modern toy and the timeless hills! A pleasanter prospect is the green strath of Gillerthwaite, but even here, man, learning nothing from nature, let loose his fancy ideas of tree planting and did his damnedest to ruin the scene. Recent felling has hardly improved things, leaving an ugly swathe of tree stumps and branch debris.
The view inland is generally confined to the mountains in the vicinity but seawards the panorama is very extensive.

Another of the Crag Fell Pinnacles (seen from above)

Fellbarrow

1363'

OS grid ref: NY132243

*from the slopes
of Burnbank Fell
above Waterend*

Waterend, a scattered hamlet,
is really mis-named. Here is
the extremity of the lake of
Loweswater, true, but this is
the head (the beginning) of
the lake, not the foot, which
is properly the end, the exit,
the place of outflow.

NATURAL FEATURES

The Vale of Lorton is sheltered on the west by a low range of grassy rounded hills uncharacteristic of Lakeland and not really part of it, this despite having southern roots in Loweswater amid scenery that is wholly typical of the district. The range has several tops of approximately the same height, none of them distinctive because the undulations are shallow, but the northern half builds up on all sides to the massive flattened dome of Fellbarrow.

The extensive slopes of grass, which serve as a vast sheep pasture, decline gradually westwards to quiet Mosser, northwards to Brandlingill and eastwards to the valley of the Cocker, all farming country. The scenery is pleasant but unexciting. The underlying rock is slate, and rarely exposed to view below its smooth green covering. There are traces of an old plantation in a basin on the east, of which a few straggly trees remain, and a still-flourishing wood on the side of the abrupt headland of Dodd near by.

Southwards, rounded humps succeed each other with little loss of height before a more distinctive shape resolves itself from the rolling acres. This is Low Fell, the subject of a separate chapter, and beyond is Loweswater.

The Fellbarrow range

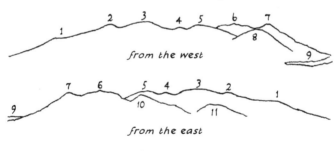

from the west

from the east

1 : Whin Fell	7 : Low Fell, main top
2 : Hatteringill Head	8 : Darling Fell
3 : Fellbarrow	9 : Loweswater
4 : Smithy Fell	10 : Watching Crag
5 : Sourfoot Fell	11 : Dodd
6 : Low Fell, north top	

The author originally wrote the following:
The traverse of the Fellbarrow range on a clear sunny day is one of the most rewarding of the simpler fellwalks, although not often undertaken. Its particular merit, apart from the easy going, is the beautiful view of the Buttermere—Crummock valley, which is seen to perfection. To enjoy it fully, walk the range from north to south.
Since then, however, access from the Low Lorton to Mosser fell road has become restricted, so the complete traverse is no longer viable.

Fellbarrow 3

MAP

Fellbarrow is extensive, its higher parts forming a vast sheep pasture and the lower slopes being cultivated for dairy farming. Woodlands and copses are a feature of the eastern flank.

The northern boundary of Fellbarrow may be regarded for fellwalking purposes as defined by the old road between Lorton and Mosser. Sometimes referred to as the Whinfell Road, this highway does not skirt the base of the fell but cuts across its shoulder at 700 feet. It is not signposted at either end, but, in spite of a rough surface, is negotiable by cars, a fact not generally known, and consequently it provides a first class terrace route for walkers with wide views northwards over the lower valley of the Cocker. It is worth noting, however, that there is no access to Fellbarrow's north flank for walkers.

Mosser Beck flows into the Cocker at Rogerscale, and is delightfully wooded throughout. The scenery along its course is pleasant and unspoilt.

The road from Mosser to Loweswater, at one time a secondary traffic route, is now signposted as unfit for cars and the surface beyond Mossergate has deteriorated, in a number of places quite badly. Cars bound for Loweswater are now directed at Mosser along a tarmac road via Sosgill and Mockerkin, a long detour that the authorities must have thought the better route as the direct road climbs to over 800 feet. Happily this change of traffic habits has left walkers in undisputed possession of a pleasant pedestrian way with grand views on the descent to Loweswater. The road is fenced, but not so as to impede wide panoramas, it is well culverted to give a good dry surface and is a splendid upland highway. A branch lane (always flooded) provides access to Fellbarrow and Low Fell.

If ascending from Mosser use any of the paths shown starting as one from the lane to Loweswater. See diagram on page 6.

COCKERMOUTH 2¾
BRANDLINGILL 3¾
PARDSHAW 1
ONE MILE
Mosser
SOSGILL 1
Chapel
Mossergate
enclosed pastures (private)
Fellside
enclosed pastures
Mosser Beck
ruin
lane
continuation on opposite page
continuation LOW FELL 2
LOWESWATER (LAKE 1; VILLAGE 2½)

MAY

Ruins of Hatteringill: the walls have severely deteriorated since this illustration was made.

The Mosser–Loweswater old road, the Whinfell Road, and the Thackthwaite by-road can be linked to provide a good circular tour around Low Fell and Fellbarrow for walkers based anywhere on the perimeter, with very little traffic interference — a 9-mile exercise for the legs very suitable for a day when cloud or bad weather puts the tops out of bounds.

Note well that this is NOT the main road along the vale of Lorton; it is the western by-road, and the bridge at Lorton is the only link.

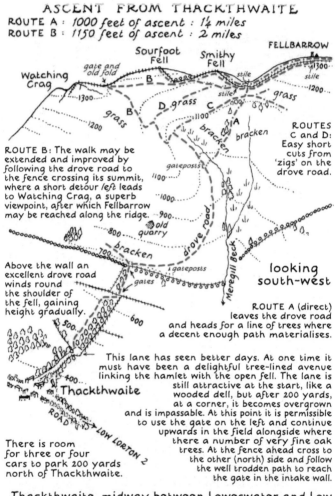

ASCENT FROM THACKTHWAITE
ROUTE A : *1000 feet of ascent : 1¼ miles*
ROUTE B : *1150 feet of ascent : 2 miles*

FELLBARROW

Sourfoot Fell

Smithy Fell

Watching Crag

gate and old fold

stile

1300

stile

B

1300

grass

1200

B

grass

D grass

C

1100

stile

1200

ROUTES C and D: Easy short cuts from 'zigs' on the drove road.

bracken

A

bracken

ROUTE B: The walk may be extended and improved by following the drove road to the fence crossing its summit, where a short detour *left* leads to Watching Crag, a superb viewpoint, after which Fellbarrow may be reached along the ridge.

gateposts

1100

1000

900

old quarry

800

bracken

700

drove road

looking south-west

Above the wall an excellent drove road winds round the shoulder of the fell, gaining height gradually.

gates

gateposts

Meregill Beck

600

ROUTE A (direct) leaves the drove road and heads for a line of trees where a decent enough path materialises.

500

This lane has seen better days. At one time it must have been a delightful tree-lined avenue linking the hamlet with the open fell. The lane is still attractive at the start, like a wooded dell, but after 200 yards, at a corner, it becomes overgrown and is impassable. At this point it is permissible to use the gate on the left and continue upwards in the field alongside where there a number of very fine oak trees. At the fence ahead cross to the other (north) side and follow the well trodden path to reach the gate in the intake wall.

400

Thackthwaite

ROAD TO LOW LORTON 2

There is room for three or four cars to park 200 yards north of Thackthwaite.

Thackthwaite, midway between Loweswater and Low Lorton on a quite by-road and peacefully carrying on its rural activities virtually undisturbed by tourists, is a good place to leave the road for the ascent of Fellbarrow; in fact, with the former route from Low Lorton impracticable, this is now the only approach from the east. The climb is simple and the views excellent if Watching Crag is visited.

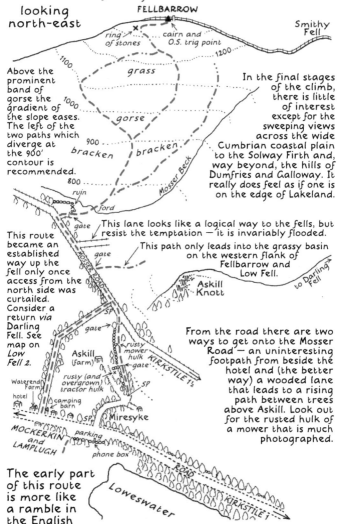

ASCENT FROM WATEREND
1000 feet of ascent : 2 miles

looking north-east

FELLBARROW

ring of stones × cairn and O.S. trig point

Smithy Fell

1100 · 1200

grass

1000

gorse

900

bracken · bracken

800

ruin · ford

gate

Mosser Beck

Above the prominent band of gorse the gradient of the slope eases. The left of the two paths which diverge at the 900' contour is recommended.

In the final stages of the climb, there is little of interest except for the sweeping views across the wide Cumbrian coastal plain to the Solway Firth and, way beyond, the hills of Dumfries and Galloway. It really does feel as if one is on the edge of Lakeland.

This lane looks like a logical way to the fells, but resist the temptation — it is invariably flooded.

gate

This path only leads into the grassy basin on the western flank of Fellbarrow and Low Fell.

Askill Knott

to Darling Fell

This route became an established way up the fell only once access from the north side was curtailed. Consider a return via Darling Fell. See map on Low Fell 2.

gate

rusty mower hulk

KIRKSTILE 1¼

Askill (farm)

SP · gate

rusty (and overgrown) tractor hulk

SP

Waterend Farm

hotel

camping barn

SP · Miresyke

MOCKERKIN and LAMPLUGH

parking

phone box

ROAD

KIRKSTILE 1

Loweswater

From the road there are two ways to get onto the Mosser Road — an uninteresting footpath from beside the hotel and (the better way) a wooded lane that leads to a rising path between trees above Askill. Look out for the rusted hulk of a mower that is much photographed.

The early part of this route is more like a ramble in the English countryside than a fell walk, and is delightful on a sunny summer's day. The latter stages, in comparison, are rather dull — although very easy going.

THE SUMMIT

HOPEGILL HEAD — WHITESIDE — EEL CRAG — GRASMOOR

Everything there is to see on the summit can be seen at a glance: a rounded swell of grass crossed by a fence (with stile), crowned with an Ordnance Survey column alongside which is a neat summit cairn. Note, 60 yards west, a collection of stones arranged in a ring. It has no special significance and no history. The pile of stones in the illustration is no longer there — they were most probably used to make the cairn.

DESCENTS: Reverse the routes of ascent or risk entanglement in fences.

The ring of stones near the summit is now overgrown

RIDGE ROUTE

To LOW FELL, 1360': 1½ miles : S
several depressions
400 feet of ascent
An easy walk towards beautiful scenery

An option is to follow the watershed, taking all the bumps (and fences) as they appear, but many fellwalkers appear to, at least, avoid Sourfoot Fell judging by the 'bypass' path. The going is easy on grass throughout. Lovely views unfold.

ONE MILE

FELLBARROW
stile
stile
1200
THACKTHWAITE
Smithy Fell
1200
Watching Crag
Sourfoot Fell
1300 gate
1200
VP
N
highest point on Low Fell
stile
LOW FELL

THE VIEW

As the diagram suggests, Fellbarrow stands on the fringe of the high country, and to north and west there is a wide and uninterrupted view over the coastal plain of Workington and district and across the Solway Firth to the Scottish hills, a scene predominantly rural but with some obvious evidences of urban development and industry (and many wind turbines). More of Lakeland is visible than the fell's low elevation of 1363' would lead one to expect. South-east the skyline is crowded with peaks (this view is better from the neighbouring Low Fell) and the best thing is the lofty ridge of the Hopegill Head range across the Vale of Lorton backed by Grasmoor.

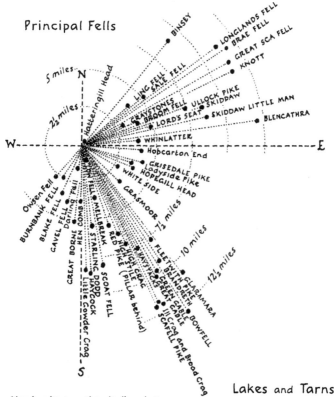

Principal Fells

Lakes and Tarns

Also in view on the skyline, but crowded out of the diagram, is ESK PIKE (just left of the top of Green Gable) and GREAT END (over Windy Gap between Green Gable, left, and Great Gable).

None, not even *Mockerkin Tarn*, which might be reasonably expected to show itself, west.

Fleetwith Pike 2126'

OS grid ref: NY206142

from Gatesgarth

• Buttermere

Gatesgarth

▲ DALE HEAD

FLEETWITH ▲
PIKE

Seatoller
•

Honister Pass

MILES

0   1   2   3

NATURAL FEATURES

Honister Crag is a landmark of renown, well known to Lakeland's visitors and as familiar to those who journey on wheels as to those who travel on foot. This precipice towers dramatically above the road between Borrowdale and Buttermere, a savage wall of rock and heather strewn with natural debris and spoil from the quarry workings high on the cliff, a place without beauty, a place to daunt the eye and creep the flesh. This huge barrier extends for two miles north-west from the top of Honister Pass, but becomes less intimidating as Gatesgarth is approached.

looking west

1 : *The summit*
2 : *Honister Crag*
3 : *Honister Pass*
4 : *Gatesgarthdale Beck*

The fell of which Honister Crag is so striking a part is Fleetwith, and its summit, overlooking Buttermere, is Fleetwith Pike, not so well known by name or shape as its illustrious subsidiary but nevertheless associated in the minds of many visitors with a conspicuous white memorial cross on its lower slopes. A smaller company of people, with better discrimination, relate the fell to a supremely beautiful view and a soaring ridge and a wild hollow rimmed by crags: the first is of the three lakes in the Buttermere valley, the second shoots into the sky like an arrow from the fields of Gatesgarth, and the third, Warnscale Bottom, is a natural amphitheatre of impressive proportions. These are the things that identify Fleetwith in the mind of the fellwalker.

looking south-east

1 : *The summit*
2 : *Honister Crag*
3 : *North-west ridge*
4 : *Gatesgarthdale Beck*
5 : *Warnscale Beck*
6 : *Warnscale Bottom*

The downward slope of the summit, away from and behind the cliffs of Honister, is gently inclined to the upland marsh of Dubs Bottom, beyond which a broad moor rises gradually to Great Gable, the dominating influence hereabouts, of which Fleetwith Pike may be described, geographically, as the northern terminus.

All the Fleetwith streams are headwaters of the River Cocker and flow north-west into Buttermere, the green colour of the water of the lake being attributed to the slate dust carried down by them from the quarries.

Fleetwith Pike 3

The Buttermere valley from the top of the north-west ridge

Honister Crag

MAP

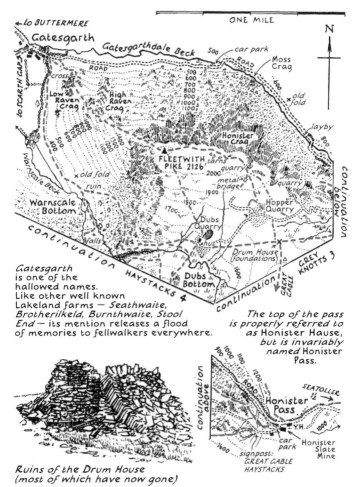

Gatesgarth is one of the hallowed names. Like other well known Lakeland farms — Seathwaite, Brotherilkeld, Burnthwaite, Stool End — its mention releases a flood of memories to fellwalkers everywhere.

The top of the pass is properly referred to as Honister Hause, but is invariably named Honister Pass.

Ruins of the Drum House (most of which have now gone)

The path between the quarry buildings on Honister Pass and Dubs Quarry is the straightest mile in Lakeland. Originally it was the permanent way for trucks conveying stone, the winding gear being accommodated in the Drum House at the highest point on the line. Since abandonment of the tramway the track of the rails has been adopted as a path (the rails have been removed, but some sleepers remain) with the blessing of the quarry management, who have signposted it for walkers.

ASCENT FROM HONISTER PASS
1000 feet of ascent : 1¾ miles

The tramway goes on beyond the Drum House, slightly descending to Dubs Quarry (disused) and is then continued by a distinct path down to Warnscale and Gatesgarth. This is a splendid alternative to the motor road for walkers bound from Borrowdale to Buttermere.

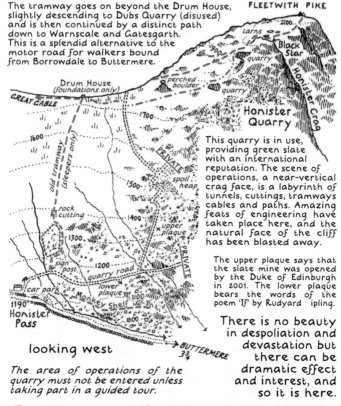

FLEETWITH PIKE

looking west

This quarry is in use, providing green slate with an international reputation. The scene of operations, a near-vertical crag face, is a labyrinth of tunnels, cuttings, tramways cables and paths. Amazing feats of engineering have taken place here, and the natural face of the cliff has been blasted away.

The upper plaque says that the slate mine was opened by the Duke of Edinburgh in 2001. The lower plaque bears the words of the poem 'If' by Rudyard Kipling.

There is no beauty in despoliation and devastation but there can be dramatic effect and interest, and so it is here.

The area of operations of the quarry must not be entered unless taking part in a guided tour.

The old tramway to the Drum House, long out of commission, has been adopted as a path and is in popular use. It leaves the quarry road beyond the second stream and is signposted to Great Gable and Haystacks. Farther along the quarry road a turning on the left follows the course of another abandoned tramway, but this is now unrecognisable as such. This is part of the public bridleway to Gatesgarth and may be followed across the shoulder of the fell to Dubs Quarry.

When opposite the Drum House, note a perched boulder on a low crag and pass to the right of this. Follow the edge of the crags, skirting two quarries, and join a higher path for the final easy half-mile to the summit cairn. The top of Honister Crag (Black Star) occurs just beyond the second of these two quarries. The ledges of Honister Crag are so rich in wild flowers they have become known as 'the hanging gardens of Honister'.

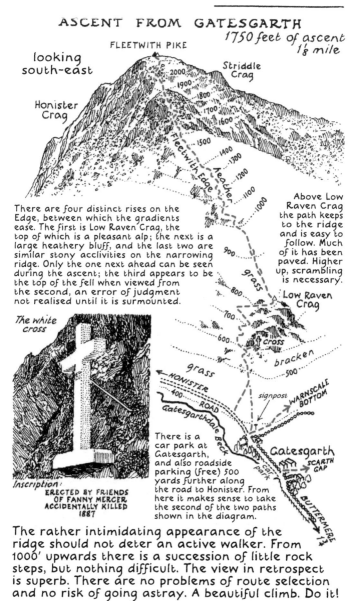

ASCENT FROM GATESGARTH

1750 feet of ascent
1¾ mile

FLEETWITH PIKE

looking
south-east

Striddle
Crag

Honister
Crag

Fleetwith Edge

There are four distinct rises on the Edge, between which the gradients ease. The first is Low Raven Crag, the top of which is a pleasant alp; the next is a large heathery bluff, and the last two are similar stony acclivities on the narrowing ridge. Only the one next ahead can be seen during the ascent; the third appears to be the top of the fell when viewed from the second, an error of judgment not realised until it is surmounted.

Above Low Raven Crag the path keeps to the ridge and is easy to follow. Much of it has been paved. Higher up, scrambling is necessary.

Low Raven Crag

The white cross

cross

bracken

grass

HONISTER
ROAD
Gatesgarthdale Beck

signpost

WARNSCALE
BOTTOM

Gatesgarth

SCARTH
GAP

BUTTERMERE 1¾

car park

Inscription:
ERECTED BY FRIENDS
OF FANNY MERCER
ACCIDENTALLY KILLED
1887

There is a car park at Gatesgarth, and also roadside parking (free) 500 yards further along the road to Honister. From here it makes sense to take the second of the two paths shown in the diagram.

The rather intimidating appearance of the ridge should not deter an active walker. From 1000' upwards there is a succession of little rock steps, but nothing difficult. The view in retrospect is superb. There are no problems of route selection and no risk of going astray. A beautiful climb. Do it!

THE SUMMIT

HIGH CRAG   HIGH STILE

RED PIKE

Standing by the cairn,
little is seen to suggest that
there is a fearful downfall only
a few score paces to the north, and the
craggy south-west declivities contributing
to Warnscale's barren and stony wilderness
are similarly unsuspected although quite close. Indeed the
environs are pleasant, with grass and heathery patches
stretching into the distance amongst rocky outcrops and a
fine company of greater hills all around. Eastwards along the
top there is little change in altitude to an uprising a third of
a mile away: this is the summit of Honister Crag.

DESCENTS: The north-west ridge is
a splendid way down to the road at
Gatesgarth, but it is necessary to
proceed slowly in several places and
to keep strictly to the track — there
is a reason for every zig-zag. The
route is safe in mist, but care is then
needed near the foot of the ridge,
where the track is faint and Low
Raven Crag forms a precipice.
Remember the cause of the white
cross and incline to the right (path
on grass) when the first rocks appear.
Under ice or snow the ridge is a
different proposition, and it may be
safer then to go down *via* Hopper
Quarry and the road to Honister or
the path to Gatesgarth.
For Honister Pass (top) the route of
ascent may be reversed, but in bad
weather wander south-east until the
unmissable quarry road is struck, and
follow it eastwards to the Pass.

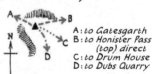

A : to Gatesgarth
B : to Honister Pass
(top) direct
C : to Drum House
D : to Dubs Quarry

RIDGE ROUTES

The neighbouring heights on the
same upland mass are Haystacks
and Grey Knotts, but connecting
ridges are absent, the journey to
either being across open country.
For Grey Knotts aim first for the
Drum House (which is in sight)
and for Haystacks aim first
for Dubs Quarry (which is not),
taking up the ascent from
there as indicated in the
chapters on those two fells.

THE VIEW

Most visitors to the cairn will consider the prospect along the Buttermere valley the best thing in view, and this is certainly remarkably fine, and exclusive to Fleetwith Pike (it is even better 100 yards down the north-west ridge).

Yet, predominantly, mountains occupy the scene. The Grasmoor fells, the High Stile and Dale Head groups, Great Gable and Pillar are all seen at close range, the latter two appearing as giants.

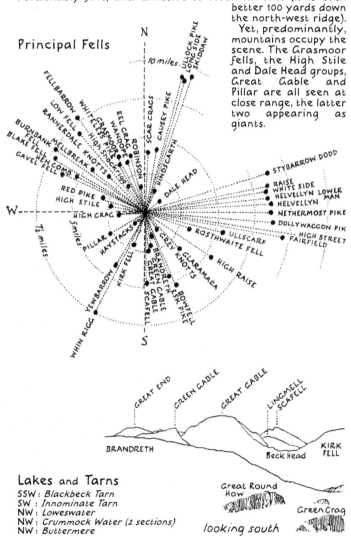

Principal Fells

Lakes and Tarns
SSW : *Blackbeck Tarn*
SW : *Innominate Tarn*
NW : *Loweswater*
NW : *Crummock Water (2 sections)*
NW : *Buttermere*

looking south

Gavel Fell

1726'

OS grid ref: NY117184

*from the terrace path
below Carling Knott*

Loweswater ●

▲ BLAKE FELL

▲ GAVEL FELL
● HEN
COMB

● Croasdale

MILES
0   1   2   3

High Nook Farm

NATURAL FEATURES

Gavel Fell is the central and second highest of the five Loweswater fells south of the lake, having Blake Fell on the west and Hen Comb on the east. It rises as a well defined ridge between Highnook Beck and Whiteoak Beck but becomes sprawling towards the summit, which is a wide grassy tableland of no particular interest and lacking a distinctive outline. Along the top is the Derwent-Ehen watershed; much of the rain that falls here, however, prefers to linger indefinitely in marshy ground and peaty pools by the side of the boundary fence, the remainder being taken down to the Loweswater valley in the two becks named above, or to Ennerdale by way of Croasdale Beck and Gill Beck. This latter watercourse rises near Floutern Tarn Pass, where there is a crossing between Ennerdale and Buttermere, and for two miles the path lies along the side of Banna Fell, a subsidiary of Gavel Fell south of the summit with some claim

looking west from the summit

to independence. On this side, too, is the curious little crest of Floutern Cop overlooking Floutern Tarn.

All the Loweswater fells have a foundation of slate and the smooth grass slopes characteristic of the type. Less characteristic is the tarn nestling in a hollow of Gavel Fell's north flank, for tarns more usually favour the harder volcanic rock. Since Gavel Fell also has a stake in Floutern Tarn it is doubly distinguished and twice blessed.

1 : The summit
2 : Ridge continuing to Blake Fell
3 : Subsidiary top
4 : Black Crag
5 : Whiteoak Beck
6 : Highnook Beck
7 : Highnook Tarn
8 : Loweswater
9 : Dub Beck
10: Park Beck
11: Banna Fell
12: Floutern Cop
13: Croasdale Beck
14: Gill Beck
15: Floutern Tarn
16: Ennerdale Water

looking south-west

looking north-east

Gavel Fell 3

MAP

Gavel Fell is the only one of the five Loweswater fells that does not reach down to Loweswater (lake) or its issuing stream. Conversely, however, Gavel Fell is the only one of the five Loweswater fells that comes down to the shore of Ennerdale Water. Its territory above Loweswater terminates at High Nook, where its boundary streams meet. The tarn north of Black Crag (surely the least known in the district) is given the convenient name of Highnook Tarn in this book, but is left nameless on maps of the Ordnance Survey.

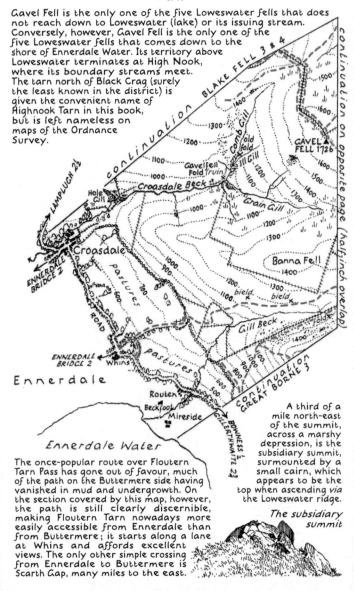

The once-popular route over Floutern Tarn Pass has gone out of favour, much of the path on the Buttermere side having vanished in mud and undergrowth. On the section covered by this map, however, the path is still clearly discernible, making Floutern Tarn nowadays more easily accessible from Ennerdale than from Buttermere; it starts along a lane at Whins and affords excellent views. The only other simple crossing from Ennerdale to Buttermere is Scarth Gap, many miles to the east.

A third of a mile north-east of the summit, across a marshy depression, is the subsidiary summit, surmounted by a small cairn, which appears to be the top when ascending via the Loweswater ridge.

The subsidiary summit

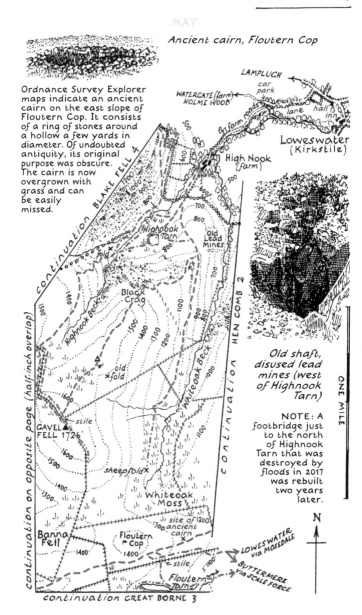

Ancient cairn, Floutern Cop

Ordnance Survey Explorer maps indicate an ancient cairn on the east slope of Floutern Cop. It consists of a ring of stones around a hollow a few yards in diameter. Of undoubted antiquity, its original purpose was obscure. The cairn is now overgrown with grass and can be easily missed.

Old shaft, disused lead mines (west of Highnook Tarn)

NOTE: A footbridge just to the north of Highnook Tarn that was destroyed by floods in 2017 was rebuilt two years later.

ONE MILE

N

ASCENT FROM LOWESWATER
1400 feet of ascent : 3 miles

looking south-west

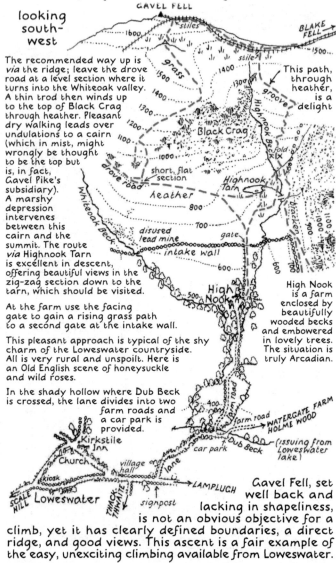

GAVEL FELL

BLAKE FELL

The recommended way up is *via* the ridge; leave the drove road at a level section where it turns into the Whiteoak valley. A thin trod then winds up to the top of Black Crag through heather. Pleasant dry walking leads over undulations to a cairn (which in mist, might wrongly be thought to be the top but is, in fact, Gavel Pike's subsidiary). A marshy depression intervenes between this cairn and the summit. The route *via* Highnook Tarn is excellent in descent, offering beautiful views in the zig-zag section down to the tarn, which should be visited.

This path, through heather, is a delight

At the farm use the facing gate to gain a rising grass path to a second gate at the intake wall.

This pleasant approach is typical of the shy charm of the Loweswater countryside. All is very rural and unspoilt. Here is an Old English scene of honeysuckle and wild roses.

In the shady hollow where Dub Beck is crossed, the lane divides into two farm roads and a car park is provided.

High Nook is a farm enclosed by beautifully wooded becks and embowered in lovely trees. The situation is truly Arcadian.

Kirkstile Inn
Church
kiosk
SCALE NILL
Loweswater
village hall
signpost
THACKTHWAITE
LAMPLUGH
car park
Dub Beck (issuing from Loweswater lake)
farm road
WATERGATE FARM
HOLME WOOD

Gavel Fell, set well back and lacking in shapeliness, is not an obvious objective for a climb, yet it has clearly defined boundaries, a direct ridge, and good views. This ascent is a fair example of the easy, unexciting climbing available from Loweswater.

THE SUMMIT

The summit is broad and gently undulating, but there is no difficulty in locating the highest point, which is decorated with a large cairn near a point where the fence is crossable. It is obvious that this is the result of much labour (for loose stones are at a premium on the all-grassy top) by an ardent member of the ancient company of Cairnbuilders Anonymous.

DESCENTS: For Croasdale head south towards Floutern Tarn and follow the bridleway to the right. For Loweswater go down east to the drove road near Whiteoak Beck, which leads pleasantly to High Nook.

THE VIEW

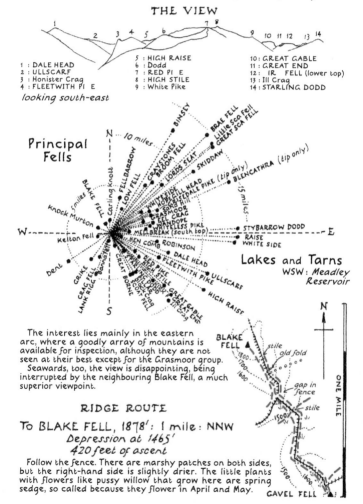

1 : DALE HEAD
2 : ULLSCARF
3 : Honister Crag
4 : FLEETWITH PIKE
5 : HIGH RAISE
6 : Dodd
7 : RED PIKE
8 : HIGH STILE
9 : White Pike
10: GREAT GABLE
11: GREAT END
12: KIRK FELL (lower top)
13: Ill Crag
14: STARLING DODD

looking south-east

Principal Fells

The interest lies mainly in the eastern arc, where a goodly array of mountains is available for inspection, although they are not seen at their best except for the Grasmoor group.

Seawards, too, the view is disappointing, being interrupted by the neighbouring Blake Fell, a much superior viewpoint.

Lakes and Tarns
WSW: Meadley Reservoir

RIDGE ROUTE

TO BLAKE FELL, 1878′: 1 mile: NNW
Depression at 1465′
420 feet of ascent

Follow the fence. There are marshy patches on both sides, but the right-hand side is slightly drier. The little plants with flowers like pussy willow that grow here are spring sedge, so called because they flower in April and May.

Great Borne

2019'

also known as Herdus

OS grid ref: NY124164

from Mosedale

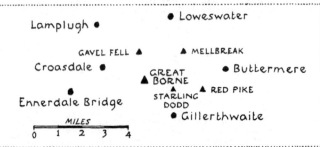

Lamplugh •

• Loweswater

GAVEL FELL ▲

▲ MELLBREAK

Croasdale •

GREAT
▲ BORNE

• Buttermere

▲ RED PIKE

Ennerdale Bridge •

▲ STARLING
DODD

• Gillerthwaite

MILES

0   1   2   3   4

NATURAL FEATURES

Great Borne is the name of the summit of the fell locally and correctly known as Herdus, an abbreviated version of the former name of Herdhouse. The fell is a familiar sight to West Cumbrians: from Ennerdale Water it rises as a massive buttress to the High Stile ridge. It is not prominent in views from other directions, however, and is not frequented by walkers.

Along its northern base, where it towers imposingly above the shy Floutern Tarn, there is a crossing of the high ground between Buttermere and Ennerdale: this is the once-popular but no-longer-popular Floutern Pass, the route having been partly submerged in the quagmire of Mosedale Head.

Facing Ennerdale the slope is steep and rough, having the name of Herdus Scaw, or Scar, and has little appeal, but on this side there is a gem of mountain architecture on a small scale in Bowness nott, which can be climbed by a short indirect path and commands a fine view of the valley but impresses most when the evening sun lights up its colourful rocks and screes. On the lower Ennerdale flanks the Forestry Commission's evergreens encroach rather patchily, there being areas of infertility.

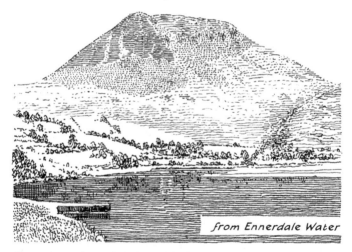

from Ennerdale Water

The viewpoint of this illustration is the lakeside path alongside the former Anglers Hotel, which was situated at the water's edge. The hotel was demolished because of a proposal by the South Cumberland Water Board to raise the level of the lake, but the plan never came to fruition and the demolition was unnecessary. If the level had been raised the pleasant lakeside path to Bowness would also have been sacrificed.

MAP

The left edge of the map has been curtailed because of shortage of space; however, the approach from Whins can be viewed in diagram form on *page 4* and map on *Gavel Fell 3*.

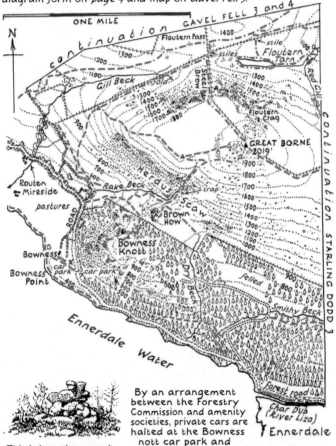

This is how the summit cairn on Bowness Knott looked back in the author's day, as illustrated in the first edition of Book Seven. There are now no trees surrounding the top rocks, although the current arrangement is rather less elaborate.

By an arrangement between the Forestry Commission and amenity societies, private cars are halted at the Bowness nott car park and prohibited from travelling further into Ennerdale by the forest road unless on business. Access to the mountains up the valley is 'not a business purpose'. The prohibition does not extend to pedestrians. It does mean that, unlike at other dale heads, access is less easy: consequently, Ennerdale is far quieter than valleys such as Great Langdale, Borrowdale and Buttermere.

ASCENT FROM ENNERDALE BRIDGE
1600 feet of ascent : 4 miles
ASCENT FROM BOWNESS CAR PARK
via THE WEST HERDUS RIDGE
1600 feet of ascent : 2½ miles

looking east

At Floutern Pass go through the gate, right over a stile, right over another stile, and left up the fence.

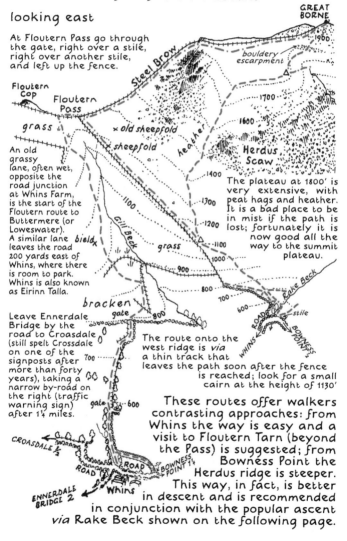

An old grassy lane, often wet, opposite the road junction at Whins Farm, is the start of the Floutern route to Buttermere (or Loweswater).
A similar lane leaves the road 200 yards east of Whins, where there is room to park. Whins is also known as Eirinn Talla.

Leave Ennerdale Bridge by the road to Croasdale (still spelt Crossdale on one of the signposts after more than forty years), taking a narrow by-road on the right (traffic warning sign) after 1¼ miles.

The plateau at 1800' is very extensive, with peat hags and heather. It is a bad place to be in mist if the path is lost; fortunately it is now good all the way to the summit plateau.

The route onto the west ridge is *via* a thin track that leaves the path soon after the fence is reached; look for a small cairn at the height of 1130'

These routes offer walkers contrasting approaches: from Whins the way is easy and a visit to Floutern Tarn (beyond the Pass) is suggested; from Bowness Point the Herdus ridge is steeper. This way, in fact, is better in descent and is recommended in conjunction with the popular ascent *via* Rake Beck shown on the following page.

ASCENT FROM BOWNESS CAR PARK
via RAKE BECK
1550 feet of ascent : 1½ miles

looking
east-
north-
east

Bowness Knott

From the public car park at Bowness this rugged subsidiary appears to be inaccessible, but easy access to the top can be found *via* the path through the bracken slope away to the left. At 900 feet the fence is crossed by a stile that comes into view as you leave the bracken.

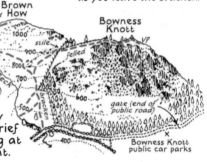

Herdus Scaw (a rough, arid and relentlessly steep area of crags, scree and boulders that straddles Rake Beck and, from the valley below, appears to be an impossible route to the summit)

This short walk is the most popular way of ascent. There is a brief section of scrambling at around the 1500' point.

. . . .

ASCENT FROM LOWESWATER

*1750 feet of ascent
4 miles (via Floutern Tarn)*

A route initially along the length of the wet Mosedale valley between Mellbreak, left, and Hen Comb, right. See the diagram, right, and *Hen Comb 2.*

ASCENT FROM BUTTERMERE

*1900 feet of ascent
4¼ miles (via Floutern Tarn)
4 miles (via Scale Beck and Gale Fell)*

This is even more of a cross-country route than that from Loweswater but at least Scale Force can be visited on the way. Please consult maps on *Red Pike 4* and *3, Starling Dodd 3, Hen Comb 2* and *Great Borne 3* — in that order.

Because of the boggy crossing of Mosedale Head these two approaches are not attractive and cannot be recommended. There are better things to do from Buttermere and Loweswater.

*from Loweswater:
the start of the
approach*

looking
south-
south-
west

THE SUMMIT

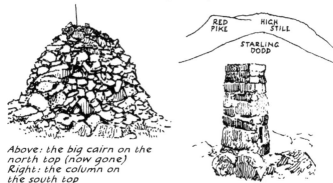

Above: the big cairn on the
north top (now gone)
Right: the column on
the south top

There are two separate tops, divided by a shallow 'valley',
which is followed by a fence. The cairn illustrated above — a
landmark for miles — was once on the north top, but its
stones have long been scattered. The south top, slightly
higher, is the one chosen by the Ordnance Survey for the site
of a triangulation column, and here too is a substantial
wind shelter; the open side faces east. The summit area is
rather unexpected on a first visit — newcomers to the fell
might reasonably anticipate a grassy top or one covered with
heather, but the field of rocks and boulders on a largely
green base is somewhat of a surprise.
  DESCENTS: Leave by way of the shallow valley between
the two tops or the easy path that starts from a cairn 350
yards west of the summit and leads to the Herdus ridge.
There should be no difficulty in clear weather, but if going
down direct to Floutern Pass descend *exactly in line* with the
fence seen crossing the pass below: it is easy to start down a
false ridge and be stopped by crags. *In mist*, make a wide
curve east to north
on easy ground,
descending into
Mosedale Head
beyond Red Gill.
The Rake Beck
path is difficult
to find unless you
came up this way;
aim south-west
towards a metal
post and then a
cairn where an
intermittent
path can be
found which
becomes clearer
as it descends
to the top of
the beck.

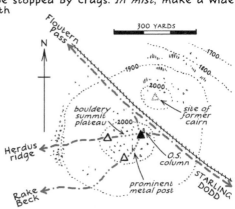

THE VIEW

Although not outstandingly good, the view has the merit of presenting old favourites from an unusual angle.

Principal Fells

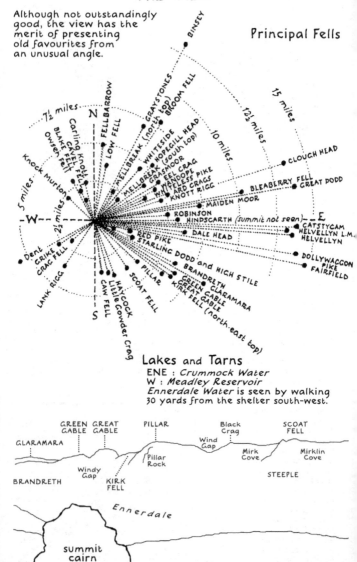

Lakes and Tarns
ENE : *Crummock Water*
W : *Meadley Reservoir*
Ennerdale Water is seen by walking 30 yards from the shelter south-west.

looking south-east

Floutern Tarn

Floutern Tarn (which according to learned authorities is pronounced *'flootern'*) is among the least visited of the named tarns high in the fells away from the valleys — and the answer to why this is most probably the case is given by the author in the Robinson chapter in BOOK SIX: THE NORTH WESTERN FELLS; describing the view, he writes: 'Robinson is one of the few fells that has the shy Floutern Tarn in its sights.'

looking south-east

Rarely seen from afar, it also is rarely visited now that the once well trodden crossing between Ennerdale and Buttermere *via* Floutern Pass has fallen out of favour. This is a shame, because the tarn is set in a rather delightful situation in a corrie overlooked by the broken cliffs of nearby Floutern Crag on Great Borne's northern flank. The tarn is unusual in shape, being long (around 340 yards) and narrow (75 yards at its widest point); only Alcock Tarn above Grasmere — which is about half its size — has a similar shape.

Near the outflow of the tarn is a collapsed entrance to a former iron mine. In the late 19th century, six years before it ceased operation, there was a proposal to link Red Gill Mine *via* a rail track to a branch line near Cogra Moss. Fortunately, this was abandoned because of the cost.

RIDGE ROUTE

To STARLING DODD, 2077'
1½ miles : ESE, E and ESE
Depression at 1625' : 480 feet of ascent

There are no difficulties even in mist once the path between the two summits of Great Borne is found (it is right beside the fence). This is a good fast walk over grass and heather across a wide depression. All gradients are easy.

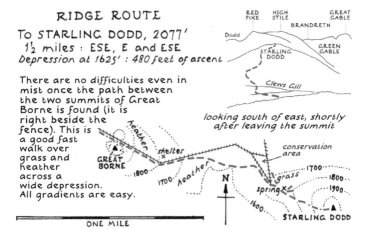

looking south of east, shortly after leaving the summit

ONE MILE

Great Gable

2949'

OS grid ref: NY211103

from Wast Water

NATURAL FEATURES

Great Gable is a favourite of all fellwalkers, and first favourite with many. Right from the start of one's apprenticeship in the hills, the name appeals magically. It is a good name for a mountain, strong, challenging, compelling, starkly descriptive, suggesting the pyramid associated with the shape of mountains since early childhood. People are attracted to it because of the name. There is satisfaction in having achieved the ascent and satisfaction in announcing the fact to others. The name has status, and confers status... Yes, the name is good, simple yet subtly clever. If Great Gable were known only as Wasdale Fell fewer persons would climb it.

continued

from Great End

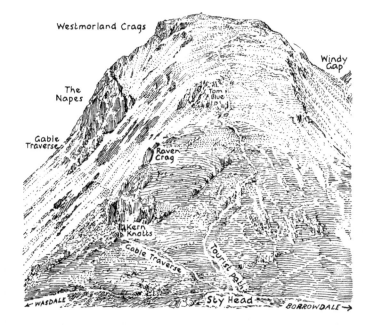

Westmorland Crags

Windy Gap

The Napes

Tom Blue

Gable Traverse

Raven Crag

Kern Knotts

Gable Traverse

Tourist Path

← WASDALE

Sty Head

BORROWDALE →

NATURAL FEATURES

continued

In appearance, too, Great Gable has the same appealing attributes. The name fits well. This mountain is strong yet not sturdy, masculine yet graceful. It is the undisputed overlord of the group of hills to which it belongs, and its superior height is emphasised tremendously by the deep gulf separating it from the Scafells and allowing an impressive view that reveals the whole of its half-mile altitude as an unremitting and unbroken pyramid: this is the aspect of the fell that earned the name. From east and west the slender tapering of the summit as seen from the south is not in evidence, the top appearing as a massive square-cut dome. From the north, where the build-up of height is more gradual, the skyline is a symmetrical arc.

continued

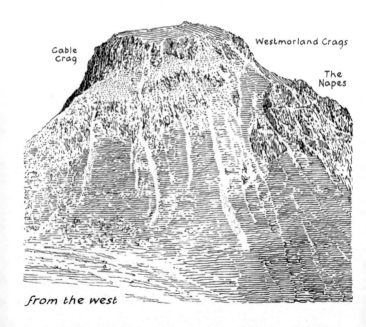

Gable Crag

Westmorland Crags

The Napes

from the west

NATURAL FEATURES

continued

Great Gable is a desert of stones. Vegetation is scanty, feeding few sheep. Petrified rivers of scree scar the southern slopes, from which stand out the bony ribs of the Napes ridges; the whole fell on this side is a sterile wilderness, dry and arid and dusty. The north face is a shadowed precipice, Gable Crag. Slopes to east and west are rough and stony. In some lights, especially in the afterglow of sunset, Great Gable is truly a beautiful mountain, but it is never a pretty one.

The view from the top is far-reaching, but not quite in balance because of the nearness of the Scafells, which, however, are seen magnificently. The aerial aspect of Wasdale is often described as the finest view in the district, a claim that more witnesses will accept than will dispute.

continued

from the north

NATURAL FEATURES

continued

The failing of Great Gable is that it holds few mysteries, all its wares being openly displayed. The explorer, the man who likes to look around corners and discover secrets and intimacies, may be disappointed, not on a first visit, which cannot fail to be interesting, but on subsequent occasions. There are no cavernous recesses, no hidden tarns, no combes, no hanging valleys, no waterfalls, no streams other than those forming the boundaries.

Yet walkers tread its familiar tracks again and again, almost as a ritual, and climbers queue to scale its familiar rocks. The truth is, Great Gable casts a spell. It starts as an honourable adversary and becomes a friend. The choice of its summit as a war memorial is testimony to the affection and respect felt for this grand old mountain.

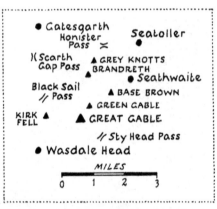

Dry Tarn

This is a tarn that Nature fashioned and forgot. It is invariably bone-dry, but it is recognisable by dark plants that can stand temporary immersion. Dry Tarn is almost unknown, and yet it is close to the main path up Great Gable from Sty Head, being situated at 2100 feet on a grass shelf.
This is Great Gable's only tarn.

MAP

Crags and other features are shown in greater detail, and named, on the larger-scale maps and diagrams appearing elsewhere in this chapter.

A curious thing about Great Gable is that, although of commanding height and so far overtopping the supporting fells as to seem to rise in isolation, it is really a huge cone resting on a high land mass. Great Gable overlooks many valleys and waters three, yet it has no roots in any except Wasdale; even here its foothold is ineffectual, being a mile beyond the true head of the valley in a side opening. On all other flanks, it is a mountain hoisted on the shoulders of supporters that have direct valley links and take over the function of principal buttresses.

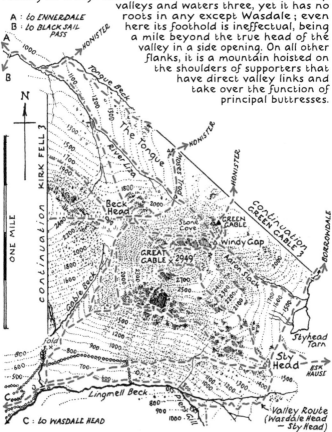

From the junction of Lingmell Beck and Piers Gill the summit is two-thirds of a mile north in lateral distance and the difference in altitude is 2,200 feet, a gradient of 1 in 1⅓. This is the longest slope in the district of such continuous and concentrated steepness.

Moses' Trod

In the years before the construction of, the gravitation tramways to convey slate from Dubs and the upper Honister quarries, when manhandled sledges were the only means of negotiating the steep slopes to the road below, it was more convenient to transport supplies destined for south Cumberland and the port of Ravenglass by packhorse directly across the high fells to Wasdale, a practice followed until the primitive highway through Honister Pass was improved for wheeled traffic. This high-level route, cleverly planned to avoid steep gradients and rough places, can still be traced almost entirely although it has had no commercial use since about 1850. Because of the past history and legend connected with it the early tourists in the district were well aware of its existence, and the path is kept in being today by discerning walkers who appreciate the easy contours, fast travel, glorious scenery and superb views.

xxxxx : line of original path, according to Ordnance maps.

N

SCALE OF MAP: Three inches = one mile

In places, the original line of the path is in doubt. The earlier Ordnance Survey maps indicated a wide divergence from the present footpath in the vicinity of Dubs Beck, but this may have been a rare error of cartography, for there are now no signs of it and it would have involved an obviously unnecessary descent and re-ascent. The route is now distinct on both sides of the Brandreth fence, and beyond to the west ridge of Great Gable above Beck Head, where the path starts the descent to Wasdale Head.

continued on next page

Unaccountably the greater part of the centuries-old Moses' Trod (i.e. from Brandreth almost to Wasdale Head) was not featured on O.S. maps until 1963!

Moses' Trod

Moses Rigg is a well established 18th century figure in local tradition, which describes him as a Honister quarryman who, after his day's work, illegally made whisky from the bog water on Fleetwith at his quarry hut, smuggling this potent produce to Wasdale with his pony-loads of slate. While historical evidence of his life is scant, many legends about him still survive in the district.

continued on previous page

GREEN GABLE

River Liza

2000

2100

WINDY GAP

Beck Head

tarns

Stone Cove

GREAT GABLE

Cable Crag

2000

1900

KIRK FELL

GREAT GABLE

2200

2400

2100

Cable Beck

1600

1500

1700

SOUTH TRAVERSE

Moses' Finger

1400

Gavel Neese

1300

1200

1100

1000

fold

900

800

700

600

STY HEAD

500

WASDALE HEAD

Lingmell Beck

SCALE OF MAP: Three inches = one mile

Also attributed to Moses was a stone hut ('the Smugglers' Retreat') hidden in the upper cliffs of Great Gable, the highest site ever used for building in England. In 1983, remains of such a hut were found, in the middle of which was a lump of wadd (graphite), one of the contraband items Moses was said to smuggle from Borrowdale over Wasdale and down to Ravenglass. By 1999 the ruins had succumbed to winter storms. Below this, in the lower part of the crag, is a rock climb known as 'Smuggler's Chimney', not climbed by Moses but so named after its first ascent in 1909 out of deference to his memory.

Moses' *Trod* (= a single-file track) is also referred to as Moses' *Sledgate* (= a way for sledges), but it seems unlikely that sledges could be used on such a journey.

Except for the boulders in Stone Cove, Moses' Trod is an exposed route without natural shelter, but a few yards from the path as it crosses the headwaters of Tongue Beck a half-hidden sheepfold gives good protection from the wind.

Moses' Finger (8 feet high)

The Gable Girdle
(linking the South Traverse and the North Traverse)

Originally a track for a privileged few (*i.e.* the early rock climbers) the South Traverse, rising across the flank of Great Gable from Sty Head, has now become a much-fancied way for lesser fry (*i.e.* modern hikers). The North Traverse passes immediately below the base of Gable Crag, and although still largely the province of climbers is equally accessible to walkers. The two traverses can be linked on the west by tracks over the scree above Beck Head; to the east the North Traverse is continued by the regular path down Aaron Slack to Sty Head. It is thus possible for walkers to make a full circuit of the mountain through interesting territory with fairly distinct tracks underfoot the whole way.

This is the finest mountain walk in the district that does not aim to reach a summit.

It is not level going: the route lies between 1500' and 2500', with many ups and downs. There are rough places to negotiate and nasty scree to cross and climb, but no dangers or difficulties. It is a doddle compared with, say, Jack's Rake or even Lord's Rake. Here one never has the feeling that the end is nigh.

1: To Summit
2: } To
3: } Wasdale Head
4: To Honister
5: } To Summit
6: }
7: To Ennerdale
8: To Green Gable
9: To Borrowdale

Beck Head

Windy Gap

Gable Crag

▲ Summit

HALF A MILE

Distance
Three miles
Time
Three hours

N

Styhead Tarn

EY TO LETTERS
and fuller detail
ON OPPOSITE PAGE

Sty Head

scramble

White Napes
Great Napes

Boots, not shoes, should be worn, and they must have soles with a firm grip, or there will be trouble on the boulders. There are few sections where the splendid views may be admired while walking: always stop to look around. The route is almost sheep-free, and dogs may be taken. So may small children, who are natural scramblers, and well behaved women — but nagging wives should be left to paddle their feet in Styhead Tarn. The journey demands and deserves concentration.

The Gable Girdle

The South Traverse leaves Sty Head near the stretcher box, by a stony path slanting left of the direct route up the mountain. At one time the start of the traverse was clearer than the direct route, and many walkers entered upon it in the belief that it would lead them to the top of the mountain. It won't, not without a lot of effort.

KEY TO THE MAP ON THE OPPOSITE PAGE

High Kern Knotts

Sty Head to Kern Knotts:

A : *Undulating path over grassy alps to bouldery depression and stony rise to the base of the crag.*

B : *Huge boulders to be negotiated along the base of the crag. (The best way to avoid these is to take the Wasdale path for a quarter of a mile and cut across from the top of the first scramble.)*

Kern Knotts to Great Hell Gate:

C : *Horizontal track over boulders leads to easier ground. A small hollow is skirted (boulders again) after which there is a short rise to a rocky corner.*

D : *A cave on the right usually provides a trickle of water. A short scramble up rocky slopes follows.*

E : *An easy rising path on scree.*

F : *The head of two gullies is crossed on rocky slabs.*

G : *Easy rising path to Great Hell Gate (a scree shoot). Tophet Wall in view ahead.*

Great Hell Gate to Little Hell Gate:

H : *A section of some confusion, to be resolved by referring to page 11.*

Little Hell Gate to Beck Head:

I : *The scree shoot of Little Hell Gate is crossed and a track picked up opposite: this trends downwards to the angle of the south and west faces. Here endeth the South Traverse. (A scree path goes down to Wasdale Head at this point.)*

J : *Around the grassy corner a thin trod contours the west slope and joins a track rising to Beck Head.*

Beck Head to Windy Gap:

The water hole (D)

: *Skirt the marshy ground ahead to a slanting scree path rising to the angle of the north and west faces. (Moses' Trod goes off to the left here by a small pool.)*

L : *The steep loose scree of the north-west ridge is climbed for 100 yds. Go between the two cairns illustrated on page 27 for the start of the path. Here commenceth the North Traverse. A track runs along the base of Gable Crag, descending to round the lowest buttress and then rising across scree to Windy Gap.*

Windy Gap to Sty Head:

M : *A popular tourist path descends Aaron Slack to Styhead Tarn, where, if women are found paddling their feet, a greeting may be unwise.*

The Great Napes

Rock climbers have played a much greater part than walkers in the selection of identifying names for natural features. All the names of the Great Napes are attributable to those who carried out the first exploration of the crags. Fortunately their choice was always appropriate, descriptive, and often inspired.

A : Sphinx Ridge
B : Arrowhead Ridge
C : Eagle's Nest Ridge
D : Needle Ridge
E : Tophet Bastion

F : Arrowhead Gully
G : Eagle's Nest Gully
H : Needle Gully
I : Dress Circle

J : rock island
 : Hell Gate Pillar

The Great Napes is a rocky excrescence high on the southern flank of Great Gable. Unlike most crags, which buttress and merge into the general slope of a mountain, the Great Napes rises like a castle above its surroundings so that there is not only a front wall of rock but side walls and a back wall too. This elevated mass is cut into by gullies to form four ridges, three of slender proportions and the fourth, and most easterly, broadly based and of substantial girth. The steepest rock occurs in the eastern part, the ground generally becoming more broken to the west. The front of the ridges, facing Wasdale, springs up almost vertically, but the gradient eases after the initial steepness to give grassy ledges in the higher reaches; the gullies, too, lose their sharp definition towards the top. Gradually the upper extremities of the Napes rise to a common apex, and here, at this point only, the Napes is undefended and a simple, grassy, and quite delightful ridge links with the main body of the fell. Here a climber may walk off the Napes and a walker may enter, with care, upon the easier upper heights. From the link ridge wide channels of scree pour down both sides of the Napes, thus defining the area clearly.

Across the westerly scree channel the rocky tower of the White Napes emphasises the angle of the south and west faces of the mountain but has no notable crags and little of interest.

The Great Napes

continued

The South Traverse reaches its highest elevation in the section of about 250 yards between the two Hell Gates and beneath the Great Napes, but it does not venture to the base of the wall of crags, preferring an easier passage 50–80 yards lower down the slope, where it maintains a horizontal course on the 2000' contour. The intervening ground is steep and rocky, especially in the vicinity of the Needle, and its exploration calls for care. The Needle is in full view from the Traverse but does not seem its usual self (as usually seen in illustrations) and on a dull day is not easily distinguished from its background of rock. To visit it, take the rising branch path from the Traverse into Needle Gully, and go up this to the base of the pinnacle; a scrambling track opposite climbs up to a ledge known as the Dress Circle, the traditional balcony for watching the ascent of the Needle. From this ledge a higher traverse can be made along the base of the crags, going below the Cat Rock into Little Hell Gate, but there is a tricky section initially and this is no walk for dogs, small children, well behaved women and the like.

Midway between the two Hell Gates Needle Gully and a branch gully, full of scree, cut across the South Traverse, which otherwise hereabouts is mainly a matter of rounding little buttresses. Another bifurcation leads off to Little Hell Gate at a higher level, near the Cat Rock. If proceeding west (*i.e.* from Sty Head) the two rising branch paths may be followed by mistake without realising that the Traverse has been left.

ROUTES TO THE SUMMIT FROM THE SOUTH TRAVERSE

It is no uncommon thing for walkers to venture upon the South Traverse, from Sty Head, in the fond hope that it will lead them in due course to the summit of Great Gable. This hope is dashed when the Napes is reached, for here the path becomes uncertain and the rocks are an impassable obstacle. The clue to further ascent is provided when it is remembered that 'gate' is a local word for 'way' and that the Napes is bounded by the two Hell Gates. Either of these will conduct the walker safely upwards, but both are chutes for loose stones and steep and arduous to climb. (In Little Hell Gate it is possible, with care, to scramble off the scree onto Sphinx Ridge at several points). The two routes converge at the little ridge below Westmorland Crags, which are rounded on the left by a good track that winds up to the summit plateau.

Napes Needle

definitely not the ←author!

The Cat Rock

The Sphinx Rock

This is the same pinnacle, shown here from the two angles that have given the two names

The Great Napes

left:
Tophet Bastion, as seen from the South Traverse on the approach from Sty Head.

The scree of Great Hell Gate runs down to the bottom left.

below:
looking steeply down on Tophet Bastion and the upper wall of the Napes, with the scree of Great Hell Gate running down to the left, from Westmorland Cairn.

The Great Napes

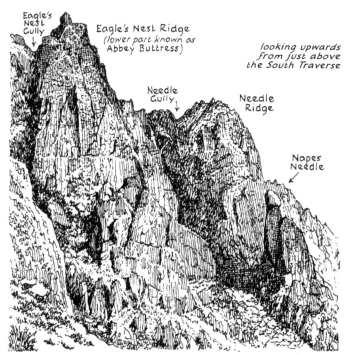

looking upwards
from just above
the South Traverse

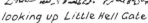

looking up Little Hell Gate

looking up Great Hell Gate

ASCENT FROM SEATHWAITE
2700 feet of ascent
2¾ miles

GREAT GABLE

Although this cannot rank as a direct ascent, Green Gable having to be surmounted first, it is to be preferred to the traditional route from Seathwaite *via* Stockley Bridge and Sty Head because of its greater interest, greater attractiveness, and *quietness*.

2800
2700
2600
Gable Crag
Windy Gap
GREEN GABLE
Stone Cove
HONISTER

Mitchell Cove

2300
2200
2100
2000
1900
1800
1700

At 1400' the view opens up ahead. To the right is Grey notts, across the hollow of Gillercomb, half-right is Brandreth, and straight in front is Green Gable.

looking south-west

2100
BASE BROWN
2000
grass
Gillercomb

1600
1500
1400

The big crag here is known to climbers as Gillercomb Buttress.

Hanging Stone

Above the wall, the path traverses the rough side of BASE BROWN; with little extra effort the journey may be improved by adding this to the day's summits. For details of the ascent, see *Base Brown 6.*

1300
1200
1100
Sourmilk Gill
gate
900
800

The hard work is all over once the intake wall is reached, with only one steepish section — from 2100' to 2300'. Beyond Windy Gap there is a rocky scramble up beside Gable Crag but this presents few problems.

This is the section of rocky scrambling that is mentioned below.

700

Seathwaite Slabs

600
500
stile
SEATOLLER

Leave Seathwaite under the arch of the farm buildings, but if travelling on foot from Seatoller, bypass the hamlet by taking the riverbank path at a gate alongside Seathwaite Bridge after three-quarters of a mile on the road. This is a charming approach that is easily overlooked.

lane
R. Derwent
parking
Seathwaite

The steep path up beside Sourmilk Gill is pitched for much of its length; note that the rounded stones are not easy to negotiate in descent. One section involves some scrambling and requires agility — as does the early stile, which is an awkward, angled ramp.

ASCENT FROM STY HEAD
1350 feet of ascent : 1 mile
(from Wasdale Head: 2750 feet : ¾ miles
from Seathwaite: 2600 feet : 3¼ miles)

GREAT GABLE

Westmorland Crags

looking north-west

GREEN GABLE

Windy Gap

MITCHELL GILL

Great Napes

grass   grass

2900
2800
2700
2600
2500
2400
2300
2200

rocky scramble

Tom Blue

Dry Tarn

2100
2000
1900

If approaching from Seathwaite consider, as an alternative, the Mitchell Gill route (quiet, pathless, no difficulties, on grass). See *Green Gable 6*

Raven Crag
Kern Knotts

grass   grass

old fold

1800
1700
1600

grass

Aaron Slack

grass

WASDALE HEAD

stretcher box

grass

1500

Sty Head

BORROWDALE

Styhead Tarn

The usual line of ascent is the original tourist path (also known as the Breast Route) from Sty Head. This path has been restructured with every stone wedged in place so that it cannot be dislodged, but in 1965 it was described as very bad underfoot (loose scree) on the steep rise by Tom Blue, where clumsy walkers had utterly ruined the path. This description inspired the following comments:

....

There are good walkers and bad walkers, and the difference between them has nothing to do with performances in mileage or speed. The difference lies in the way they put their feet down.

A good walker is a *tidy* walker. He moves quietly, places his feet where his eyes tell him to, on beaten tracks treads firmly, avoids loose stones on steep ground, disturbs nothing. He is, by habit, an improver of paths.

A bad walker is a *clumsy* walker. He moves noisily, disturbs the surface and even the foundations of paths by kicking up loose stones, tramples the verges until they disintegrate into debris. He is, by habit a maker of bad tracks and a spoiler of good ones.

A good walker's special joy is zig-zags, which he follows faithfully. A bad walker's special joy is in shortcutting and destroying zig-zags. *All fellwalking accidents are the result of clumsiness.*

....

The author lived to see the restructuring of the paths and to express his disapproval, but many who read his description of this path then and see it as it is now would agree that there has been an improvement. The route has been expertly repaired.

ASCENT FROM HONISTER PASS
1950 feet of ascent : 3 miles

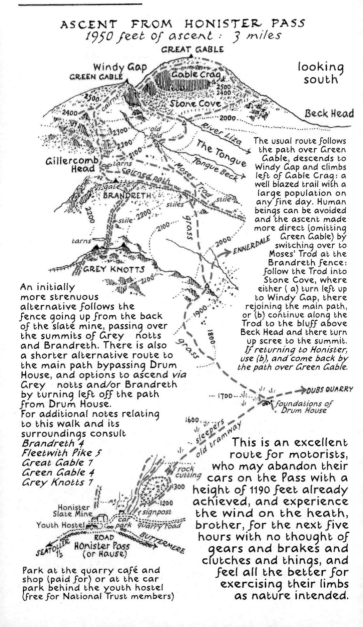

GREAT GABLE

Windy Gap
GREEN GABLE
Gable Crag

looking south

2500
2400
cairns
2400
2500
2400

Stone Cove

2000

Beck Head

2300
old fold
river Liza

2100
The Tongue

Gillercomb Head
tarns
cairned path
Tongue Beck

Moses' Trod

BRANDRETH

gate
2200
stiles
stile

stile 2200
grass
2100

The usual route follows the path over Green Gable, descends to Windy Gap and climbs left of Gable Crag: a well blazed trail with a large population on any fine day. Human beings can be avoided and the ascent made more direct (omitting Green Gable) by switching over to Moses' Trod at the Brandreth fence: follow the Trod into Stone Cove, where either (a) turn left up to Windy Gap, there rejoining the main path, or (b) continue along the Trod to the bluff above Beck Head and there turn up scree to the summit. If returning to Honister, use (b), and come back by the path over Green Gable.

tarns

GREY KNOTTS
2100

2000
➤ ENNERDALE

grass

1900

An initially more strenuous alternative follows the fence going up from the back of the slate mine, passing over the summits of Grey Knotts and Brandreth. There is also a shorter alternative route to the main path bypassing Drum House, and options to ascend via Grey Knotts and/or Brandreth by turning left off the path from Drum House.
For additional notes relating to this walk and its surroundings consult
Brandreth 4
Fleetwith Pike 5
Great Gable 7
Green Gable 4
Grey Knotts 7

1800

grass

1700
➤ DUBS QUARRY
foundations of Drum House

1600
sleepers
old tramway

Honister Slate Mine
Youth Hostel
car park
signpost
quarry road
rock cutting
1300
1200

SEATOLLER 1½
ROAD
Honister Pass
(or Hause)
BUTTERMERE

Park at the quarry café and shop (paid for) or at the car park behind the youth hostel (free for National Trust members)

This is an excellent route for motorists, who may abandon their cars on the Pass with a height of 1190 feet already achieved, and experience the wind on the heath, brother, for the next five hours with no thought of gears and brakes and clutches and things, and feel all the better for exercising their limbs as nature intended.

ASCENT FROM GATESGARTH
2800 feet of ascent : 4 miles

looking
south-
south-east

There are three distinct stages in this walk. The first is the rough climb out of Warnscale in a striking surround of crags, the second is the easy tramp across the Brandreth plateau, and finally the steep scramble on Great Gable. Alternative routes from the Brandreth west fence are described on the opposite page.

A cairn indicates the route of Moses' Trod where it leaves the Brandreth fence.

From the front Great Round How looks very imposing — from the back it's a green hummock.

A : Dubs Hut
B : Warnscale Bothy

Cross Warnscale Beck by the footbridge where Black Beck joins in, and use the old path on the far bank, an interesting route on a clear path over rough ground. Alternatively the beck may be crossed by the stepping stones below Dubs Hut. In addition there is a third crossing point between the two, but this is more difficult. The three routes unite below Little Round How.
Elsewhere, Warnscale Beck runs deep in an impassable and dangerous ravine.

There is sustained interest all the way, the scenery being unusually varied and the route ingenious and a delight to follow. This is the finest of the many approaches to Great Gable: a splendid mountain walk.

ASCENT FROM ENNERDALE
(BLACK SAIL YOUTH HOSTEL)
2000 feet of ascent : 2¼ miles

GREAT GABLE

Gable
Crag

GREEN GABLE
Windy
Gap

White
Napes

2800
2700
2600
2500
2400
2300

North Traverse

2300
2200

Stone
Cove

WASDALE
HEAD

KIRK
FELL

HONISTER — Moses Trod 2000

Beck Head

1900

1800

River Liza

1700

1600

1500

1400

1300
1200

1100

The Tongue

Tongue Beck

moraines

1000

Sail Beck

WASDALE
HEAD

Black Sail
Youth Hostel

ENNERDALE

SCARTH
GAP

With Great Gable in full view, directly in front all the way, there are no difficulties of route finding. Another advantage, which will appeal to hikers with tender hooves, is that, unlike most ways up Gable, grass may be kept underfoot to the last third of a mile. Only then, above Beck Head, are the characteristic slopes of shifting scree encountered. From here on, stones are unavoidable (the firmest footing is found at the angle of this north-west ridge) and the slope is relentlessly rough and steep to the edge of the summit plateau. Here, a short detour along the rim of Gable Crag is more rewarding in scenery and views than a direct course.

Estate, parish and local government boundaries in open fell country are invariably plotted in a series of straight lines — absolutely straight as if drawn on a map with a ruler, not in curves. The men whose job it was to indicate the boundaries on the ground by the erection of wire fences or stone walls were faithful to their instructions to proceed in dead straight lines, whatever the natural obstacles encountered. There was a good example of their fidelity at Beck Head, where a wire fence, now gone, originally passed through the middle of the two tarns in the depression.

looking south-east

Difficulties of access to the lonely head of Ennerdale for walkers based elsewhere make this ascent almost the exclusive preserve of those staying at Black Sail Youth Hostel (open to all but it is advisable to book well in advance).

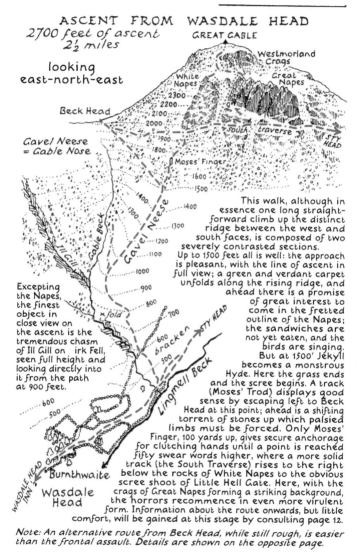

ASCENT FROM WASDALE HEAD
2700 feet of ascent
2½ miles

**looking
east-north-east**

GREAT GABLE

Westmorland
Crags

White
Napes

Great
Napes

2300
2200
2100
2000
1900
1800

Beck Head

SOUTH traverse

STY
HEAD

Gavel Neese
= Gable Nose

Moses' Finger

1600
1500

1400

1400

1300

1300

Gable Beck

Gavel Neese

1200

1100

1000

900

800

× fold

700

Ill Gill

STY HEAD

600

500

bracken

Lingmell Beck

Excepting
the Napes,
the finest
object in
close view on
the ascent is the
tremendous chasm
of Ill Gill on Kirk Fell,
seen full height and
looking directly into
it from the path
at 900 feet.

600

500

Burnthwaite

Wasdale
Head

WASDALE HEAD INN

This walk, although in essence one long straight-forward climb up the distinct ridge between the west and south faces, is composed of two severely contrasted sections.
Up to 1500 feet all is well: the approach is pleasant, with the line of ascent in full view; a green and verdant carpet unfolds along the rising ridge, and ahead there is a promise of great interest to come in the fretted outline of the Napes; the sandwiches are not yet eaten, and the birds are singing.
But at 1500' Jekyll becomes a monstrous Hyde. Here the grass ends and the scree begins. A track (Moses' Trod) displays good sense by escaping left to Beck Head at this point; ahead is a shifting torrent of stones up which palsied limbs must be forced. Only Moses' Finger, 100 yards up, gives secure anchorage for clutching hands until a point is reached fifty swear words higher, where a more solid track (the South Traverse) rises to the right below the rocks of White Napes to the obvious scree shoot of Little Hell Gate. Here, with the crags of Great Napes forming a striking background, the horrors recommence in even more virulent form. Information about the route onwards, but little comfort, will be gained at this stage by consulting page 12.

Note: An alternative route from Beck Head, while still rough, is easier than the frontal assault. Details are shown on the opposite page.

From Wasdale Head this route is clearly seen to be the most direct way to the summit. It is also the most strenuous. (Its conquest is more wisely announced at supper, *afterwards*, than at breakfast, *in advance*).

THE SUMMIT

There is no longer a post on the highest point.

Great Gable's summit is held in special respect by the older generation of fellwalkers, because here, set in the rocks that bore the top cairn, is the bronze War Memorial tablet of the Fell and Rock Climbing Club, dedicated in 1924, and ever since the inspiring scene of an annual Remembrance Service in November; it was replaced with an updated replica in 2013. It is a fitting place to pay homage to men who once loved to walk on these hills and gave their lives defending the right of others to enjoy the same happy freedom, for the ultimate crest of Gable is truly characteristic of the best of mountain Lakeland: a rugged crown of rock and boulders and stones in chaotic profusion, a desert without life, a harsh and desolate peak thrust high in the sky above the profound depths all around.

Gable, tough and strong all through its height, has here made a final gesture by providing an outcrop of rock even in its last inches, so that one must climb to reach the highest point. Sometimes there is a cairn, sometimes not, despite an entreaty by the author that no man tear it asunder lest a thousand curses accompany his guilty flight. On three sides the slopes fall away immediately, but to the north there extends a small plateau, with a little vegetation, before the summit collapses in the sheer plunge of Gable Crag. The rim of this precipice, and also the top of Westmorland Crags to the south, should be visited for their superlative views.

There are few days in the year when no visitors arrive on the summit. Snow and ice and severe gales may defy those who aspire to reach it in winter, but in the summer months there is a constant parade of perspiring pedestrians across the top from early morning to late evening.

To many fellwalkers this untidy bit of ground is Mecca.

continued

THE SUMMIT

continued

DESCENTS: Except for the improved path to Sty Head, all ways off the summit are paved with loose stones and continue so for most of the descent. Allied to roughness is steepness, particularly on the Wasdale side, and care is needed to avoid involuntary slips. In places, where scree runners have bared the underlying ground, surfaces are slippery and unpleasant. Never descend Gable in a mad rush!

In fine weather there should be no trouble in distinguishing the various cairned routes; in mist their direction is identified by the memorial tablet, which faces north overlooking the path to Windy Gap. Not all cairns can be relied upon; some are not route markers but indicators of viewpoints. Generally, however, the principal traffic routes are well blazed by boots.

In bad conditions the safest line is down the breast of the mountain to Sty Head. Care is needed in locating the descent to Beck Head, which keeps closely to the angle of the north and west faces and does not follow any of the inviting scree runs on the west side, which end in fields of boulders. Caution is also advised in attempting direct descents of the Wasdale face if the topography of the Napes is not already familiar.

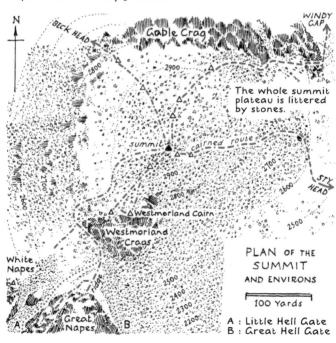

N

BECK HEAD

WINDY GAP

Gable Crag

2800

2900

The whole summit plateau is littered by stones.

2700

summit

cairned route

2900

2100

2800

STY HEAD

2600

2500

△Westmorland Cairn

Westmorland Crags

White Napes

2500

2400

2300

2200

A   Great   B
Napes

PLAN OF THE
SUMMIT
AND ENVIRONS

100 Yards

A : Little Hell Gate
B : Great Hell Gate

Great Gable 23

THE VIEW
(with distances in miles)

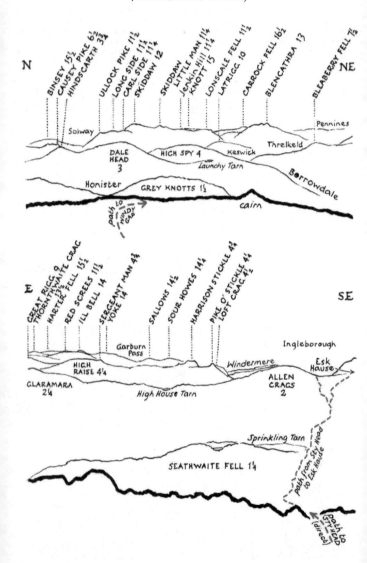

THE VIEW

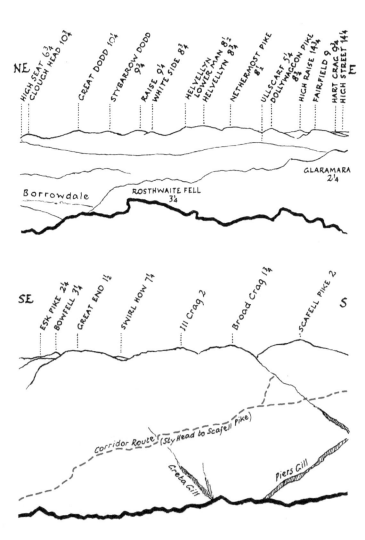

The thick line marks the visible boundaries
of the summit from the cairn

THE VIEW

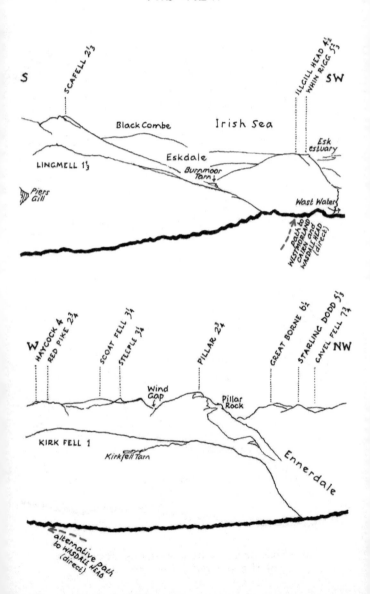

S

SCAFELL 2½

Black Combe

Irish Sea

ILLGILL HEAD 4½
WHIN RIGG 5½

SW

LINGMELL 1⅓

Eskdale

Esk estuary

Burnmoor Tarn ↓

Piers Gill

West Water

Path to WESTMORLAND CAIRN and NASDALE HEAD (direct)

W

HAYCOCK 4
RED PIKE 2¾

SCOAT FELL 3¼
STEEPLE 3¼

PILLAR 2¾

GREAT BORNE 6½
STARLING DODD 5½
GAVEL FELL 7¾

NW

Wind Gap ↓

Pillar Rock

KIRK FELL 1

Kirkfell Tarn

Ennerdale

alternative path to WASDALE HEAD (direct)

THE VIEW

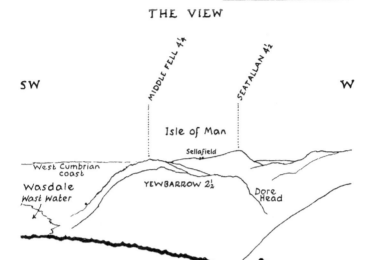

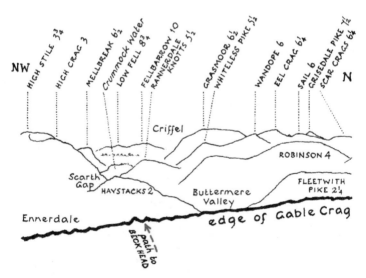

RIDGE ROUTES

To GREEN GABLE, 2628': NNE, then E and NNE : ½ mile
Depression (Windy Gap) at 2460'
150 feet of ascent

Rough and stony all the way.
The best that can be said for the path
is that it is clearly defined throughout,
which is as well, there being unseen
precipices in the vicinity. One section,
where Gable Crag is rounded to reach
Windy Gap, is particularly objectionable and needs care on
smooth rocky steps, particularly when wet or under ice.

To KIRK FELL, 2630': NW, then W and SW : 1½ miles
Depression (Beck Head) at 2040'   700 feet of ascent

A passing from the sublime to the less sublime, better done the other way.
Pick a way carefully down the north-west ridge, avoiding
false trails that lead only to boulder slopes and keeping
generally near the angle of the ridge, where the footing is
firmest. When a line of fence posts is joined, the remainder of
the route is assured, the posts leading across the depression
of Beck Head, up the steep facing slope of Rib End, and
visiting first the lower and then the top summit of Kirk Fell
across a wide grassy plateau.

A place to remember.......

Some quite ordinary patches of fellside have
extraordinary significance when they indicate
important route junctions occurring in rough
terrain and not clearly defined by paths
on the ground. The best example is the
upper exit of Lord's Rake on Scafell,
and there are many others.

*Illustrated here is
the place where the
North Traverse leaves
the north-west ridge
to cross below Gable
Crag to Windy Gap.*

*Pass between the two cairns
and the track comes into view*

Westmorland Cairn

Erected in 1876 by two brothers of the name of Westmorland to mark what they considered to be the finest mountain viewpoint in the district, this soundly built and tidy cairn is well known, to climbers and walkers alike, and has always been respected. The cairn has maintained its original form throughout the years quite remarkably: apart from visitors who like to add a pebble, it has suffered neither from the weather nor from human despoilers. It stands on the extreme brink of the south face, above steep crags, and overlooks Wasdale. Rocky platforms around make the place ideal for a halt after climbing Great Gable. The cairn is not in sight from the summit but is soon reached by walking 150 yards across the stony top in the direction of Wast Water.

Green Gable

2628'

OS grid ref: NY215107

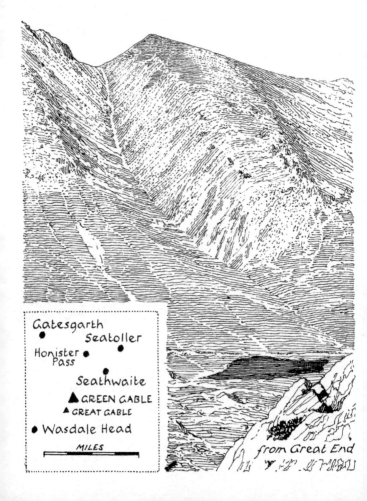

Gatesgarth
Seatoller
Honister Pass
Seathwaite
▲ GREEN GABLE
▲ GREAT GABLE
Wasdale Head

MILES

from Great End

NATURAL FEATURES

Several thousand people reach the summit cairn of Green Gable every year, yet it is probably true to say that no visitor to Lakeland ever announced at breakfast that this fell was his day's objective; and, if he did, his listeners would assume a slip of the tongue: of course he must mean Great Gable. The two Gables are joined like Siamese twins, but they are not likenesses of each other. Great Gable is the mighty mountain that every walker wants to climb; Green Gable is a stepping stone to it but otherwise of no account. All eyes are fixed on Great Gable; Green Gable is merely something met en route. So think most folk who pass from one to the other.

But Green Gable is not at all insignificant. At 2628' its altitude, by Lakeland standards, is considerable. A sharp peaked summit, more delicately wrought than Great Gable's, adds distinction. Rock climbers' crags adorn its western fringe. Important paths reach it on all sides. Unsought though the top may be, nevertheless it is much used and well known through the accident of its position. There are two main slopes, one going down to Styhead Gill, the other gaining a slender footing in Ennerdale.

It is a crowning misfortune for Green Gable, however, that the volcanic upheaval ages ago stopped upheaving at a moment when this fell was in a position completely subservient to a massive neighbour, and so fashioned the summit that it is forever destined to look up into the pillared crags of Great Gable as a suppliant before a temple. It is because of the inferiority induced by Big Brother that Green Gable cannot ever expect to be recognised as a fine mountain in its own right.

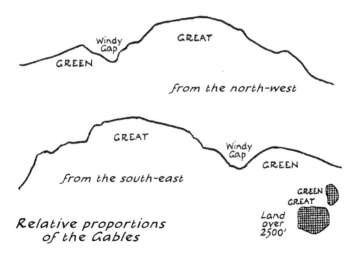

from the north-west

from the south-east

Relative proportions of the Gables

Green Gable 3

MAP

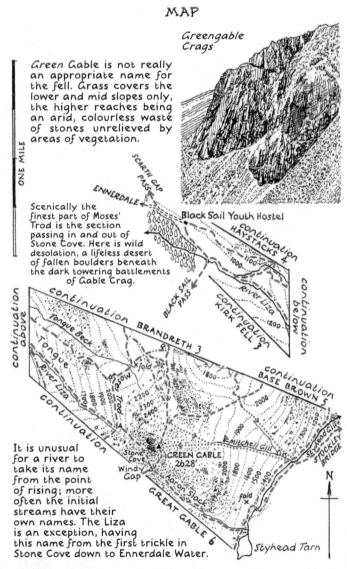

Greengable Crags

Green Gable is not really an appropriate name for the fell. Grass covers the lower and mid slopes only, the higher reaches being an arid, colourless waste of stones unrelieved by areas of vegetation.

ONE MILE

SCARTH GAP PASS

ENNERDALE ←

Black Sail Youth Hostel

continuation HAYSTACKS 4

continuation below

Scenically the finest part of Moses' Trod is the section passing in and out of Stone Cove. Here is wild desolation, a lifeless desert of fallen boulders beneath the dark towering battlements of Gable Crag.

BLACK SAIL PASS

River Liza

continuation KIRK FELL 3

continuation above

continuation BRANDRETH 3

Tongue Beck

Tongue

Moses' Trod

River Liza

continuation

continuation BASE BROWN 5

Mitchell Gill

STOCKLEY BRIDGE

Stone Cove

GREEN GABLE 2628'

Windy Gap

Aaron Slack

GREAT GABLE 6

N

It is unusual for a river to take its name from the point of rising; more often the initial streams have their own names. The Liza is an exception, having this name from the first trickle in Stone Cove down to Ennerdale Water.

Styhead Tarn

For more information about the pathless route north-west from the confluence of Styhead Gill and Mitchell Gill see Base Brown 5.

ASCENT FROM HONISTER PASS
1550 feet of ascent : 2½ miles

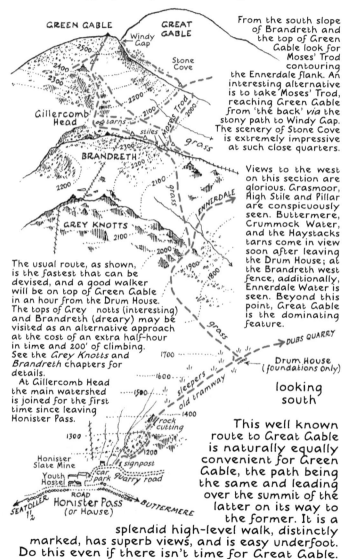

From the south slope of Brandreth and the top of Green Gable look for Moses' Trod contouring the Ennerdale flank. An interesting alternative is to take Moses' Trod, reaching Green Gable from 'the back' via the stony path to Windy Gap. The scenery of Stone Cove is extremely impressive at such close quarters.

Views to the west on this section are glorious. Grasmoor, High Stile and Pillar are conspicuously seen. Buttermere, Crummock Water, and the Haystacks tarns come in view soon after leaving the Drum House; at the Brandreth west fence, additionally, Ennerdale Water is seen. Beyond this point, Great Gable is the dominating feature.

The usual route, as shown, is the fastest that can be devised, and a good walker will be on top of Green Gable in an hour from the Drum House. The tops of Grey Knotts (interesting) and Brandreth (dreary) may be visited as an alternative approach at the cost of an extra half-hour in time and 200' of climbing. See the *Grey Knotts* and *Brandreth* chapters for details.

At Gillercomb Head the main watershed is joined for the first time since leaving Honister Pass.

looking south

This well known route to Great Gable is naturally equally convenient for Green Gable, the path being the same and leading over the summit of the latter on its way to the former. It is a splendid high-level walk, distinctly marked, has superb views, and is easy underfoot. Do this even if there isn't time for Great Gable.

ASCENT FROM SEATHWAITE
2250 feet of ascent : 2¼ miles

looking south-west

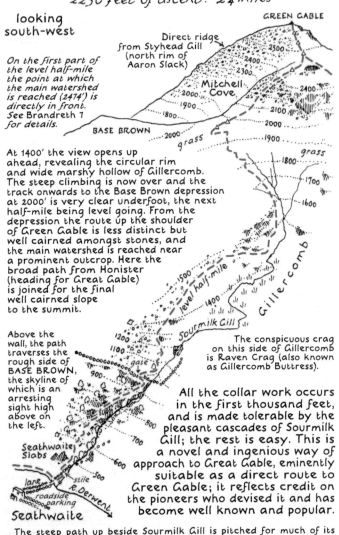

GREEN GABLE

Direct ridge from Styhead Gill (north rim of Aaron Slack)

Mitchell Cove

BASE BROWN

grass

grass

Gillercomb

Sourmilk Gill

gate

Seathwaite Slabs

lane
roadside parking
stile
R. Derwent

Seathwaite

On the first part of the level half-mile the point at which the main watershed is reached (2474') is directly in front. See Brandreth 7 for details.

At 1400' the view opens up ahead, revealing the circular rim and wide marshy hollow of Gillercomb. The steep climbing is now over and the track onwards to the Base Brown depression at 2000' is very clear underfoot, the next half-mile being level going. From the depression the route up the shoulder of Green Gable is less distinct but well cairned amongst stones, and the main watershed is reached near a prominent outcrop. Here the broad path from Honister (heading for Great Gable) is joined for the final well cairned slope to the summit.

Above the wall, the path traverses the rough side of BASE BROWN, the skyline of which is an arresting sight high above on the left.

The conspicuous crag on this side of Gillercomb is Raven Crag (also known as Gillercomb Buttress).

All the collar work occurs in the first thousand feet, and is made tolerable by the pleasant cascades of Sourmilk Gill; the rest is easy. This is a novel and ingenious way of approach to Great Gable, eminently suitable as a direct route to Green Gable; it reflects credit on the pioneers who devised it and has become well known and popular.

The steep path up beside Sourmilk Gill is pitched for much of its length; note that the rounded stones are not easy to negotiate in descent. One section involves some scrambling and requires agility — as does the early stile, which is an awkward, angled ramp.

ASCENT FROM STYHEAD GILL
1200 feet of ascent : ¾ mile

looking north-west

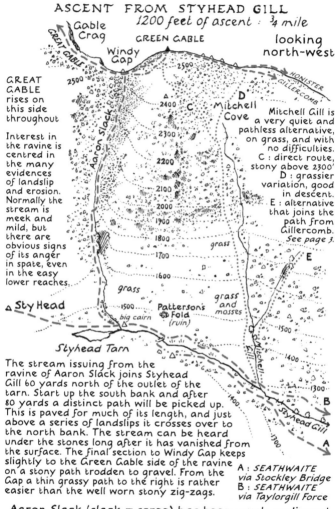

GREAT GABLE rises on this side throughout

Interest in the ravine is centred in the many evidences of landslip and erosion. Normally the stream is meek and mild, but there are obvious signs of its anger in spate, even in the easy lower reaches.

Mitchell Gill is a very quiet and pathless alternative, on grass, and with no difficulties. C: direct route, stony above 2300' D: grassier variation, good in descent. E: alternative that joins the path from Gillercomb. See page 3.

The stream issuing from the ravine of Aaron Slack joins Styhead Gill 60 yards north of the outlet of the tarn. Start up the south bank and after 80 yards a distinct path will be picked up. This is paved for much of its length, and just above a series of landslips it crosses over to the north bank. The stream can be heard under the stones long after it has vanished from the surface. The final section to Windy Gap keeps slightly to the Green Gable side of the ravine on a stony path trodden to gravel. From the Gap a thin grassy path to the right is rather easier than the well worn stony zig-zags.

A: SEATHWAITE via Stockley Bridge
B: SEATHWAITE via Taylorgill Force

Aaron Slack (slack = scree) has been much maligned, even in verse, as an abomination of stones, but there are worse places (for instance, Stone Cove on the other side of Windy Gap). The route is enclosed and without views, but in its favour it may be fairly described as direct, sheltered, foolproof in mist, and of a steady (not steep) gradient.

ASCENT FROM ENNERDALE
(BLACK SAIL YOUTH HOSTEL)
1650 feet of ascent : 2¼ miles

looking
south-east

GREEN GABLE   Windy   Gable
Gap   Crag

Gillercomb
Head

2400
2300
2200
2100

Stone
Cove

HONISTER   grass   fold

HONISTER 2000   Moses Trod   A   BECK HEAD

GREAT GABLE

1900
1800
1700
1600
1500
1400
1300
1200
1100

falls

Tongue Beck   grass   The Tongue   River Liza

HONISTER PASS

Sail Beck   WASDALE
fell

1000

moraines
1000

River Liza

Black Sail
Youth Hostel

Arrival at Moses' Trod marks a sharp change from one phase of the climb to another. Up to this point the route has followed an easy grass incline; beyond, all vegetation ceases in a concentration of stones so thickly littering the ground that they lay yards deep. Progress to Windy Gap would be extremely arduous without the help of a beaten track that keeps slightly to the Green Gable side of the hollow, where the debris is rather more tractable than the blocks and boulders fallen from Gable Crag. This track is found by going straight up from the cairn on Moses' Trod 15 yards left of the infant Liza. When Windy Gap is reached — after much slipping and sliding — turn left up a scree path to the summit, or take the easier grassy alternative to the right, and there find a position (a few yards west of the cairn) where a striking downwards view is obtained of the track in Stone Cove just ascended.

A pleasant variation to the direct way alongside the Liza is provided by the grassy crest of the Tongue, which meets Moses' Trod at an outcrop. Here turn right along the Trod to join the direct way, or cross to Gillercomb Head and finish by the path from Honister Pass.

The undoubted highlight of this walk is the close-up view of Great Gable's northern precipice, Gable Crag, dramatically seen from the devastation of Stone Cove.

THE SUMMIT

It is a pity that most visitors to the summit are in a hurry to get off it, for the narrow strip of rough ground between the cairn and the rim of the western crags is a fine perch to study the massive architecture of Gable Crag and the deep pit of stones below it: this is a tremendous scene. A wide gravelly path crosses the top, which is uncomplicated, making a sharp angle at the cairn. There are windshelters.

DESCENTS: Honister Pass can be reached at a fast exhilarating pace by the good cairned path northwards *via* the Drum House (where turn left for Buttermere, right for Borrowdale). The Gillercomb route to Seathwaite is the best direct way down to Borrowdale in clear weather, although the final steep section needs care. The Windy Gap and Aaron Slack descent for Sty Head is not recommended as a way down except in mist, when it is very safe; this route is the best for Wasdale, however. For Ennerdale it is palpably necessary first to go down to Windy Gap to avoid crags, there turning to the right on a scree path.

RIDGE ROUTES

TO BRANDRETH, 2344´ : NE, then N : 1 mile
Depression (Gillercomb Head) at 2160´
200 feet of ascent

On the descent from Green Gable it is easy to take the Seathwaite path by mistake, and it is necessary to bear left to stay on the ridge.

TO GREAT GABLE, 2949´
SE, then SW : ½ mile
Depression (Windy Gap) at 2460´
500 feet of ascent

Follow everybody else. Rocks soon after Windy Gap entail scrambling.

HALF A MILE

THE VIEW

It might almost be thought that the summit had been expressly constructed for observing the northern crags of Great Gable, so convenient a platform is it for this purpose. The scene calls for first attention; wander west a few yards from the cairn (not too many!) to appreciate the full proportions of the cliff above Stone Cove. Elsewhere the view is very comprehensive, little of the district being hidden by Great Gable. The best picture, a beautiful one, is north-west, where four sheets of water nestle in the folds of rugged and colourful mountains: note how Blackbeck Tarn appears to spill into Buttermere, although in fact there is an unseen mile between.

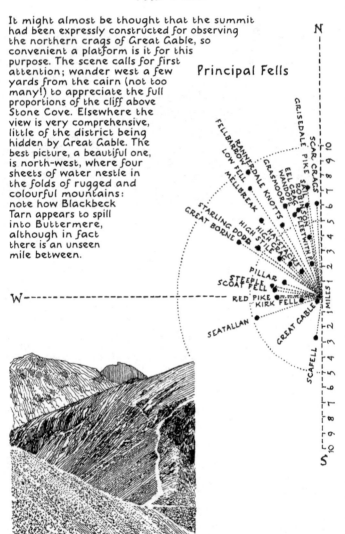

Principal Fells

Windy Gap (bottom right), showing the start of the path therefrom to the top of Great Gable, and Scafell Pike (left) and Scafell in the background, from the summit of Green Gable

THE VIEW

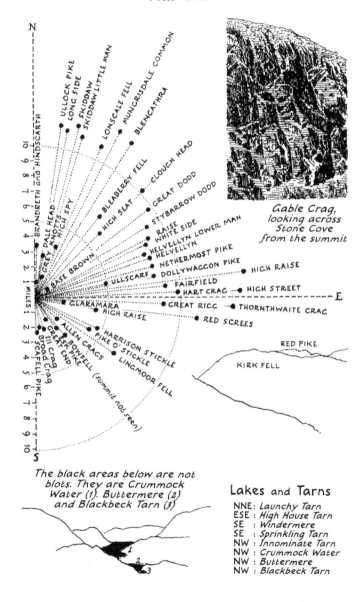

*Gable Crag,
looking across
Stone Cove
from the summit*

*The black areas below are not
blots. They are Crummock
Water (1), Buttermere (2)
and Blackbeck Tarn (3)*

Lakes and Tarns

NNE : *Launchy Tarn*
ESE : *High House Tarn*
SE : *Windermere*
SE : *Sprinkling Tarn*
NW : *Innominate Tarn*
NW : *Crummock Water*
NW : *Buttermere*
NW : *Blackbeck Tarn*

Grey Knotts

2287'

OS grid ref: NY217126

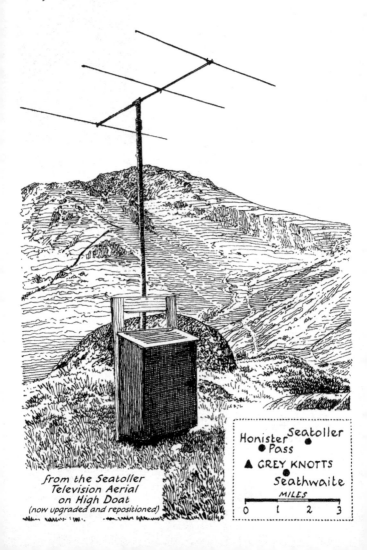

*from the Seatoller
Television Aerial
on High Doat*
(now upgraded and repositioned)

Honister Seatoller
● Pass ●

▲ GREY KNOTTS

Seathwaite
●

MILES

0   1   2   3

NATURAL FEATURES

Grey Knotts has an interesting situation, rising as a long narrow wedge between upper Borrowdale and an entrant valley half-concealed on the west that carries the motor road over Honister to Buttermere. So thin is this wedge of high ground that, at the dreary and desolate summit of Honister Pass, sylvan Seathwaite in Borrowdale is still only a straight mile distant.

The ridge of Grey Knotts starts to rise at once, quite steeply, from the woods of Seatoller, levels out at mid height, and finally climbs roughly amongst crags to a broad summit decorated with rock turrets and tarns. The Honister side of the ridge is plainly unattractive, the Borrowdale side pleasant and interesting, having several notable features: chiefly, high up, the massive buttress of Raven Crag and the scarped hanging valley of Gillercomb. Unique in Lakeland, a once-famous wad or plumbago mine pierces deeply into the Borrowdale flank above Seathwaite. Here, too, is yet another Sourmilk Gill, a leaping white cascade, and not far, away is the location of the celebrated 'fraternal four', the Borrowdale Yews written of by Wordsworth — 'joined in one solemn and capacious grove' — and named on maps of Lakeland. One of them was blown down in 1866 and another was damaged during storms in 2005.

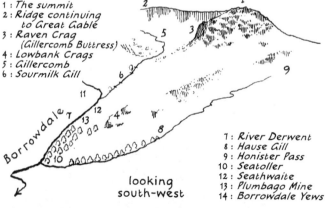

1 : The summit
2 : Ridge continuing to Great Gable
3 : Raven Crag (Gillercomb Buttress)
4 : Lowbank Crags
5 : Gillercomb
6 : Sourmilk Gill

7 : River Derwent
8 : Hause Gill
9 : Honister Pass
10 : Seatoller
12 : Seathwaite
13 : Plumbago Mine
14 : Borrowdale Yews

looking south-west

Grey Knotts is geographically the first stepping stone to Great Gable from the north (although not commonly used as such), the connection being a high ridge that runs over the two intermediate summits of Brandreth and Green Gable. The western slope descends easily to halt in the marshes of Dubs Bottom and is redeemed from dreariness only by the fine views it commands.

MAP

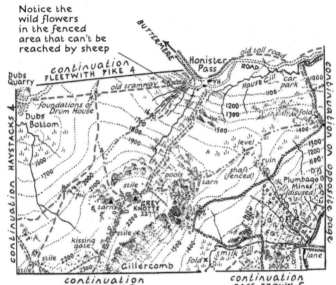

Notice the wild flowers in the fenced area that can't be reached by sheep

BUTTERMERE

continuation
FLEETWITH PIKE 4

Dubs Quarry

old tramway

Honister Pass

YH

old toll road

ROAD

Hause Gill

car park

1000

foundations of Drum House

Dubs Bottom

1100

1200

1300

1500

1400

1300

1200

1100

continuation on opposite page

1600

1700

1800

1900

2000

2100

level

ruin

shaft (fenced)

Plumbago Mines (disused)

continuation HAYSTACKS 4

pools

tarn

stile

tarns

GREY KNOTTS
2287'

stile

kissing gate

stile

stile

2200

2300

1500

1400

fold

milk Gill

lane

Gillercomb

continuation
BRANDRETH 3

continuation
BASE BROWN 5

Hause Gill

MAP

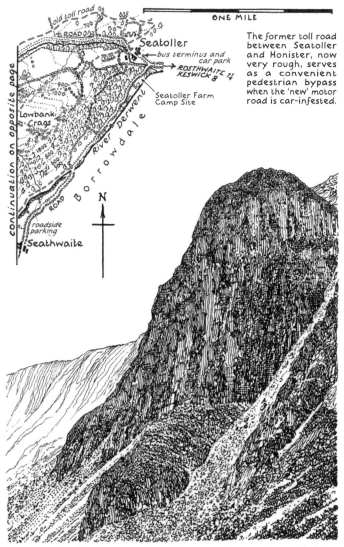

The former toll road between Seatoller and Honister, now very rough, serves as a convenient pedestrian bypass when the 'new' motor road is car-infested.

Raven Crag (known to climbers as Gillercomb Buttress)

ASCENT FROM SEATHWAITE
1900 feet of ascent: 1½ miles

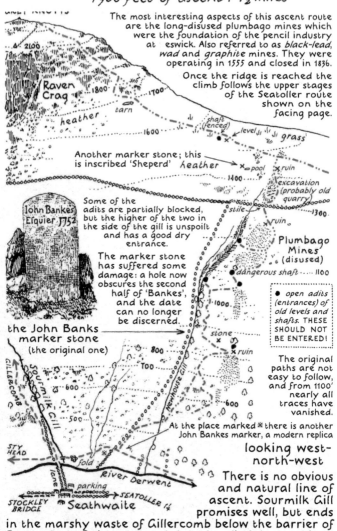

The most interesting aspects of this ascent route are the long-disused plumbago mines which were the foundation of the pencil industry at eswick. Also referred to as *black-lead*, *wad* and *graphite* mines. They were operating in 1555 and closed in 1836.

Once the ridge is reached the climb follows the upper stages of the Seatoller route shown on the facing page.

Another marker stone; this is inscribed 'Sheperd'

Some of the adits are partially blocked, but the higher of the two in the side of the gill is unspoilt and has a good dry entrance.

The marker stone has suffered some damage: a hole now obscures the second half of 'Bankes', and the date can no longer be discerned.

the John Banks marker stone (the original one)

John Bankes Esquier 1752

excavation (probably old quarry)

Plumbago Mines (disused)

dangerous shaft

● open adits (entrances) of old levels and shafts. THESE SHOULD NOT BE ENTERED!

The original paths are not easy to follow, and from 1100' nearly all traces have vanished.

At the place marked ✳ there is another John Bankes marker, a modern replica

looking west-north-west

There is no obvious and natural line of ascent. Sourmilk Gill promises well, but ends in the marshy waste of Gillercomb below the barrier of Raven Crag. It is suggested that the climb be combined with a surface exploration of the plumbago mines, above which the ridge from Seatoller may be joined.

ASCENT FROM SEATOLLER
1950 feet of ascent : 2½ miles

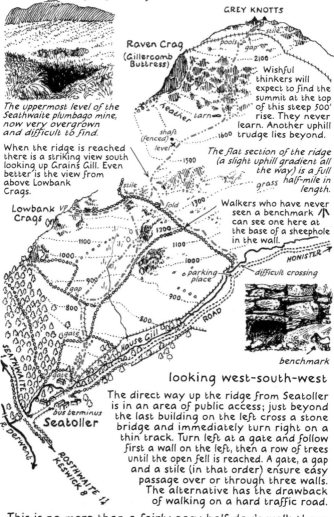

GREY KNOTTS

Raven Crag
(Gillercomb Buttress)

The uppermost level of the Seathwaite plumbago mine, now very overgrown and difficult to find.

Wishful thinkers will expect to find the summit at the top of this steep 500' rise. They never learn. Another uphill trudge lies beyond.

When the ridge is reached there is a striking view south looking up Grains Gill. Even better is the view from above Lowbank Crags.

The flat section of the ridge (a slight uphill gradient all the way) is a full half-mile in length.

Lowbank Crags

Walkers who have never seen a benchmark /|\ can see one here at the base of a sheephole in the wall.

HONISTER

difficult crossing

parking place

ROAD

Hause Gill

SEATHWAITE

R. Derwent

bus terminus
Seatoller

ROSTHWAITE
KESWICK 8

benchmark

looking west-south-west

The direct way up the ridge from Seatoller is in an area of public access; just beyond the last building on the left cross a stone bridge and immediately turn right on a thin track. Turn left at a gate and follow first a wall on the left, then a row of trees until the open fell is reached. A gate, a gap and a stile (in that order) ensure easy passage over or through three walls. The alternative has the drawback of walking on a hard traffic road.

This is no more than a fairly easy half-day's walk there and back, with a delightful start direct from Seatoller; the route makes a good alternative to the more usual starts for Great Gable from Borrowdale.

ASCENT FROM HONISTER PASS
1150 feet of ascent : 1 mile

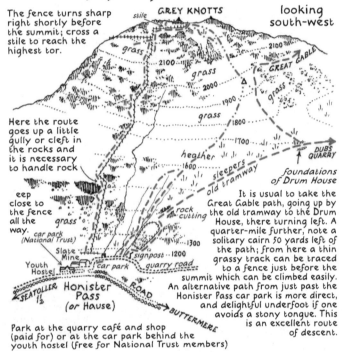

looking
south-west

The fence turns sharp right shortly before the summit; cross a stile to reach the highest tor.

GREY KNOTTS
stile

grass
2100
GREAT GABLE
grass
2000
grass
1900
grass
1800
grass
1700
heather
1600
sleepers
old tramway

Here the route goes up a little gully or cleft in the rocks and it is necessary to handle rock

DUBS QUARRY

foundations
of Drum House

eep close to the fence all the way.

grass

rock cutting

car park
(National Trust)

Slate Mine

Youth Hostel

signpost
car park
quarry road
1300
1200

SEATOLLER 1½

Honister Pass
(or Hause)

ROAD

BUTTERMERE

It is usual to take the Great Gable path, going up by the old tramway to the Drum House, there turning left. A quarter-mile further, note a solitary cairn 50 yards left of the path; from here a thin grassy track can be traced to a fence just before the summit which can be climbed easily. An alternative path from just past the Honister Pass car park is more direct, and delightful underfoot if one avoids a stony tongue. This is an excellent route of descent.

Park at the quarry café and shop (paid for) or at the car park behind the youth hostel (free for National Trust members)

A rather gloomy start, a tedious middle distance, and an excellent finish are features of this mild exercise for the cramped legs of motorists who park their cars at the top of the Pass.

The rock cutting

The skyline of Great Knotts from the Drum House, which now only consists of its rocky foundations

THE SUMMIT

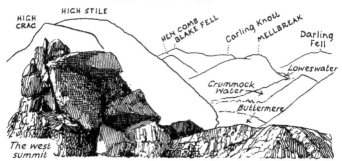

HIGH CRAG · HIGH STILE · HEN COMB · BLAKE FELL · Carling Knott · MELLBREAK · Darling Fell · Loweswater · Crummock Water · Buttermere

The west summit

Five grey tors of rock, all looking much alike, and four small sheets of water make the top of the fell very attractive, but in mist this would be a most confusing place were it not crossed by a post-and-wire fence from which it is possible to take direction. Two tors compete for the distinction of being the highest: one within the angle of the fence and another 180 yards west and apparently at the same elevation or within inches of it. Only the west summit is given an altitude on the 2008 edition of the Ordnance Survey Explorer map, yet on the east summit can be found an O.S. triangulation bolt. So which of the tors *is* the summit? It seems walkers have decided upon the eastern, which *does* seem to be slightly higher — although the western tor has the finer view.

DESCENTS: If the fence is being followed east from the angle, it is essential to watch for the junction of the Honister fence — the other branch, still going east, heads for sudden death over the edge of Gillercomb Buttress. For Seatoller, strike a course midway between the two fences, picking a way down among low crags to the level ridge below, and when a wall is reached it is preferable to follow it left to the Honister road. The easiest way off the summit is *via* the grass slope (a thin track) to the Gable—Honister path.

The west summit from the east summit

The east summit, looking to Glaramara

PLAN OF SUMMIT

100 yards

HONISTER (direct) · gap in fence · fence (easy to cross) · stile · HONISTER · SEATOLLER · tarn · SUDDEN DEATH · BRANDRETH GREAT GABLE · N · 2200' · tarn

The name 'Grey Knotts' is apt, and appropriate to the scenery of the top. But it clearly refers only to the summit, this being yet another example of a summit name commonly but quite wrongly, adopted for the whole fell from the roots up. Compare 'Great Gable', another descriptive name, which obviously applies to the mountain in its entirety, the summit having no separate name.

THE VIEW

The view is good on all sides, with a skyline of giants to the south. The finest prospect lies north-west, where the Buttermere district, seen over a foreground of rock, is of superlative beauty. *The diagram is based on the view from the west cairn.*

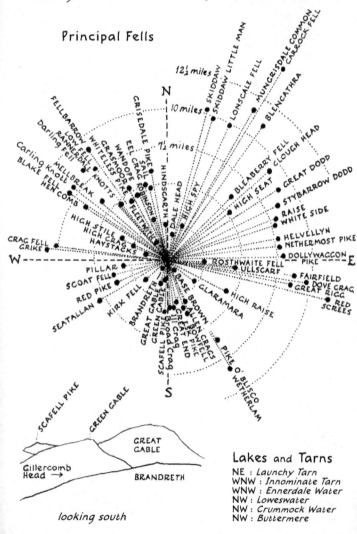

Principal Fells

looking south

Lakes and Tarns

NE : *Launchy Tarn*
WNW : *Innominate Tarn*
WNW : *Ennerdale Water*
NW : *Loweswater*
NW : *Crummock Water*
NW : *Buttermere*

RIDGE ROUTE

To BRANDRETH, 2344′ : ½ mile : SW
Depression at 2250′ : 100 feet of ascent

Only those of unusual talent could go astray on this simple walk, the fence leading most of the way to the top of Brandreth. Some interest may be added by a detour leftwards to look down into Gillercomb.

There are paths on both sides of the fence and a stile where one can switch sides. In periods of heavy rain the tarn on the eastern side of the fence encroaches on the path and some desperate boulder hopping may be needed to avoid getting wet feet.

ONE MILE

Gillercomb and Raven Crag

Grike

1601'

OS grid ref: NY085141

from Lanefoot

cows
sitting down
(explanatory note)

Ennerdale Bridge

● Cleator Moor

CRAC
FELL

GRIKE ▲   ▲

MILES

0   1   2   3   4

from Kinniside Stone Circle

NATURAL FEATURES

Grike is the beginning of Lakeland from the west. Approaching from Whitehaven an industrial belt has first to be crossed to Cleator Moor, after which follows an attractive undulating countryside watered by the Ehen, until, quite sharply, Grike and Crag Fell dominate the view ahead, with a glimpse of greater fells beyond closing in the valley of Ennerdale.

Grike, with its smooth grass and forestry plantations, is not a typical forerunner, although the north side overlooking the valley is seamed and scarred with huge ravines, and only its position makes the fell interesting. It is a good viewpoint, and the summit boasts a large cairn and a wind shelter, which can be seen for some distance around. The indefinite top forms a watershed, the southern slopes draining into the Calder, which, curiously, shares the same estuary near Sellafield as the Ehen, coming round from the north.

Over the past fifty years Grike has undergone a transformation. The Forestry Commission, denied further activity in the central areas of the district after making such a mess of Ennerdale, acquired more land along the western fringe, where they were less subject to public outcry, and Grike, like Murton Fell and Blake Fell, was festooned with fences and decorated with little trees, that have now grown into big ones, all looking exactly the same, trees without character. This process of afforestation has turned Grike into another fox sanctuary, as the first edition of this guide predicted, although the sanctuary is shrinking, with much felling in 2018 and 2019 south of the old mine road to the east of Blakeley Rise.

the Kinniside Stone Circle

looking north-east

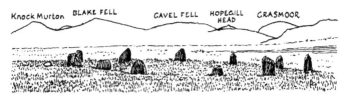

It is a remarkable fact that the Kinniside Stone Circle, although a well known local monument, was for many years omitted from Ordnance Survey maps. The popular explanation for this was that at the time of the first, and early subsequent, surveys, the Kinniside Stone Circle was non-existent, all twelve stones having long before been taken by local farmers for use as gateposts and building materials. Then in the 1920s a grand job of restoration was supposedly accomplished by an enterprising working party who located and recovered all twelve stones and completely restored the site. It eventually transpired, however, that the Kinniside Stone Circle is a modern creation, erected in 1925 by a local archaeologist. (See *A Coast to Coast Walk*, page 10.)

Grike 3

MAP

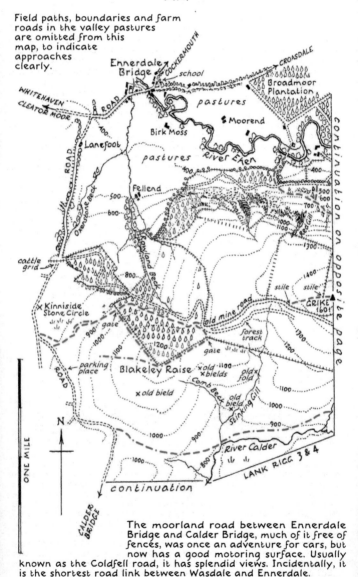

Field paths, boundaries and farm roads in the valley pastures are omitted from this map, to indicate approaches clearly.

ONE MILE

The moorland road between Ennerdale Bridge and Calder Bridge, much of it free of fences, was once an adventure for cars, but now has a good motoring surface. Usually known as the Coldfell road, it has splendid views. Incidentally, it is the shortest road link between Wasdale and Ennerdale.

ASCENT FROM KINNISIDE STONE CIRCLE
850 feet of ascent : 2 miles

From the stile where a clear path on grass leaves the old mine road (a gate here is invariably locked) the higher stile is clearly visible ahead, and the summit is only a short distance further. It is visible from the top stile.

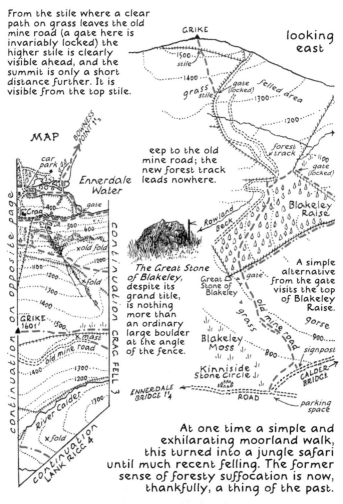

looking east

MAP

The Great Stone of Blakeley, despite its grand title, is nothing more than an ordinary large boulder at the angle of the fence.

eep to the old mine road; the new forest track leads nowhere.

A simple alternative from the gate visits the top of Blakeley Raise.

At one time a simple and exhilarating moorland walk, this turned into a jungle safari until much recent felling. The former sense of foresty suffocation is now, thankfully, a thing of the past.

An alternative start (not shown on the diagram on this page, but shown on *Caw Fell 9* and also on the map opposite) leaves the Coldfell road at the cattle grid north of the stone circle and keeps to the forest road until it meets the route shown here at 1150 feet.

ASCENT FROM ENNERDALE BRIDGE
1250 feet of ascent : 2½ miles

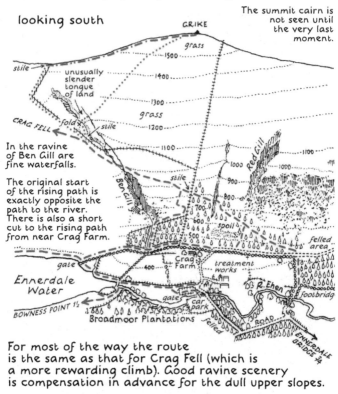

looking south

The summit cairn is
not seen until
the very last
moment.

GRIKE

grass

1500

1400

1300

1200

grass

stile

unusually
slender
tongue of land

CRAG FELL

fold

stile

1100

1000

900

800

700

600

500

Red Gill

1100

1000

In the ravine
of Ben Gill are
fine waterfalls.

The original start
of the rising path is
exactly opposite the
path to the river.
There is also a short
cut to the rising path
from near Crag Farm.

Ben Gill

stile

spoil

felled
area

gate

400

Crag
Farm

treatment
works

Ennerdale
Water

R. Ehen

BOWNESS POINT 1½

gate

car
park

ROAD

footbridge

ENNERDALE BRIDGE ¾

Broadmoor Plantations

felled

For most of the way the route
is the same as that for Crag Fell (which is
a more rewarding climb). Good ravine scenery
is compensation in advance for the dull upper slopes.

THE SUMMIT

RED PIKE

HIGH STILE

CRAG FELL

PILLAR

Wind Gap
Black Crag
STEEPLE

SCOAT FELL

continued

THE SUMMIT

continued

The summit is remarkable for its large cairn and even larger wind shelter, cairn building here being an easy task thanks to a rash of stones on the highest part of the fell, an eruption quite out of character: all around is uninterrupted grass. Diligent search will not reveal anything else of interest. A forest fence crosses the western shoulder very close to the summit, but a stile has been provided.

DESCENTS: Head east to a junction of fences, then left along the far side of the fence to the north to join the path from Crag Fell. This crosses Ben Gill and descends through the plantation to a forest road. Turn sharp right for the car park, or take the path directly opposite for Ennerdale Bridge. (See the diagram on page 5.) The descent by the mine road is a fast walk and the best way down in mist; head west to a stile and continue in the same direction to join the mine road at a gate. On reaching tarmac, turn right along it for Ennerdale Bridge.

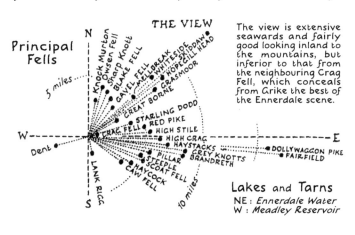

THE VIEW

Principal Fells

The view is extensive seawards and fairly good looking inland to the mountains, but inferior to that from the neighbouring Crag Fell, which conceals from Grike the best of the Ennerdale scene.

Lakes and Tarns
NE : *Ennerdale Water*
W : *Meadley Reservoir*

RIDGE ROUTE

To CRAG FELL, 1716':
1 mile : E, then NE
Depression at 1450'
260 feet of ascent

An easy stroll.

The old mine road cannot be utilised because of the fence, and it is impossible to avoid marshy ground. Note the anemometer and other equipment in a fenced enclosure close to the mast.

ONE MILE

Haycock

2618'

OS grid ref: NY145107

from Winscale Hows, Seatallan

NATURAL FEATURES

Haycock rises in a massive dome on the Wasdale and Ennerdale watershed, and its comparative neglect by walkers must be ascribed more to its remote position on the fringe of the dreary and unattractive moors of innside and Copeland than to its own shortcomings, which are few. The fell, indeed, has all the qualities of ruggedness and cragginess characteristic of the Wasdale mountains, and the approaches to it have charm of surroundings not usually associated with such rough terrain.

Despite its considerable height, however, Haycock is not rooted in valleys, being instead hoisted on the shoulders of Caw Fell and Seatallan, supporting fells of lesser altitude but greater extensiveness; between Haycock and Seatallan to the south the upland depression known as Pots of Ashness (1640') marks the boundary of the fell in this direction. Pleasant streams flow north to Ennerdale and to Wasdale southwards, but the biggest waterway leaving the fell, a great natural channel, is that occupied by the River Bleng, south-west. Seen from this latter direction, Haycock is a giant in stature, completely dominating the head of the valley and unchallenged by other peaks. Here, at least, it is supreme; it cannot be neglected.

Ennerdale Bridge

CRAG FELL ▲

Gillerthwaite

LANK RIGG ▲

CAW FELL

▲ PILLAR
▲ SCOAT FELL
▲ HAYCOCK

Coldfell Gate

▲

Thornholme

SEATALLAN
▲

Scalderskew

Wasdale Head

Bowderdale

Calder Bridge

Greendale

Gosforth

Strands

MILES

0 1 2 3 4

Haycock 3

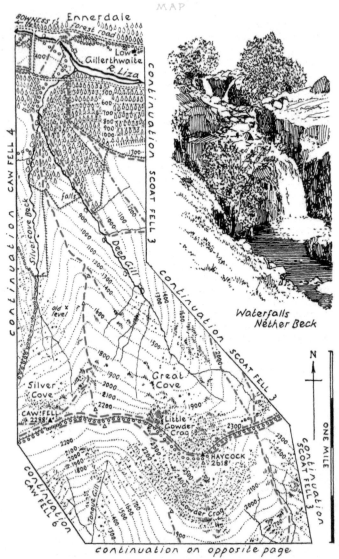

continuation on opposite page

Waterfalls
Nether Beck

N

ONE MILE

The fence beside the broken wall over the summit and east (to Scoat Fell) and west (to Little Gowder Crag) has been added as part of the Wild Ennerdale project. West of Caw Fell the wall has been rebuilt.

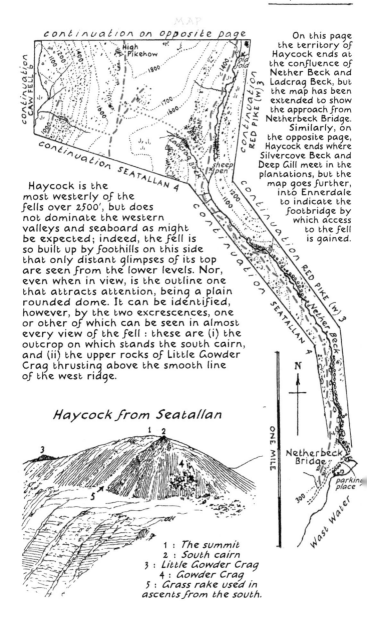

continuation on opposite page

MAP

High Pikehow

continuation CAWFELL 6

continuation SEATALLAN 4

continuation RED PIKE (W) 3

continuation RED PIKE (W) 3

continuation SEATALLAN 4

Ladcrag Beck

Nether Beck

sheep pen

On this page the territory of Haycock ends at the confluence of Nether Beck and Ladcrag Beck, but the map has been extended to show the approach from Netherbeck Bridge. Similarly, on the opposite page, Haycock ends where Silvercove Beck and Deep Gill meet in the plantations, but the map goes further, into Ennerdale to indicate the footbridge by which access to the fell is gained.

Haycock is the most westerly of the fells over 2500', but does not dominate the western valleys and seaboard as might be expected; indeed, the fell is so built up by foothills on this side that only distant glimpses of its top are seen from the lower levels. Nor, even when in view, is the outline one that attracts attention, being a plain rounded dome. It can be identified, however, by the two excrescences, one or other of which can be seen in almost every view of the fell: these are (i) the outcrop on which stands the south cairn, and (ii) the upper rocks of Little Gowder Crag thrusting above the smooth line of the west ridge.

Haycock from Seatallan

N

ONE MILE

Netherbeck Bridge

parking place

300

Wast Water

1 : The summit
2 : South cairn
3 : Little Gowder Crag
4 : Gowder Crag
5 : Grass rake used in ascents from the south.

ASCENT FROM WASDALE
(GREENDALE)

2500 feet of ascent : 4¼ miles

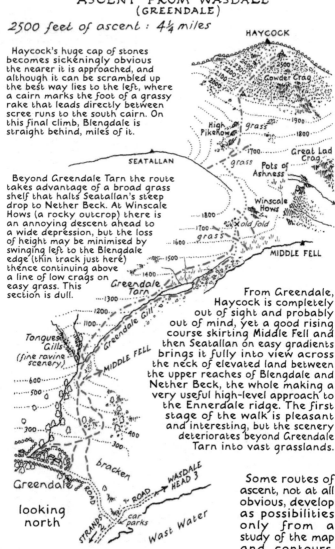

Haycock's huge cap of stones becomes sickeningly obvious the nearer it is approached, and although it can be scrambled up the best way lies to the left, where a cairn marks the foot of a grassy rake that leads directly between scree runs to the south cairn. On this final climb, Blengdale is straight behind, miles of it.

Beyond Greendale Tarn the route takes advantage of a broad grass shelf that halts Seatallan's steep drop to Nether Beck. At Winscale Hows (a rocky outcrop) there is an annoying descent ahead to a wide depression, but the loss of height may be minimised by swinging left to the Blengdale edge (thin track just here) thence continuing above a line of low crags on easy grass. This section is dull.

HAYCOCK

Gowder Crag

High Pikehow

grass

Great Lad Crag

SEATALLAN

grass

Pots of Ashness

Winscale Hows

old fold

grass

MIDDLE FELL

Greendale Tarn

Greendale Gill

MIDDLE FELL

Tongues Gills (fine ravine scenery)

bracken

Greendale

ROAD

WASDALE HEAD 3

looking north

STRANDS

car parks

Wast Water

From Greendale, Haycock is completely out of sight and probably out of mind, yet a good rising course skirting Middle Fell and then Seatallan on easy gradients brings it fully into view across the neck of elevated land between the upper reaches of Blengdale and Nether Beck, the whole making a very useful high-level approach to the Ennerdale ridge. The first stage of the walk is pleasant and interesting, but the scenery deteriorates beyond Greendale Tarn into vast grasslands.

Some routes of ascent, not at all obvious, develop as possibilities only from a study of the map and contours, and this way up Haycock is one such. The walk is a simple one throughout, and fast progress can be made.

ASCENT FROM WASDALE
(NETHERBECK BRIDGE)
2400 feet of ascent : 4 miles

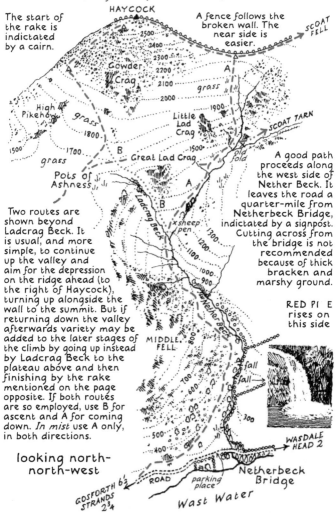

The start of the rake is indicated by a cairn.

HAYCOCK

A fence follows the broken wall. The near side is easier.

SCOAT FELL

Cowder Crag

High Pikehow

grass

grass

Little Lad Crag

grass

SCOAT TARN

Great Lad Crag

Pots of Ashness

Old fold

A good path proceeds along the west side of Nether Beck. It leaves the road a quarter-mile from Netherbeck Bridge, indicated by a signpost. Cutting across from the bridge is not recommended because of thick bracken and marshy ground.

Two routes are shown beyond Ladcrag Beck. It is usual, and more simple, to continue up the valley and aim for the depression on the ridge ahead (to the right of Haycock), turning up alongside the wall to the summit. But if returning down the valley afterwards variety may be added to the later stages of the climb by going up instead by Ladcrag Beck to the plateau above and then finishing by the rake mentioned on the page opposite. If both routes are so employed, use B for ascent and A for coming down. *In mist* use A only, in both directions.

Ladcrag Beck

sheep pen

Nether Beck

MIDDLE FELL

RED PI E rises on this side

fall
fall

looking north-north-west

WASDALE HEAD 2

GOSFORTH 6½
STRANDS 2¾

ROAD

parking place

Netherbeck Bridge

Wast Water

An interesting expedition with particularly good scenery in the early sections of the Nether Beck valley. The latter stages of the climb are rather dull in comparison.

ASCENT FROM ENNERDALE
(LOW GILLERTHWAITE)
2300 feet of ascent : 3 miles

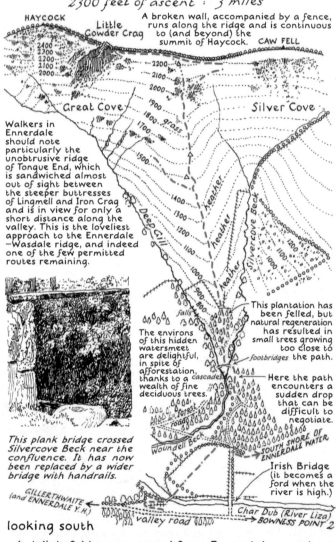

HAYCOCK

Little Cowder Crag

A broken wall, accompanied by a fence, runs along the ridge and is continuous to (and beyond) the summit of Haycock.

CAW FELL

2400
2300
2200
2100
2000

2200
2100
2000
1900 grass
1800

Great Cove

Silver Cove

Walkers in Ennerdale should note particularly the unobtrusive ridge of Tongue End, which is sandwiched almost out of sight between the steeper buttresses of Lingmell and Iron Crag and is in view for only a short distance along the valley. This is the loveliest approach to the Ennerdale—Wasdale ridge, and indeed one of the few permitted routes remaining.

1700
1600
1500
1400
1300
1200
1100
1000
900
800 falls

Deep Gill

heather

heather

heather

Silvercove Beck

1200
1100
1000

This plantation has been felled, but natural regeneration has resulted in small trees growing too close to *footbridges* the path.

The environs of this hidden watersmeet are delightful, in spite of afforestation, thanks to a wealth of fine deciduous trees.

cascades

forest road

Woundell Beck

Here the path encounters a sudden drop that can be difficult to negotiate.

This plank bridge crossed Silvercove Beck near the confluence. It has now been replaced by a wider bridge with handrails.

SOUTH SHORE OF ENNERDALE WATER

Irish Bridge (it becomes a ford when the river is high.)

GILLERTHWAITE (and ENNERDALE Y.H.)

valley road

Char Dub (River Liza)
BOWNESS POINT 2

looking south

A delightful 'escape route' from Ennerdale — make a note of the hidden watersmeet near the footbridges.

THE SUMMIT

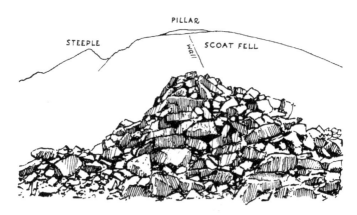

There are two summit cairns, one on each side of the ruined stone wall running over the top of the fell. That on the north side has slightly the greater elevation and has been made into a wind shelter with its entrance facing east. The top is stony everywhere and without paths: it is usual not to stray far from the wall. 150 yards south is another cairn, prominent on an outcrop of rock and commanding a better view of the Wasdale scene.

DESCENTS:

For Wasdale, the quickest route lies alongside the wall to the east depression, there turning right at a cairn onto a distinct path down an easy grass slope. eep to the right of an incipient stream. Nether Beck is joined on its way down from Scoat Tarn, and from here on the path, distinct nearly all the way, can be followed down to the Wasdale road at Netherbeck Bridge. This is a simple and straightforward way off the fell, the best for a party that has already had enough for one day, and the safest route in mist, but the time required for it should not be underestimated.

For Ennerdale, follow the north side of the wall north-west over Little Gowder Crag and on the grass beyond turn down an indefinite ridge that soon becomes more pronounced, and, when heather is reached, provides a good ridge path down Tongue End into the plantations, gaining the valley road across the footbridge a few fields east of the head of Ennerdale Water.

The second (slightly lower) summit cairn. Beyond the old wall is a wind shelter.

THE VIEW

Although the view of Lakeland tends to deteriorate on the long decline to the west from Pillar, that from the summit of Haycock is still remarkably good in all directions. The full length of the Scafell range is seen, but, curiously, only the uppermost feet of Pillar and Great Gable are visible above the intervening heights of Scoat Fell and Red Pike.

Principal Fells

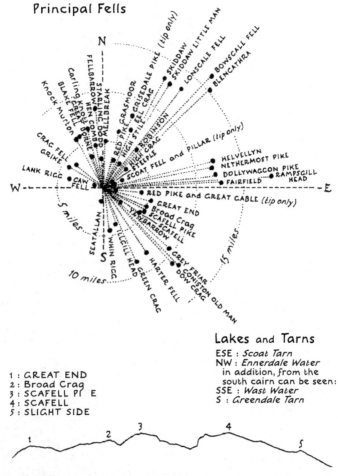

Lakes and Tarns

ESE : *Scoat Tarn*
NW : *Ennerdale Water*
in addition, from the
south cairn can be seen:
SSE : *Wast Water*
S : *Greendale Tarn*

1 : GREAT END
2 : Broad Crag
3 : SCAFELL PI E
4 : SCAFELL
5 : SLIGHT SIDE

The outline of the Scafell range, from Haycock

RIDGE ROUTES

To SCOAT FELL, 2760': 1 mile : ENE
Depression at 2315': 450 feet of ascent
Just a matter of following the wall.

The wall, accompanied by a fence, connects
the two summits and there is no possibility
of going astray. Starting east, the
south side of the wall is rather
less stony down to the
depression, but
here, with the
remainder of
the walk on grass,
it is preferable to change
sides to get the striking
views into Mirklin Cove and across to Steeple.

To SEATALLAN, 2266': 2 miles
S, then SW, SE and SSW
Depression at 1610': 670 feet of ascent
Not recommended in mist.

Haycock is defended to the south by a
semi-circular barrier of broken rock and
scree, but has one weakness — a grassy rake
that leaves the top 10 yards short of the
south cairn, on the right, in the direction
of Blengdale. Go down this to the hummocky
grassland, a mile of it, between the two fells.
There is no difficulty in crossing over to
Seatallan in clear weather, but the absence of
landmarks makes this a confusing area in mist.

To CAW FELL, 2288': 1 mile
NW, then W
Depression at 2210': 120 feet of ascent
The scenery deteriorates with every step.

The wall leads over the
top rocks of Little
Gowder Crag.

Follow the wall
north-west down
a stony slope to
a grassy saddle,
where a slight ascent is made to the
top rocks of Little Gowder Crag. Here,
vertical steps, easily avoided, interrupt
the continuity of the wall, which then
resumes its aim for Caw Fell. Alternatively, the wall route
can be avoided by paths on the left, initially from the top of Haycock
and later 400 yards west, and the rocky summit of Little Gowder Crag
can be bypassed on grass. A choice of stiles follows soon after.

Haystacks

1959'

OS grid ref: NY193131

properly
Hay Stacks
(two words)
as on
Ordnance maps

from Gamlin End, High Crag

Gatesgarth ●
HIGH ▲
CRAC
HAYSTACKS
▲
Black ●Sail Y.H.
MILES
0   1   2

NATURAL FEATURES

Haystacks stands unabashed and unashamed in the midst of a circle of much loftier fells, like a shaggy terrier in the company of foxhounds, some of them known internationally, but not one of this distinguished group of mountains around Ennerdale and Buttermere can show a greater variety and a more fascinating arrangement of interesting features. Here are sharp peaks in profusion, tarns with islands and tarns without islands, crags, screes, rocks for climbing and rocks not for climbing, heather tracts, marshes, serpentine trails, tarns with streams and tarns with no streams. All these, with a background of magnificent landscapes, await every visitor to Haystacks but they will be appreciated most by those who go there to linger and explore. It is a place of surprises around corners, and there are many corners. For a man trying to get a persistent worry out of his mind, the top of Haystacks is a wonderful cure.

The fell rises between the deep hollow of Warnscale Bottom near Gatesgarth, and Ennerdale: between a valley familiar to summer motorists and a valley reached only on foot. It is bounded on the west by Scarth Gap, a pass linking the two. The Buttermere aspect is the better known, although this side is often dark in shadow and seen only as a silhouette against the sky: here, above Warnscale, is a great wall of crags. The Ennerdale flank, open to the sun, is friendlier but steep and rough nevertheless.

Eastwards, beyond the tangle of tors and outcrops forming the boundary of Haystacks on this side, a broad grass slope rises easily and unattractively to Brandreth on the edge of the Borrowdale watershed; beyond is Derwent country.

The spelling of Haystacks as one word is a personal preference of the author (and others), and probably arises from a belief that the name originated from the resemblance of the scattered tors on the summit to *stacks* of hay in a field. If this were so, the one word *Haystacks* would be correct (as it is in *Haycock*). But learned authorities state that the name derives, from the Icelandic 'stack', meaning 'a columnar rock', and that the true interpretation is *High Rocks*. This is logical and appropriate. *High Rocks* is a name of two words and would be wrongly written as *Highrocks*.

The summit tarn

Big Stack,
looking east from a point near the path to the summit from Scarth Gap.

In the picture below Big Stack appears on the extreme right.

The north crags,
looking west from the slopes of Green Crag.

The path is seen skirting the cliff on the left.

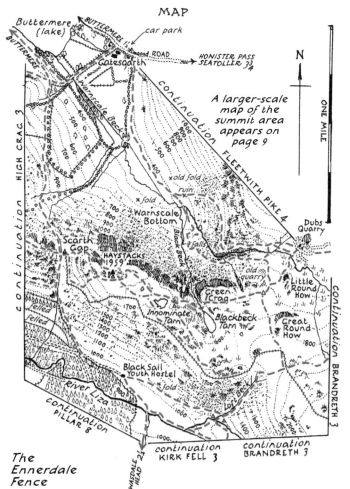

MAP

Buttermere (lake)

BUTTERMERE 1½

car park

Gatesgarth

ROAD

HONISTER PASS 3
SEATOLLER 3¾

N

continuation FLEETWITH PIKE 4

A larger-scale map of the summit area appears on page 9

ONE MILE

continuation HIGH CRAG 3

BUTTERMERE

Warnscale Beck

× old fold

ruin

× fold

Warnscale Bottom

Black Beck

falls

Dubs Quarry

Scarth Gap

HAYSTACKS 1959

old quarry

Little Round How

Green Crag

continuation BRANDRETH 3

Innominate Tarn

Blackbeck Tarn

Great Round How

felled

felled

Black Sail Youth Hostel

× fold

Loft Beck

river Liza

continuation PILLAR 8

WASDALE HEAD 2½

continuation KIRK FELL 3

continuation BRANDRETH 3

The Ennerdale Fence

At one time Ennerdale was enclosed by a fence nearly twenty miles in length, running along both watersheds and around the head of the valley. The fence was mainly of post and wire, and in most places only the posts survive. On Haystacks the fence has been restored, but it comes to a curiously abrupt end at Scarth Gap. In general, the line of the fence followed parish boundaries but on Haystacks there is considerable deviation. Here the series of iron stakes embedded in rock (erected to mark the boundary of the Lonsdale estate) coincides with the parish boundary, but the fence keeps well to the south of this line.

ASCENT FROM GATESGARTH
1550 feet of ascent : 1¼ miles

via SCARTH GAP   HAYSTACKS

Big Stack

Stack Rake

From Scarth Gap a well constructed path leads up to the summit, avoiding all scree, though in places it is necessary to handle rock.

HIGH CRAG

Scarth Gap

1500 HIGH CRAG

1400

1300

1200

gap

1100

High Wax Knott

Low Wax Knott

looking south

Scarth Gap is one of the pleasantest of the foot passes. Apart from the steep section above the old sheepfold, the gradients are gentle and the views both ahead and behind are full of interest. The path is generally good — well repaired in many sections — and the roughness that was formerly encountered on the early stages of the climb is buried underneath a new conifer plantation.

Leave Gatesgarth by the bridge, at a signpost to Ennerdale.

It is a test of iron discipline to pass without halting several large *comfortable* boulders athwart the path.

Coupled with a return by the Warnscale route to make a full 'round' journey, the ascent of Haystacks *via* the pass of Scarth Gap is a prelude of much merit and beauty to a mountain walk of unique character, the whole distance being no more than five miles. Save it, however, for a fine clear day.

1000

stile and gate

bracken

900

700

800

600

500

400

gap

old sheepfold

BUTTERMERE via BURTNESS WOOD

Gatesgarth

kissing gate

ROAD

car park

Buttermere

There is a car park (not free) at Gatesgarth which fills quickly at busy times of the year; also, there are roadside parking spaces further along the road to Honister barely five minutes' walk away.

ASCENT FROM GATESGARTH
via WARNSCALE
1600 feet of ascent : 2¾ miles

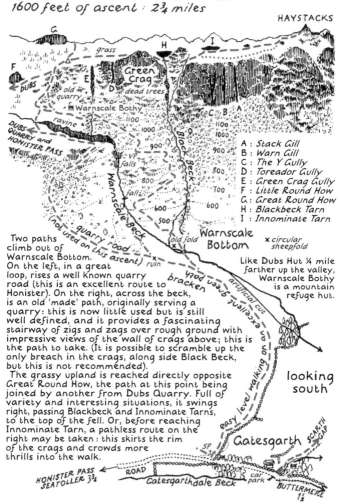

HAYSTACKS

A : Stack Gill
B : Warn Gill
C : The Y Gully
D : Toreador Gully
E : Green Crag Gully
F : Little Round How
G : Great Round How
H : Blackbeck Tarn
I : Innominate Tarn

Like Dubs Hut ¼ mile farther up the valley, Warnscale Bothy is a mountain refuge hut.

Two paths climb out of Warnscale Bottom. On the left, in a great loop, rises a well known quarry road (this is an excellent route to Honister). On the right, across the beck, is an old 'made' path, originally serving a quarry: this is now little used but is still well defined, and it provides a fascinating stairway of zigs and zags over rough ground with impressive views of the wall of crags above; this is the path to take. (It is possible to scramble up the only breach in the crags, along side Black Beck, but this is not recommended).

The grassy upland is reached directly opposite Great Round How, the path at this point being joined by another from Dubs Quarry. Full of variety and interesting situations, it swings right, passing Blackbeck and Innominate Tarns, to the top of the fell. Or, before reaching Innominate Tarn, a pathless route on the right may be taken: this skirts the rim of the crags and crowds more thrills into the walk.

looking south

For sustained interest, impressive crag scenery, beautiful views, and a most delightful arrangement of tarns and rocky peaks, this short mountain excursion ranks with the very best.

Gatesgarth is served by no. 77 buses from Keswick in summer.

ASCENT FROM HONISTER PASS
1050 feet of ascent : 2¼ miles

A note of explanation is required. This ascent route does not conform to the usual pattern, being more in the nature of an upland cross-country walk than a mountain climb: there are two pronounced descents before foot is set on Haystacks. The wide variety of scene and the fascinating intricacies of the path are justification for the inclusion of the route in this book.

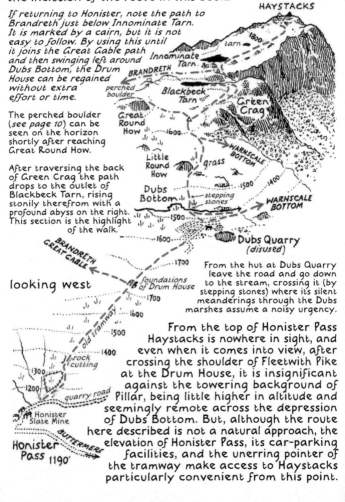

If returning to Honister, note the path to Brandreth just below Innominate Tarn. It is marked by a cairn, but it is not easy to follow. By using this until it joins the Great Gable path and then swinging left around Dubs House, the Drum House can be regained without extra effort or time.

The perched boulder (*see page 10*) can be seen on the horizon shortly after reaching Great Round How.

After traversing the back of Green Crag the path drops to the outlet of Blackbeck Tarn, rising stonily therefrom with a profound abyss on the right. This section is the highlight of the walk.

looking west

From the hut at Dubs Quarry leave the road and go down to the stream, crossing it (by stepping stones) where its silent meanderings through the Dubs marshes assume a noisy urgency.

From the top of Honister Pass Haystacks is nowhere in sight, and even when it comes into view, after crossing the shoulder of Fleetwith Pike at the Drum House, it is insignificant against the towering background of Pillar, being little higher in altitude and seemingly remote across the depression of Dubs Bottom. But, although the route here described is not a natural approach, the elevation of Honister Pass, its car-parking facilities, and the unerring pointer of the tramway make access to Haystacks particularly convenient from this point.

ASCENT FROM ENNERDALE
(BLACK SAIL YOUTH HOSTEL)

970 feet of ascent
1¼ miles

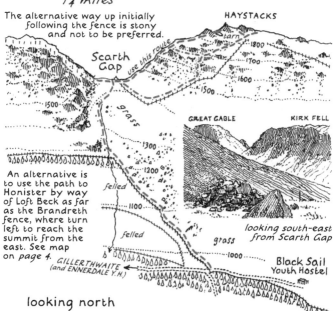

The alternative way up initially following the fence is stony and not to be preferred.

HAYSTACKS

Scarth Gap

use this route

grass

An alternative is to use the path to Honister by way of Loft Beck as far as the Brandreth fence, where turn left to reach the summit from the east. See map on *page 4*.

felled

felled

GILLERTHWAITE
(and ENNERDALE Y.H.)

GREAT GABLE   KIRK FELL

looking south-east from Scarth Gap

grass

Black Sail Youth Hostel

looking north

This route is likely to be of interest only to those staying at the magnificently situated Black Sail Youth Hostel. This hostel is open to everyone, but those intending to use it are advised to book well in advance.

formerly a shepherd's hut.....

Black Sail Youth Hostel

THE SUMMIT

NOTE: Haystacks has far too many paths to fit on a map; those shown below are the main ones, but there are many others. A large number of small tarns and pools have also been omitted.

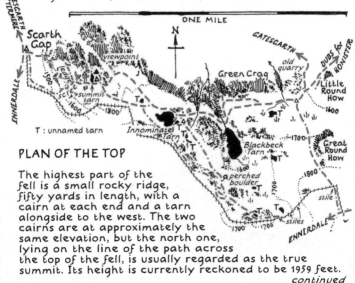

T : unnamed tarn

PLAN OF THE TOP

The highest part of the fell is a small rocky ridge, fifty yards in length, with a cairn at each end and a tarn alongside to the west. The two cairns are at approximately the same elevation, but the north one, lying on the line of the path across the top of the fell, is usually regarded as the true summit. Its height is currently reckoned to be 1959 feet.

continued

THE SUMMIT

continued

Haystacks fails to qualify for inclusion in the authors 'best half-dozen' only because of inferior height, a deficiency in vertical measurement. Another thousand feet would have made all the difference.

But for beauty, variety and interesting detail, for sheer fascination and unique individuality, the summit area of Haystacks is supreme. This is in fact the best fell top of all — a place of great charm and fairyland attractiveness. Seen from a distance, these qualities are not suspected: indeed, on the contrary, the appearance of Haystacks is almost repellent when viewed from the higher surrounding peaks: black are its bones and black is its flesh. With its thick covering of heather it is dark and sombre even when the sun sparkles the waters of its many tarns, gloomy and mysterious even under a blue sky. There are fierce crags and rough screes and outcrops that will be grittier still when the author's ashes are scattered here. ✳

Yet the combination of features, of tarn and tor, of cliff and cove, the labyrinth of corners and recesses, the maze of old sheepwalks and paths, form a design, or a lack of design, of singular appeal and absorbing interest. One can forget even a raging toothache on Haystacks.

✳ *After his death in 1991, the author's ashes were duly scattered on Haystacks.*

perched boulder on a rock platform

Note the profile in shadow. Some women have faces like that.

On a first visit, learn thoroughly the details of the mile-long main path across the top, a magnificent traverse, because this serves as the best introduction to the geography of the fell.

Having memorised this, several interesting deviations may be made: the parallel alternative above the rim of the north face, the scramble onto Big Stack, the 'cross-country' route around the basin of Blackbeck Tarn, the walk alongside the fence, and so on.

typical summit tors

DESCENTS: A well made path starts just west of the summit and leads down to Scarth Gap. An alternative path farther south is marred by loose stones and should be avoided. It is advisable to regard the whole of the north edge as highly dangerous. The only advice that can be given to a novice lost on Haystacks *in mist* is that he should kneel down and pray for safe deliverance.

THE VIEW

This is not a case of distance lending enchantment to the view, because apart from a glimpse of Skiddaw above the Robinson—Hindscarth depression and a slice of the Helvellyn range over Honister, the scene is predominantly one of high mountains within a five-mile radius. And really good they look — the enchantment is close at hand. Set in a tight surround, they are seen in revealing detail: a rewarding study deserving leisurely appreciation.

Principal Fells

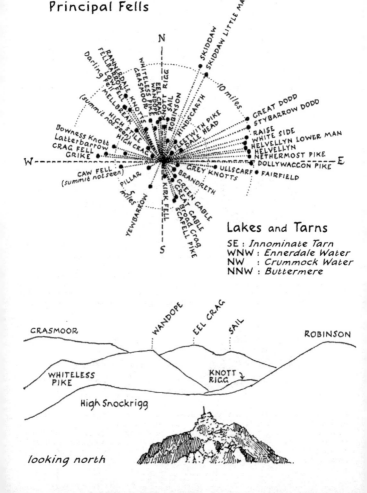

Lakes and Tarns

SE : *Innominate Tarn*
WNW : *Ennerdale Water*
NW : *Crummock Water*
NNW : *Buttermere*

looking north

RIDGE ROUTES

To BRANDRETH, 2344': 2 miles
Depression at 1540'
850 feet of ascent
ESE, E, S and SE

The first mile is excellent.

On a clear day a route of one's own choice may be taken over the top of Haystacks, aiming for the corner of the Brandreth fence. But the regular path off Haystacks, by way of Innominate and Blackbeck Tarns, passes through the finest scenery and should certainly be preferred by those to whom it is new, in which case the indefinite junction of the Brandreth path below Great Round How should be watched for carefully — it occurs just before the main path swings left and starts to descend towards Dubs Quarry. From the corner of the fence there is no cause for further deviation, the fence leading most of the way to the summit of Brandreth up an easy grass slope and crossing two well known paths in the course of doing so.

To HIGH CRAG, 2443'
1¼ miles : W, then NW
Depression at 1425' (Scarth Gap)
1100 feet of ascent

A fine walk in spite of scree.

Follow faithfully the well made path to the west from the summit, a delightful game of ins and outs and ups and downs. An alternative path south of the summit encounters an area of loose stones and should be avoided. From Scarth Gap a beautiful path

High Crag, from Scarth Gap

climbs through the heather to Seat; then a good ridge follows to the final tower of High Crag: this deteriorates badly into slippery scree on the later stages of the ascent.

HALF A MILE

Hen Comb

1670'

OS grid ref: NY132181

from Mosedale

Following the general pattern of the Loweswater Fells, Hen Comb rises as a long ridge from the valley to a round summit set well back. It is a grassy fell, almost entirely, with a rocky knuckle, Little Dodd, midway on the ridge, and there is very little of interest on the flanks apart from slight traces of former mining activity. The main mass of the fell rises on three sides from a desolate moorland with extensive tracts of marsh that serve as a moat and effectively discourage a close acquaintance. It is the sort of fell sometimes climbed, but rarely twice. It is unfortunate in having Mellbreak as a neighbour.

Loweswater ●

BLAKE FELL ▲

GAVEL FELL ▲   MELLBREAK ▲

HEN COMB ▲

GREAT BORNE ▲   Buttermere

MILES

0   1   2   3   4

MAP

The map shows Hen Comb's simple structure — a long ridge rising from a main valley (Loweswater) between side valleys that carry streams down from a wide upland morass, a desolate tract of marshland and bog encircling the extremity of the fell like a moat, out of which rise the summit slopes as an island from the sea. The two becks, fed from such an unfailing source, bring down water in considerable volume, and, being without bridges above the intakes, make access to Hen Comb from the north difficult in wet weather. In fact the only way up after heavy rain is from Ennerdale *via* the path beside the site of an ancient cairn — a circle of stones around a pit. Barely a trace of this structure will be found, it being hidden by moss, reeds and grass.

ASCENT FROM LOWESWATER
1300 feet of ascent : 2½ miles

HEN COMB

1600
1500
1400
1300

grass
1200

The ridge route over Little Dodd is the better of the two shown. At the first fence there is evidence that walkers scale it (there is a clear path on the far side), but it is just as easy to follow a sketchy track up to a stile where the fence turns half left. If making a round trip by the two routes shown the Little Dodd route offers the best view of Loweswater when used in descent.

Little Dodd

heather
grass

three posts around a bog 1100

bracken

1000

old mine

900

stile
fold

grass

bracken

800

Mosedale Beck

bracken

700

bracken

FLOUTERN TARN or
BUTTERMERE or
ENNERDALE

600

The alternative to the Little Dodd route is obstructed by two fences and hindered by summer bracken. From the remains of the old mine traces of a former zig-zag path on the flank of the fell can be found. In fact, this part of the route is the easiest way through the bracken that clogs this side of the fell.

MELLBREAK

HIGHPARK

gate

grassy lane

Normally it is just possible, by a feat of daring, to cross the beck without taking off boots and stockings

500

ancient earthwork

look over the wall to see it. (Indistinct at eye-level but clearly seen aerially)

Kirkgate (farm)

looking south-south-west

HIGHPARK

Kirkstile Inn

Church

Loweswater

Little Dodd

Not an exciting walk, but pleasant enough on a sunny day for anybody who doesn't want to get excited.

THE SUMMIT

The summit is a small grassy dome with a neat cairn but nothing of interest.

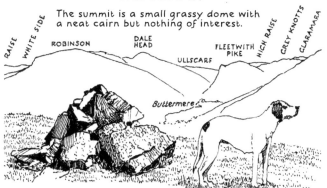

The bystander, patiently waiting while details are noted but eager to be off, is Barmaid of the Melbreak Foxhounds.

THE VIEW

Principal Fells

The view is better than anticipated, with one aspect in particular, that of Buttermere valley in a frame of fells, of classic beauty.

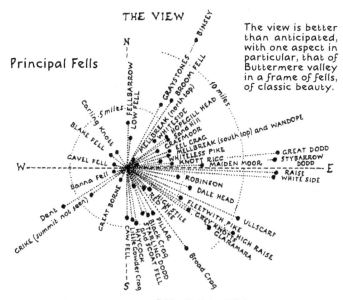

Lakes and Tarns

N : Loweswater
ESE : Crummock Water (small part of head of lake)
ESE : Buttermere

RIDGE ROUTES:

There are no ridges connecting with other fells. However, the ascent of Hen Comb is commonly combined with that of Mellbreak. Gavel Fell and Great Borne can both be easily visited, too.

High Crag

2443'

OS grid ref: NY180140

from Haystacks

- Buttermere

HIGH
STILE ▲

- Gatesgarth

▲ HIGH CRAG

Scarth }{ HAYSTACKS
Gap ▲

Black Sail ● Y.H.

MILES

0   1   2   3

NATURAL FEATURES

High Crag is the least known of the three linked peaks of the High Stile range towering above the Buttermere valley and is the lowest in elevation, but it concedes nothing in grandeur and ruggedness to the other two, High Stile and Red Pike, its formidable northern buttress being the finest object in the group. To the west of this buttress lies deeply inurned the stony rock-girt hollow of Burtness (or Birkness) Comb, a favourite climbing ground, with High Stile soaring beyond, the two summits being connected by a narrow ridge overlooking the Comb. Eastwards are vast scree runs, where few men venture; the continuation of the ridge on this side is at first unpleasantly stony until an easier slope of grass leads down to a depression beyond which the ridge reasserts itself as a distinctive crest and then falls abruptly in crags and scree to the top of Scarth Gap Pass. The fell's aspect from Buttermere is exceedingly impressive, giving an air of complete inaccessibility, but the opposite flank falling to Ennerdale's new forests lacks distinctive features although everywhere rough. The summit commands a glorious view of mountainous country, a deserved reward for it is neither easily attained nor easily left, its defence of battlemented crags and hostile stones being breached only by the narrow ridge connecting with High Stile, a mountain with difficulties of its own. Indeed, if it were not for this ridge (which goes on to and beyond Red Pike) the summits of both would be almost unattainable by the ordinary pedestrian. With the help of the ridge they should certainly be visited, the scenery being of the highest order and the situations exciting.

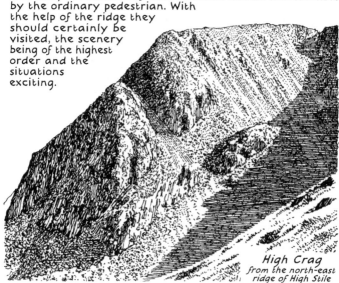

High Crag
from the north-east
ridge of High Stile

MAP

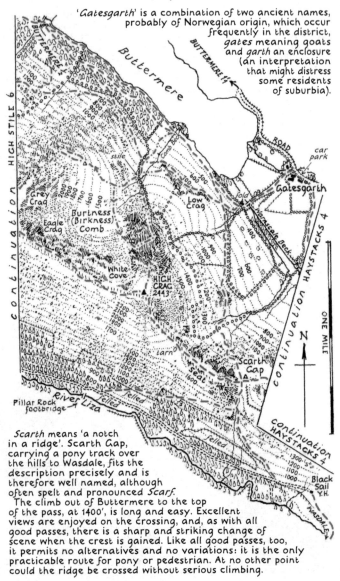

'Gatesgarth' is a combination of two ancient names, probably of Norwegian origin, which occur frequently in the district, *gates* meaning goats and *garth* an enclosure (an interpretation that might distress some residents of suburbia).

Scarth means 'a notch in a ridge'. Scarth Gap, carrying a pony track over the hills to Wasdale, fits the description precisely and is therefore well named, although often spelt and pronounced *Scarf*.

The climb out of Buttermere to the top of the pass, at 1400', is long and easy. Excellent views are enjoyed on the crossing, and, as with all good passes, there is a sharp and striking change of scene when the crest is gained. Like all good passes, too, it permits no alternatives and no variations: it is the only practicable route for pony or pedestrian. At no other point could the ridge be crossed without serious climbing.

ASCENT FROM ENNERDALE
(BLACK SAIL YOUTH HOSTEL)
1500 feet of ascent : 1¾ miles

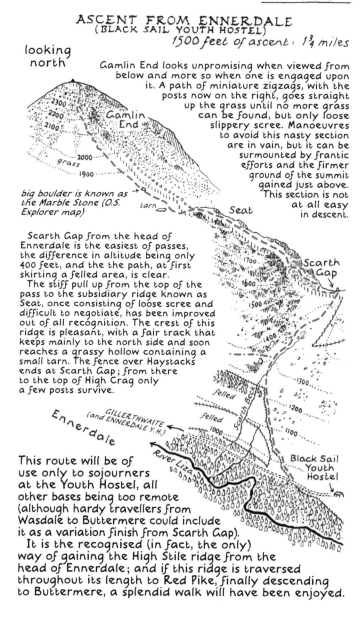

looking north

Gamlin End looks unpromising when viewed from below and more so when one is engaged upon it. A path of miniature zigzags, with the posts now on the right, goes straight up the grass until no more grass can be found, but only loose slippery scree. Manoeuvres to avoid this nasty section are in vain, but it can be surmounted by frantic efforts and the firmer ground of the summit gained just above. This section is not at all easy in descent.

big boulder is known as the Marble Stone (O.S. Explorer map)

Scarth Gap from the head of Ennerdale is the easiest of passes, the difference in altitude being only 400 feet, and the the path, at first skirting a felled area, is clear.

The stiff pull up from the top of the pass to the subsidiary ridge known as Seat, once consisting of loose scree and difficult to negotiate, has been improved out of all recognition. The crest of this ridge is pleasant, with a fair track that keeps mainly to the north side and soon reaches a grassy hollow containing a small tarn. The fence over Haystacks ends at Scarth Gap; from there to the top of High Crag only a few posts survive.

This route will be of use only to sojourners at the Youth Hostel, all other bases being too remote (although hardy travellers from Wasdale to Buttermere could include it as a variation finish from Scarth Gap).

It is the recognised (in fact, the only) way of gaining the High Stile ridge from the head of Ennerdale; and if this ridge is traversed throughout its length to Red Pike, finally descending to Buttermere, a splendid walk will have been enjoyed.

ASCENT FROM GATESGARTH
2100 feet of ascent : 1¾ miles

looking south-west

The loose and nasty slope of scree leading up from Scarth Gap to the pleasant ridge of Seat has been transformed into a beautiful path winding up through rocks and heather. Before the improvements were made an alternative route was formed that turned up by the last wall and reached the ridge at the foot of Gamlin End; this is still in use as a short cut but has no particular charms.

Gamlin End, seen from Seat; line of path indicated (the short cut is shown coming in from the right).

There is a car park opposite Gatesgarth

More often used for the purpose of gaining a foothold on the High Stile ridge, this popular route is well worth doing if the sole object is to climb High Crag only.

ASCENT FROM BUTTERMERE
(DIRECT)

2100 feet of ascent
2½ miles

looking south

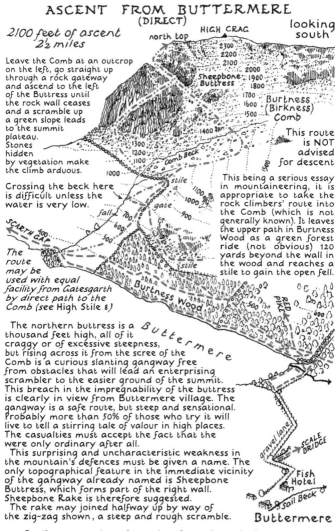

Leave the Comb at an outcrop on the left, go straight up through a rock gateway and ascend to the left of the Buttress until the rock wall ceases and a scramble up a green slope leads to the summit plateau.
Stones hidden by vegetation make the climb arduous.

Crossing the beck here is difficult unless the water is very low.

The route may be used with equal facility from Gatesgarth by direct path to the Comb (see High Stile 8)

This route is NOT advised for descent

This being a serious essay in mountaineering, it is appropriate to take the rock climbers' route into the Comb (which is not generally known). It leaves the upper path in Burtness Wood as a green forest ride (not obvious) 120 yards beyond the wall in the wood and reaches a stile to gain the open fell.

The northern buttress is a thousand feet high, all of it craggy or of excessive steepness, but rising across it from the scree of the Comb is a curious slanting gangway free from obstacles that will lead an enterprising scrambler to the easier ground of the summit. This breach in the impregnability of the buttress is clearly in view from Buttermere village. The gangway is a safe route, but steep and sensational. Probably more than 50% of those who try it will live to tell a stirring tale of valour in high places. The casualties must accept the fact that the were only ordinary after all.

This surprising and uncharacteristic weakness in the mountain's defences must be given a name. The only topographical feature in the immediate vicinity of the gangway already named is Sheepbone Buttress, which forms part of the right wall. Sheepbone Rake is therefore suggested.

The rake may joined halfway up by way of the zig-zag shown, a steep and rough scramble.

Ordinary pedestrians, having already been warned (page 2) that direct access to High Crag is virtually impossible, are here provided with a route that, if safely accomplished, will establish their right to be classed as better than ordinary.

THE SUMMIT

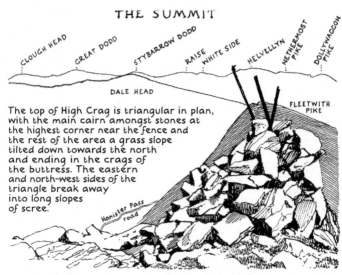

CLOUGH HEAD   GREAT DODD   STYBARROW DODD   RAISE   WHITE SIDE   HELVELLYN   NETHERMOST PIKE   DOLLYWAGGON PIKE

DALE HEAD

FLEETWITH PIKE

The top of High Crag is triangular in plan, with the main cairn amongst stones at the highest corner near the fence and the rest of the area a grass slope tilted down towards the north and ending in the crags of the buttress. The eastern and north-west sides of the triangle break away into long slopes of scree.

Honister Pass road

DESCENTS: The orthodox way off goes down by the fence posts in a south-easterly direction (descend the loose scree with care) and reaches Scarth Gap (Buttermere left, Black Sail right). Distance can be saved, if Buttermere is the destination, by inclining left at the first depression to follow a path beside an old wall: this meets the Scarth Gap path well below the top of the pass. This route is loose and stony, and it is much better to use the improved path to Scarth Gap. *From the north end of the summit plateau a cairned line of descent skirts the north crags on the east scree, but it is rough and bumpy, and dangerous in mist. So is Sheepbone Rake. Neither is recommended as a way down.*

HIGH STILE

2500 2400

Eagle Crag   Burtness Comb

HIGH CRAG

2300
2200
2100
2000
1900
1800

BUTTERMERE

tarn

N

RIDGE ROUTES

To HIGH STILE, 2644': 1 mile
NW : 300 feet of ascent

This magnificent traverse has no difficulties of route finding, the way being precisely defined by the line of fence posts and the steep ground on the right hand side. The good path is distinct most of the way.

To HAYSTACKS, 1959': 1¼ miles : SE 550 feet of ascent

This is an interesting walk with never a dull moment but it lies over rough ground and care should be taken beyond Scarth Gap in mist. A well constructed path avoids the need to negotiate scree on the steep ascent of Haystacks.

700
600
500
1400
1300

Scarth Gap

HAYSTACKS

ONE MILE

THE VIEW

The view is less comprehensive than that from High Stile, but the outlook towards the heart of the district is even better. Wander north a little for some good camera shots not apparent from the top cairn.

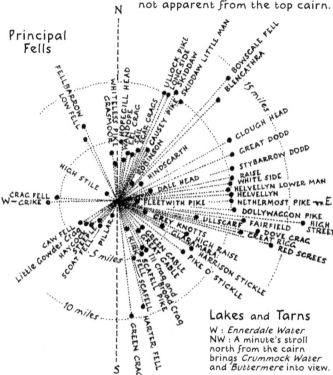

Principal Fells

Lakes and Tarns

W : *Ennerdale Water*
NW : A minute's stroll north from the cairn brings *Crummock Water* and *Buttermere* into view.

This is the best place for viewing the head of Ennerdale. Backed by Great Gable and overtopped by the Scafells, here is a splendid mountain landscape.

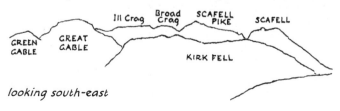

looking south-east

High Stile

2644'

OS grid ref: NY168148

from Buttermere

Buttermere ●
RED PIKE ▲   Gatesgarth ●
        HIGH STILE ▲   HIGH CRAG ▲
Gillerthwaite ●   Scarth)(Gap
        Black Sail Y.H. ●

MILES
0   1   2   3

from Gatesgarth

NATURAL FEATURES

The Buttermere valley is robbed of winter sunshine by a rugged mountain wall exceeding two thousand feet in height and of unusual steepness, its serrated skyline seeming almost to threaten the green fields and dark lake and homesteads far below in its shadow. No mountain range in Lakeland is more dramatically impressive than this, no other more spectacularly sculptured, no other more worth climbing and exploring. Here the scenery assumes truly Alpine characteristics, yet without sacrifice of the intimate charms, the romantic atmosphere, found in Lakeland and nowhere else. From the level strath of the valley the wall rises steeply at once, initially through forests, above which, without respite, buttresses spring upwards from the bare fellside to lose themselves high above in the battlemented crags of the long summit ridge. Three summits rise from this ridge, a trinity of challenging peaks, and of these the central one is the loftiest and grandest.
This is High Stile.

1 : High Stile
2 : Red Pike
3 : High Crag
4 : Burtness Comb
5 : Bleaberry Comb
6 : Ling Comb
7 : Burtness Wood
8 : Buttermere
9 : Crummock Water

looking south

The range is magnificently carved to a simple design on a massive scale. Each of the three summits sends down to the valley a broad buttress, steep, rough, untrodden. To the north of each buttress natural forces ages ago eroded a great hollow, leaving a rim of broken crags. A stream cascades from each hollow. A tarn lies in the central recess like a jewel.
This is superb architecture.

NATURAL FEATURES

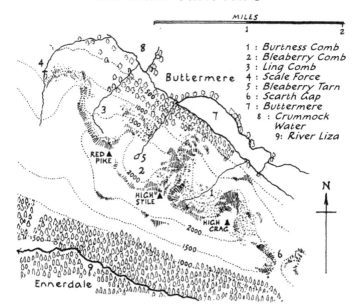

1 : Burtness Comb
2 : Bleaberry Comb
3 : Ling Comb
4 : Scale Force
5 : Bleaberry Tarn
6 : Scarth Gap
7 : Buttermere
8 : Crummock Water
9 : River Liza

Most mountains have a good side and a not-so-good side, and High Stile and its lesser companions, Red Pike and High Crag, conform to the rule. The Buttermere side of the ridge is tremendously exciting and darkly mysterious, compelling attention, but the other flank, by comparison, is plain and dull, without secrets, falling to the new forests of Ennerdale steeply but lacking attractive adornment; for here the contours do not twist and leap about, they run evenly in straight lines. Ennerdale, repeating the Buttermere design, concentrates its finest features on the southern wall of the valley.

North-flowing streams from the High Stile range contribute to the Cocker river system, so reaching the sea at Workington, but the sparser drainage southwards joins the River Ehen * on its remarkable journey from Great Gable to the sea at Sellafield — remarkable because of its obvious hesitation before taking the final plunge.

* née Liza

*Chapel Crags
from
Bleaberry
Tarn*

*Dale Head
and
Fleetwith
Pike
from
Grey Crag,
north-east
spur*

MAP

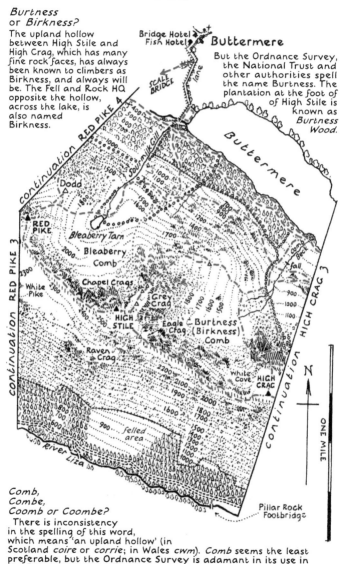

Burtness or *Birkness?*
The upland hollow between High Stile and High Crag, which has many fine rock faces, has always been known to climbers as Birkness, and always will be. The Fell and Rock HQ opposite the hollow, across the lake, is also named Birkness.

But the Ordnance Survey, the National Trust and other authorities spell the name Burtness. The plantation at the foot of High Stile is known as *Burtness Wood*.

Comb, Combe, Coomb or Coombe?
There is inconsistency in the spelling of this word, which means 'an upland hollow' (in Scotland *coire* or *corrie*; in Wales *cwm*). *Comb* seems the least preferable, but the Ordnance Survey is adamant in its use in the Buttermere area. The pronunciation is *coom*.

ASCENT FROM BUTTERMERE
2350 feet of ascent : 2¼ miles

HIGH STILE

looking south-west

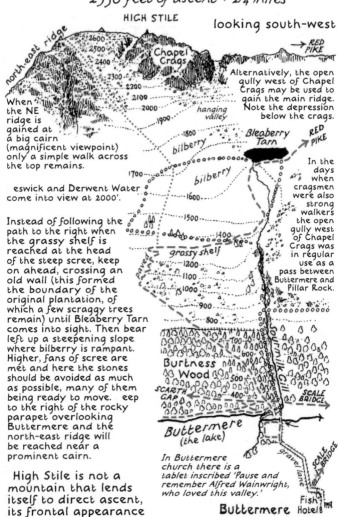

→ RED PIKE

north-east ridge

2600
2500
2400
2300
2200
2100
2000
1900

Chapel Crags

hanging valley

1800

bilberry

Bleaberry Tarn

RED PIKE

Alternatively, the open gully west of Chapel Crags may be used to gain the main ridge. Note the depression below the crags.

When the NE ridge is gained at a big cairn (magnificent viewpoint) only a simple walk across the top remains.

eswick and Derwent Water come into view at 2000'.

Instead of following the path to the right when the grassy shelf is reached at the head of the steep scree, keep on ahead, crossing an old wall (this formed the boundary of the original plantation, of which a few scraggy trees remain) until Bleaberry Tarn comes into sight. Then bear left up a steepening slope where bilberry is rampant. Higher, fans of scree are met and here the stones should be avoided as much as possible, many of them being ready to move. eep to the right of the rocky parapet overlooking Buttermere and the north-east ridge will be reached near a prominent cairn.

1700

bilberry

1600

1500

1400

grassy shelf

1200
1100
1000

900
800
700
600
500
400

paved

In the days when cragsmen were also strong walkers the open gully west of Chapel Crags was in regular use as a pass between Buttermere and Pillar Rock.

Burtness Wood

Sourmilk Gill

SCARTH GAP ←

SCALE BRIDGE →

Buttermere (the lake)

gravel lane

SCALE BRIDGE

In Buttermere church there is a tablet inscribed 'Pause and remember Alfred Wainwright, who loved this valley.'

Buttermere

Fish Hotel

High Stile is not a mountain that lends itself to direct ascent, its frontal appearance being grimly forbidding, and the top is invariably reached along the ridge from Red Pike or High Crag. The route shown here, however, although pathless above 1250', in quite practicable.

ASCENT FROM GATESGARTH
2300 feet of ascent : 2 miles

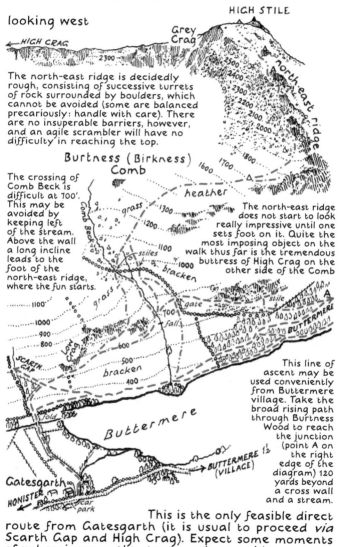

looking west

HIGH STILE

Grey Crag

← HIGH CRAG

2300

north-east ridge

2500
2400
2300
2200
2100
2000

1800
1700
1600

The north-east ridge is decidedly rough, consisting of successive turrets of rock surrounded by boulders, which cannot be avoided (some are balanced precariously: handle with care). There are no insuperable barriers, however, and an agile scrambler will have no difficulty in reaching the top.

Burtness (Birkness) Comb

heather

The crossing of Comb Beck is difficult at 700'. This may be avoided by keeping left of the stream. Above the wall a long incline leads to the foot of the north-east ridge, where the fun starts.

grass

1300
1200
1100
1000

stiles

bracken

The north-east ridge does not start to look really impressive until one sets foot on it. Quite the most imposing object on the walk thus far is the tremendous buttress of High Crag on the other side of the Comb

1100
1000
900
800

grass

gate
700
fall
600
500
400
bracken

stile
BUTTERMERE

SCARTH GAP

Lord Crag

fold

Buttermere

This line of ascent may be used conveniently from Buttermere village. Take the broad rising path through Burtness Wood to reach the junction (point A on the right edge of the diagram) 120 yards beyond a cross wall and a stream.

Gatesgarth

HONISTER →

car park

BUTTERMERE (VILLAGE) 1½ →

This is the only feasible direct route from Gatesgarth (it is usual to proceed *via* Scarth Gap and High Crag). Expect some moments of unhappiness on the steep north-east ridge.

ASCENT FROM ENNERDALE
(HIGH GILLERTHWAITE)
2200 feet of ascent : 2½ miles

Access to the Ennerdale slopes of High Stile is completely barred by fenced forests, and the only public right of way up the fellside is a narrow strip of unplanted ground further to the west provided for the ascent of Red Pike. This route may also be adopted for High Stile, following the ridge path south-east when it is reached at 2400'; up to this point the route is identical with that for Red Pike and suffers from the same demerits and disabilities. A diagram is given on page *Red Pike (B) 9*, and there is no point in repeating it.

Let's have some pictures of Burtness Comb instead.

Two scenes in Burtness Comb

Left : Looking across the Comb to Eagle Crag from Sheepbone Rake.
Right : Looking up the Comb to Eagle Crag.

Burtness Comb has no tarn, and cannot compete with Bleaberry Comb in popular favour. Yet it is the finer of the two, as cragsmen have long realised, and is a grand place to spend a quiet day.

Unlike most mountain hollows its floor is bone-dry and even the beck is partly subterranean; it is notable for a rich July harvest of bilberries, which grow in lush carpets among the tumbled boulders.

THE SUMMIT

The location of the highest point is in doubt. The main ridge (that followed by the fence) rises sharply on the Red Pike side, gradually on the High Crag side, to a rocky eminence crowned with two cairns immediately over the abrupt fall to Chapel Crags, and it is customary to consider the climb ended when this point is reached. The cairns are only a few yards apart. The more northerly of the two, shown left, comes and goes — but what never changes is its magnificent situation with a dramatic view downwards to Bleaberry Tarn. Away to the east, however, a large cairn indicates the Ordnance Survey station, the height of which, 2644', is accepted as the altitude of the fell*, but this cairn, situated where the north-east spur takes shape before narrowing to the north-east ridge, does not seem to be quite so elevated as the two first mentioned, perhaps because the latter occupy a more pronounced rise, nor are its environs so attractive. Just north of this large cairn, a smaller one marks the highest point of the north-east spur. Without measuring instruments it is not possible to say definitely where the highest inches are, and better not to worry about it but to enjoy the sublime surroundings instead.

Stones and boulders litter the top everywhere, and, as all visitors prefer to pick their own way amongst these obstacles, no clear path has been formed.

* *In recent years the height of High Stile (measured at the survey station) has been reassessed as being 2648', but this book will continue to use the traditional figure quoted by the author, above.*

DESCENTS: A woebegone series of fence posts, shorn of all connecting strands, pursues an erratic course across the stony top. The posts are too far apart to guide woebegone walkers to zones of safety, but the ridge is easy enough to follow. To the east, it leads over High Crag to Scarth Gap; west, to Red Pike, and these are the best ways off. The direct routes of ascent (*pages 7 and 8*) from Buttermere and Gatesgarth respectively are not recommended for descent, but Ennerdale (page 9 — diagram on *Red Pike (B) 9*) is a good, fast route.

In emergency, the gully between the ridge top and the north-east spur, shown on the diagram below, may be resorted to — it is a rough and steep but safe descent to Bleaberry Tarn, for Buttermere.

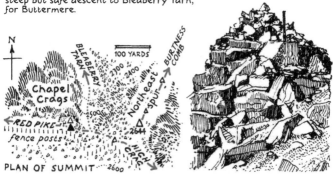

PLAN OF SUMMIT

THE VIEW
(with distances in miles)

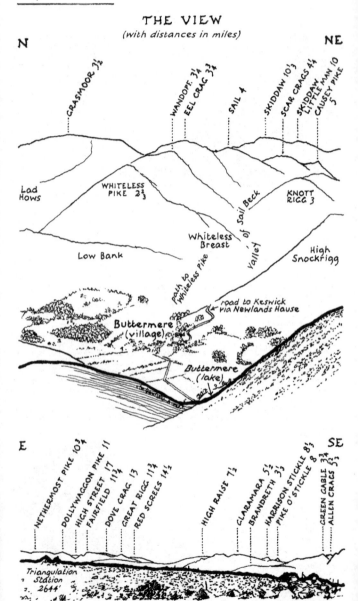

N

NE

GRASMOOR 3½
WANDOPE 3¼
EEL CRAG 3¾
SAIL 4
SKIDDAW 10½
SCAR CRAGS 4¼
SKIDDAW LITTLE MAN 10
CAUSEY PIKE 5

Lad Hows

WHITELESS PIKE 2⅔

Low Bank

Whiteless Breast

Valley of Sail Beck

KNOTT RIGG 3

High Snockrigg

path to Whiteless Pike

road to Keswick via Newlands Hause

Buttermere (village)

Buttermere (lake)

E

SE

NETHERMOST PIKE 10¾
DOLLYWAGGON PIKE 11
HIGH STREET 17
FAIRFIELD 11¾
DOVE CRAG 13
GREAT RIGG 11¾
RED SCREES 14½
HIGH RAISE 7½
GLARAMARA 5½
BRANDRETH 3⅓
HARRISON STICKLE 8⅓
PIKE O'STICKLE 8⅜
GREEN GABLE 3¾
ALLEN CRAGS 5⅓

Triangulation Station 2644'

THE VIEW

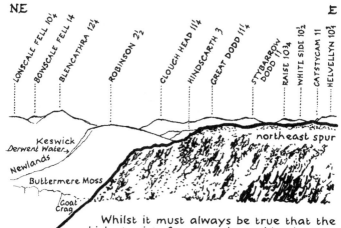

NE

LONSDALE FELL 10¼
BOWSCALE FELL 14
BLENCATHRA 12¼
ROBINSON 2½
CLOUGH HEAD 11¼
HINDSCARTH 3
GREAT DODD 11¼
STYBARROW DODD 11
RAISE 10¾
WHITE SIDE 10½
CATSTYCAM 11
HELVELLYN 10¾

E

Keswick
Derwent Water
Newlands
Buttermere Moss
Goat Crag

northeast spur

Whilst it must always be true that the highest point of a mountain provides the most extensive view it by no means follows that it must therefore be the best station for surveying the surrounding landscape, nor even that it must be most prominently seen in views of the mountain from other heights in the vicinity. On the map of Lakeland there are several instances where the triangulation stations of the Ordnance Survey are sited some distance away from the actual summit.

On High Stile the highest point appears to occur on the main ridge coming up from Red Pike, and this elevation has been selected for the panorama here given, but the Ordnance Survey station is a furlong to the east and not quite on the highest point of the north-east spur, which, in the view above, cuts into the horizon between White Side and Catstycam.

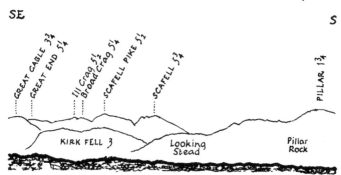

SE

GREAT GABLE 3¾
GREAT END 5¼
ILL CRAG 5½
BROAD CRAG 5¼
SCAFELL PIKE 5½
SCAFELL 5¾
PILLAR 1¾

S

KIRK FELL 3
Looking Stead
Pillar Rock

THE VIEW

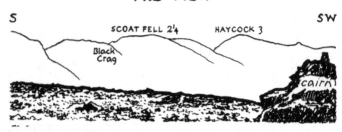

S

SCOAT FELL 2¼   HAYCOCK 3

SW

Black Crag

cairn

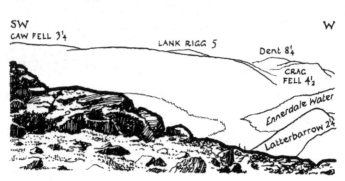

SW
CAW FELL 3¼

W

LANK RIGG 5

Dent 8¼

CRAG FELL 4½

Ennerdale Water

Latterbarrow 2¼

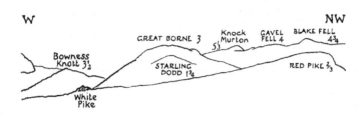

W

NW

GREAT BORNE 3

Knock Murton 5⅓

GAVEL FELL 4

BLAKE FELL 4¾

Bowness Knott 3½

STARLING DODD 1¾

RED PIKE ⅔

White Pike

The thick black line marks the visible boundaries of the fell from the viewpoint

In clear weather, the Isle of Man appears over Lank Rigg, Scotland and the Solway Firth above Crummock Water, and the Irish Sea extends across the western horizon.

THE VIEW

NW   N

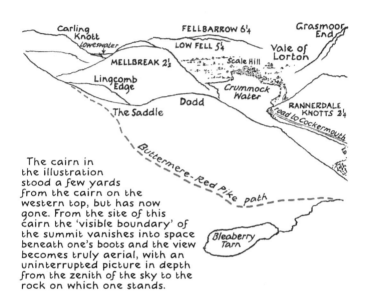

The cairn in the illustration stood a few yards from the cairn on the western top, but has now gone. From the site of this cairn the 'visible boundary' of the summit vanishes into space beneath one's boots and the view becomes truly aerial, with an uninterrupted picture in depth from the zenith of the sky to the rock on which one stands.

RIDGE ROUTE

TO RED PIKE, 2479' : ¾ mile : NW

Depression at 2300' : 200 feet of ascent

Very easy walking after initial roughness.

The line of fence posts that follows the ridge and skirts the summit of Red Pike survives only in places. Elsewhere the posts are too far apart to be followed in mist, but there is a good path for most of the way, and the last part of the route is cairned. The route passes the gaping mouth of the Chapel Crags gully and there are fine views down into Bleaberry Comb along its whole length.

RED PIKE

Bleaberry Comb

2300

Chapel Crags

N

2200 2400 2300

HIGH STILE

ONE MILE

Red Pike from High Stile

RIDGE ROUTE

To HIGH CRAG, 2443' : 1 mile : SE
80 feet of ascent.
Minor depressions only.
Simple, but grand.

There is no path at first, but one forms when the ridge narrows. The line of fence posts is continuous to High Crag, and it is important to keep them in sight in bad weather.

N

HIGH STILE   Grey Crag

Burtness Comb   Eagle Crag

2500 2400 2300 2200

HIGH CRAG

ONE MILE

Looking back to High Stile from the ridge, a view of Eagle Crag in profile, and Grey Crag, more distant across the depths of the Comb, is seen.

The escarpment here falls away suddenly and vertically; this danger, fortunately, lurks some distance below the path used by walkers along the ridge.

Kirk Fell

2630'

OS grid ref: NY195105

from Green Gable

NATURAL FEATURES

irk Fell is the patron fell of Wasdale Head, a distinction little recognised. To most visitors in this grandest of all daleheads, Great Gable so catches the eye that irk Fell, next to it, is hardly looked at; and even the other two fells enclosing the valley, Lingmell and Yewbarrow, win more glances. irk Fell, although bulking large in the scene, is in fact plain and unattractive, a vast wall of bracken and grass, every yard of it much like the rest. Everybody's camera points to Great Gable, nobody's to irk Fell. But look at the map. The streams coming down each side of irk Fell, Lingmell Beck and Mosedale Beck, are long in meeting: for a mile or more at valley level they enclose a flat tongue of land at the foot of irk Fell. Every building in the little hamlet of Wasdale Head — cottages, farmhouses, church and inn, and all the valley pastures, lie in the lap of irk Fell on this flat extension between the two streams. The fell takes its name from the church. irk Fell accommodates the community of Wasdale Head, but the footings in the valley of Great Gable and Lingmell and Yewbarrow are barren.

Bland the southern aspect may be, but the dark north face is very different. Here, shadowed cliffs seam the upper slopes in a long escarpment, a playground for climbers, above rough declivities that go down to the Liza in Ennerdale. Linking with Great Gable is the depression of Beck Head to the east; westwards is a counterpart in Black Sail Pass, linking with Pillar. And between is a broad undulating top, with tarns, the ruins of a wire fence, and twin summits: on the whole a rather disappointing ornamentation, a poor crown for so massive a plinth.

Gatesgarth

Seatoller

Black Sail Y.H.   Seathwaite

▲ PILLAR

KIRK FELL
▲ GREAT GABLE

● Wasdale Head

MILES

0   1   2   3

MAP

irkfell Crags occur in two
series, the first overlooking
Black Sail Pass in a broken cliff and the other, steeply
buttressing the north-east summit and exhibiting cleaner
rock faces, having the adopted name of Boat How Crags.

ASCENT FROM WASDALE HEAD
2330 feet of ascent : 1¼ miles

A straight line is the shortest
distance between two points.
This route is the straightest
and therefore the most direct
ascent in Lakeland. It is also
the steepest — a relentless
and unremitting treadmill,
a turf-clutching crawl, not a
walk. There are only three
opportunities of standing
upright, three heaven-sent
bits of horizontal, before the
slope eases into the summit
plateau. Apart from steepness,
there are no difficulties or
hazards of any sort.

KIRK FELL

natural dykes

2500
2400

*third halting
place (small
delectable
grass ridge
at the top
of the
scree)*

2300
2200
2100
2000
1900
1800

grass
1700
1600

Highnose Head
1500

*second halting place
(crest of steep
grass slope)*

grass
1400
1300

1200

*Back buttons
cannot stand
the strain, and
wearers of braces
are well advised to
profit from a sad
experience of the
author on this climb
and take a belt as
reserve support.*

1100

grass
1000

900

*first halting place
(top of small crag)*

800
*Looking backwards
(between one's legs)
there is a superb
upside-down view
of Wasdale Head*

700

600

bracken
500

Two alternative routes
are available and more
generally used. Either (a)
proceed to the top of
Black Sail Pass, thence
climbing the north ridge
— see map on facing page —
or (b) go up to Beck Head
and ascend Rib End. In
both cases the top of the
fell is reached after an
interesting scramble on
a stony track alongside
the watershed fence.

BLACK SAIL PASS

looking
north

Wasdale
Head

Inn   Row Head

Leave Wasdale Head by the Black
Sail path, first passing through the yard of the
Wasdale Head Inn and then following Mosedale Beck upstream.

ASCENT FROM ENNERDALE
(BLACK SAIL YOUTH HOSTEL)

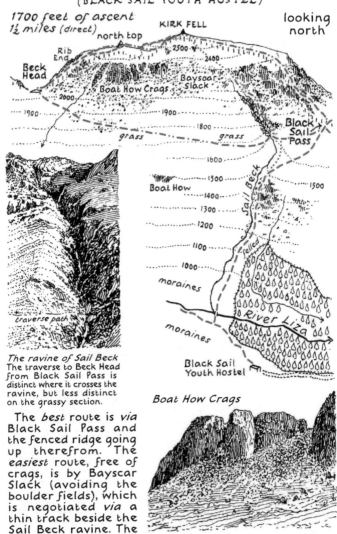

1700 feet of ascent
1½ miles (direct)

looking
north

KIRK FELL

north top

2500

2400

Rib
End

Beck
Head

Boat How Crags

Baysoar
Slack

2000

1900

1900

1800

grass

grass

Black
Sail
Pass

1600

1500

1500

Boat How

1400

1300

1200

1100

1000

moraines

Sail Beck

felled

moraines

River Liza

Black Sail
Youth Hostel

traverse path

The ravine of Sail Beck
The traverse to Beck Head
from Black Sail Pass is
distinct where it crosses the
ravine, but less distinct
on the grassy section.

Boat How Crags

The *best* route is *via*
Black Sail Pass and
the fenced ridge going
up therefrom. The
easiest route, free of
crags, is by Bayscar
Slack (avoiding the
boulder fields), which
is negotiated *via* a
thin track beside the
Sail Beck ravine. The
most interesting route,
which passes beneath Boat How Crags, is along the grassy
traverse and up from Beck Head *via* the Rib End ridge.

THE SUMMIT

irk Fell has two separate tops, the higher being at the head of the Wasdale slope in an area of stones. Here is the main cairn, which takes the form of a wind shelter, and there is a second wind shelter 30 yards further north. The fence, which otherwise follows the water shed strictly, rather oddly does not quite visit the highest point at 2630'. The other top, north east, is appreciably lower, the cairn here surmounting a rocky outcrop. In a hollow between the two summits are two unattractive tarns, named as one, irkfell Tarn. (One of the tarns has dried up.)

DESCENTS: The top of the fell is usually left with the guidance of the fence, which, after a long crossing of the summit plateau, goes down northwards to Black Sail Pass; or, eastwards, over the lesser summit and down Rib End to Beck Head. Either route may be used for Wasdale Head or Ennerdale and both descend roughly on distinct stony tracks amongst crags although the top of the fell is pathless. For Wasdale Head direct, wander south, where a line of cairns leads down to a small and dainty grass ridge (it is important to find this). Below starts the very steep and straight descent, stony at first. Grass is reached at 2000', and from this point onwards a badly shod walker will suffer many slips and spills, none fatal, and it is not a bad plan to continue in bare or stockinged feet, which give a better grip than boots.

the north-east summit

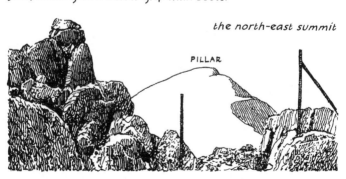

THE VIEW

Great Gable dominates the scene but does not rob the view of detail, which is well distributed over all sectors. The Scafells look magnificent, and the path up to the Pike from the Lingmell *col* is clearly seen. Criffel appears over High Crag.

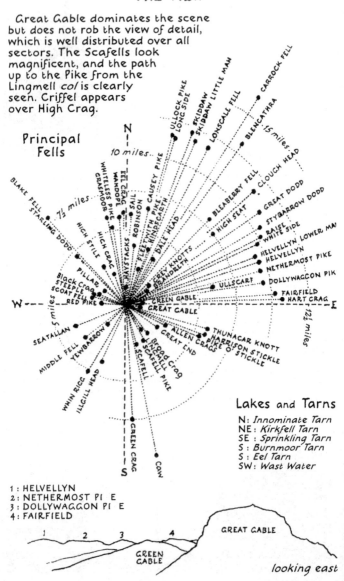

Principal Fells

Lakes and Tarns

N : *Innominate Tarn*
NE : *Kirkfell Tarn*
SE : *Sprinkling Tarn*
S : *Burnmoor Tarn*
S : *Eel Tarn*
SW : *Wast Water*

1 : HELVELLYN
2 : NETHERMOST PI E
3 : DOLLYWAGGON PI E
4 : FAIRFIELD

looking east

RIDGE ROUTES

To PILLAR, 2927′ : 2½ miles : NW, then N and WNW
Depression at 1800′ (Black Sail Pass)
1150 feet of ascent

A walk full of interest, but a long one.
Check there is sufficient time to do it.

PILLAR
2800 2700 2600 2500 2400 2300 2200 2100 2000 1900 1800

HIGH-LEVEL ROUTE

ONE MILE

N

▲ Looking Stead

Tarn

WASDALE HEAD

Black Sail Pass

1800 1900 2000 2100 2200 2300 2400 2500

Kirkfell Crags

KIRK FELL

Very easy walking
by the fence leads to a
steepening slope, and here
a track materialises amongst the
stones. When crags are reached the
fence does a bit of rock climbing, but
prefer to keep the track underfoot, and,
after one awkward step, Black Sail Pass
will be duly reached. An opportunity of
changing one's mind and beating a quick
retreat to Wasdale Head or into Ennerdale
here arises. In front there is a splendid walk
across Looking Stead (detour to the cairn for
the view) before the first of the three stony
rises on the ridge is tackled. The whole climb
from Black Sail Pass is quite easy.

To GREAT GABLE, 2949′ : 1⅓ miles : NE, then E and SE
Depression at 2040′ (Beck Head) : 990 feet of ascent.
Rough going, but well worth the effort.

2500 Beck Head
Rib End
KIRK FELL ▲ 2500 Kirkfell Tarn 2200 2100 2000 2100 1800
▲ GREAT GABLE

Follow the fence over the lower summit to join a stony
track down the craggy declivity
of Rib End to Beck Head.
Beyond, up the steep
facing slope, keep
left to find the
best footing.

Great Gable from Kirkfell Tarn

Lank Rigg

1775'

OS grid ref: NY092120

from Friar Moor
near Coldfell Gate

• Ennerdale Bridge

GRIKE ▲   ▲ CRAG FELL

▲ LANK RIGG
CAW FELL ▲
• Coldfell Gate
• Thornholme
• Scalderskew

• Calder Bridge

MILES
0   1   2   3   4

Water Intake Works, Worm Gill
(now derelict)

NATURAL FEATURES

Ridgewalkers on the more frequented western fells will occasionally notice the isolated summit of Lank Rigg appearing on the skyline and almost certainly will need to refer to a map to determine its identity, for this is a fell most visitors have never heard of and few know sufficiently well to recognise on sight. The map will confirm further that Lank Rigg is an outsider, beyond the accepted limits of Lakeland, too remote to bother about. If Pillar and High Stile haven't yet been climbed, there is admittedly no case to be made out for this humble fell, but walkers already familiar with the district might well devote a day to this lonely outpost of innside; they will do so with especial advantage if of an enquiring turn of mind for things ancient. A column on the summit shows that the Ordnance men have a regard for the place. And Lank Rigg is, after all, within the Lake District National Park boundary.

The fell has wide sprawling slopes and is extensive. It calls for a full day's expedition even if the problem of reaching its environs can be overcome by car or helicopter, for it is distant from tourist centres. To walk all round it, having got there, is a rough tramp of ten miles. Meeting another human is outside the realms of possibility. Die here, unaccompanied, and your disappearance from society is likely to remain an unsolved mystery.

Lank Rigg is bounded by two streams that quickly assume the proportions of rivers. One of them, the Calder, has the name of river from birth; the other, Worm Gill, at one time tapped for water supplies, is a fast flowing torrent that has carved a wide course through the hills.

Some prehistoric remains suggest that the fell was probably better known in ages past. More recent, but still many centuries old, is a packhorse bridge spanning a ravine of the Calder, a thing of beauty.

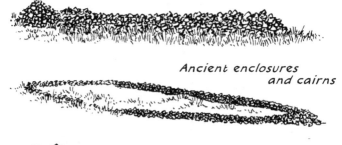

Ancient enclosures
and cairns

on Tongue How,
Town Bank

Lank Rigg 3

MAP

In conversation Lank Rigg becomes one word, pronounced *Lan-krigg*.

Matty Benn's Bridge, although known thus locally, is named Monks Bridge on maps of the Ordnance Survey. 'Matty' was Martha Benn, a late 1800s farmer's wife well known for her enjoyment of alcohol.

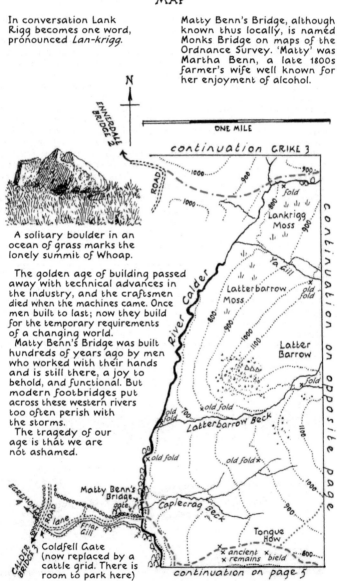

A solitary boulder in an ocean of grass marks the lonely summit of Whoap.

The golden age of building passed away with technical advances in the industry, and the craftsmen died when the machines came. Once men built to last; now they build for the temporary requirements of a changing world.

Matty Benn's Bridge was built hundreds of years ago by men who worked with their hands and is still there, a joy to behold, and functional. But modern footbridges put across these western rivers too often perish with the storms.

The tragedy of our age is that we are not ashamed.

continuation CRIKE 3

continuation on opposite page

continuation on page 5

Coldfell Gate (now replaced by a cattle grid. There is room to park here)

MAP

The pathless route from Tongue How (shown on the facing page) leading to Boat How and then on to the summit (this page) is pointed out on *page 6* as ways of ascent from Coldfell Gate and Calder Bridge.

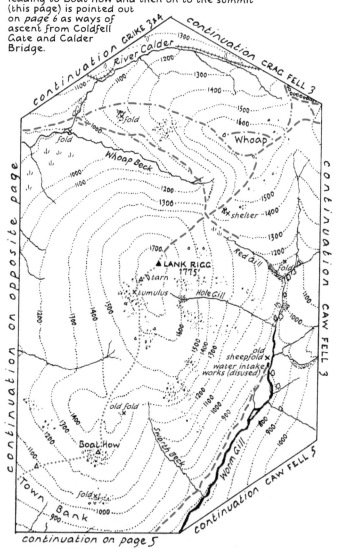

continuation CRIKE 3&4
continuation CRAG FELL 3
continuation on opposite page
continuation CAW FELL 3
continuation CAW FELL 5
continuation on page 5

River Calder

fold

fold

Whoap Beck

Whoap

shelter

Red Gill

▲ LANK RIGG 1775

tarn

tumulus

Hole Gill

fold

old sheepfold

water intake works (disused)

Worm Gill

old fold

Swath Beck

Boat How △

fold

Town Bank

MAP

continuation on pages 3 and 4

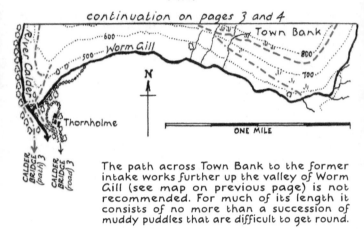

The path across Town Bank to the former
intake works further up the valley of Worm
Gill (see map on previous page) is not
recommended. For much of its length it
consists of no more than a succession of
muddy puddles that are difficult to get round.

Matty Benn's Bridge

The valley of
the River Calder
near Thornholme

ASCENT FROM THE COLDFELL ROAD
1400 feet of ascent : 2½ miles

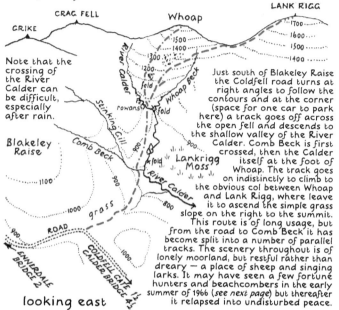

Note that the crossing of the River Calder can be difficult, especially after rain.

Just south of Blakeley Raise the Coldfell road turns at right angles to follow the contours and at the corner (space for one car to park here) a track goes off across the open fell and descends to the shallow valley of the River Calder. Comb Beck is first crossed, then the Calder itself at the foot of Whoap. The track goes on indistinctly to climb to the obvious col between Whoap and Lank Rigg, where leave it to ascend the simple grass slope on the right to the summit. This route is of long usage, but from the road to Comb Beck it has become split into a number of parallel tracks. The scenery throughout is of lonely moorland, but restful rather than dreary — a place of sheep and singing larks. It may have seen a few fortune hunters and beachcombers in the early summer of 1966 (*see next page*) but thereafter it relapsed into undisturbed peace.

looking east

For the man who wants to get away from it all, alone.

ASCENT FROM COLDFELL GATE
via Boat How — 1800 feet of ascent : 4 miles

Rather less conveniently, a footing may be gained on Lank Rigg from Coldfell Gate (3 miles from Calder Bridge; 4¼ from Ennerdale Bridge, on the Coldfell road). Here a lane goes down to ford the Calder, and upstream 120 yards of this point, reached from a gate in the field wall, is Matty Benn's Bridge, which must be visited even though its function has been taken over by a modern footbridge alongside the ford. Across the river rise the long gentle slopes of Lank Rigg and they may be tackled anywhere, but the most interesting plan is to go via Tongue How and Boat How, both of which have many ancient remains in the vicinity. The summit is a mile north of Boat How.

This route is indicated on the map on *pages 3 and 4*.

ASCENT FROM CALDER BRIDGE
via Boat How — 2000 feet of ascent : 6 miles

Now that there is a footbridge across Worm Gill just short of its confluence with the Calder at Thornholme, a very pleasant approach can be made from Calder Bridge, visiting the Abbey on the way. In fact, there is also a footbridge over the Calder at Thornholme, which means that the public footpath from Stakes Bridge can be used. The route is practicable and pleasant, but there is no continuous path. Refer to *pages 3 and 4* which show the suggested route from the River Calder over first Tongue How and then (pathless) over Boat How.

THE SUMMIT

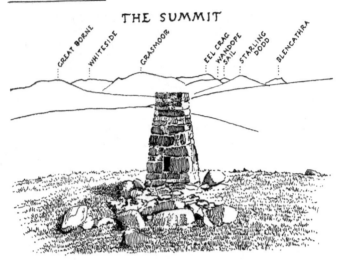

The highest point on the grassy summit is indicated by a column of the Ordnance Survey, S 5647. South-west across the flat top is a small tarn and beyond this a rough outcrop and cairn from which is seen, further south-west, a large tumulus of antiquarian interest. DESCENTS: In dry weather the best way down is by way of Whoap Beck, but after rain it is better to head south to Tongue How.

Buried Treasure on Lank Rigg

The only exciting experience in the lonely life of the Ordnance column occurred on a gloriously sunny day in April 1965, when it was a mute and astonished witness to an unparalleled act of generosity. In an uncharacteristic mood of magnanimity which he subsequently regretted, the author decided on this summit to share his hard won royalties with one of his faithful readers and placed a two-shilling piece under a flat stone four feet from the column: it awaited the first person to read this note and act upon it. The finder was invited to write in c/o the publishers and confirm his claim by stating the year of the coin's issue. If nobody had done so by the end of 1966 the author intended to go back and retrieve it for the purchase of fish and chips. It is reported that the coin was recovered the day after publication, and it has become a tradition for visitors to the summit to leave a coin here for others to find.

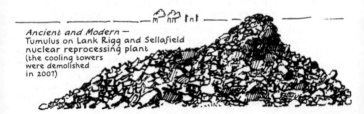

Ancient and Modern —
Tumulus on Lank Rigg and Sellafield nuclear reprocessing plant (the cooling towers were demolished in 2007)

THE VIEW

Except for an unexpected appearance by Blencathra, the scene inland to the mountains is unremarkable, and it is the villages and towns of West Cumbria, seen as on a map, that provide most interest. The distant height overtopping Grike is Criffel in Scotland.

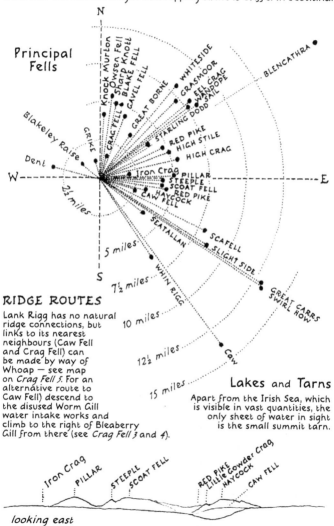

Principal Fells

N

Knock Murton
Owsen Fell
Sharp Knoll
Blake Fell
Gavel Fell
GREAT BORNE
WHITESIDE
GRASMOOR
EEL CRAG
WANDOPE
SAIL
STARLING DODD
BLENCATHRA
RED PIKE
HIGH STILE
HIGH CRAG

Blakeley Raise
GRIKE
CRAG FELL
Dent

W

Iron Crag
PILLAR
STEEPLE
SCOAT FELL
RED PIKE
HAYCOCK
FELL

E

2½ miles

SEATALLAN
SCAFELL
SLIGHT SIDE

S

5 miles

WHIN RIGG

7½ miles

GREAT CARRS
SWIRL HOW

10 miles

Caw

12½ miles

15 miles

RIDGE ROUTES

Lank Rigg has no natural ridge connections, but links to its nearest neighbours (Caw Fell and Crag Fell) can be made by way of Whoap — see map on *Crag Fell 5*. For an alternative route to Caw Fell) descend to the disused Worm Gill water intake works and climb to the right of Bleaberry Gill from there (see *Crag Fell 3 and 4*).

Lakes and Tarns

Apart from the Irish Sea, which is visible in vast quantities, the only sheet of water in sight is the small summit tarn.

Iron Crag
PILLAR
STEEPLE
SCOAT FELL
RED PIKE
Little Gowder Crag
HAYCOCK
CAW FELL

looking east

Low Fell

1352'

OS grid ref: NY136223

from Lanthwaite Hill

The lesser heights and foothills of Lakeland, especially those on the fringe, are too much neglected in favour of the greater mountains, yet many of these unsought and unfashionable little hills are completely charming. In this category is Low Fell, north of Loweswater and west of the Vale of Lorton. It has many tops, uniformly around 1350 feet, rising from a ridge. The most southerly eminence has the main cairn and a perfectly composed view of mountain and lake scenery, a connoisseur's piece.

Low Fell and Fellbarrow together form a separate range, a final upthrust of land between Lakeland and the sea. The underlying rock is slate, and the hills exhibit smooth rounded slopes in conformity to pattern; but they deny conformity to the lake of Loweswater, forcing its issuing stream, by a freak of contours, to flow inland, away from the sea, in compliance with the inexorable natural law that water always obeys.

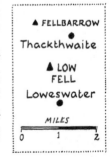

MAP

ONE MILE

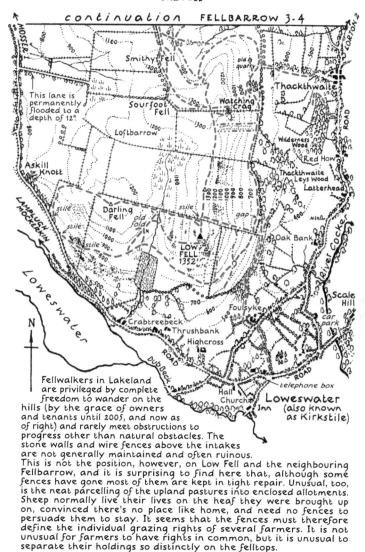

continuation FELLBARROW 3-4

Fellwalkers in Lakeland
are privileged by complete
freedom to wander on the
hills (by the grace of owners
and tenants until 2005, and now as
of right) and rarely meet obstructions to
progress other than natural obstacles. The
stone walls and wire fences above the intakes
are not generally maintained and often ruinous.
This is not the position, however, on Low Fell and the neighbouring
Fellbarrow, and it is surprising to find here that, although some
fences have gone most of them are kept in tight repair. Unusual, too,
is the neat parcelling of the upland pastures into enclosed allotments.
Sheep normally live their lives on the heaf they were brought up
on, convinced there's no place like home, and need no fences to
persuade them to stay. It seems that the fences must therefore
define the individual grazing rights of several farmers. It is not
unusual for farmers to have rights in common, but it is unusual to
separate their holdings so distinctly on the felltops.

ASCENT FROM LOWESWATER
1050 feet of ascent : 2 miles (direct route)
1350 feet of ascent : 3 miles (via Darling Fell)

From the top of Crabtree Beck it is usual to follow the steep path up beside the fence to the depression on the ridge, there turning right towards the summit. However, an easier alternative has appeared in recent years utilising a chink in Low Fell's stony armour on this flank — a thin but fairly clear path follows a grassy route all the way to the *col* between the summit and the south top. This is especially good in descent.

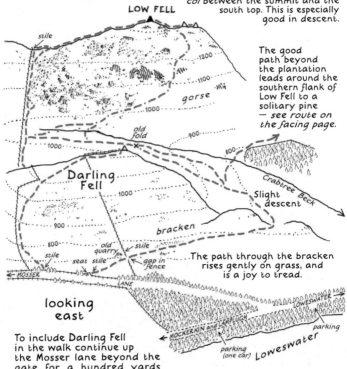

The good path beyond the plantation leads around the southern flank of Low Fell to a solitary pine — *see route on the facing page.*

The path through the bracken rises gently on grass, and is a joy to tread.

looking east

To include Darling Fell in the walk continue up the Mosser lane beyond the gate for a hundred yards and turn right at a stile just beyond a small cluster of bushes (look for a signpost). This route is easy to follow and pleasant underfoot, but there is a quite considerable depression between Darling Fell and Low Fell. The summit of Darling Fell offers beautiful views over Loweswater.

A wide belt of cultivated land in private occupation and without public paths lies between the valley road and the open fell. The easiest way to reach rough ground is to go up the lane towards Mosser (most definitely unsuitable for motor vehicles) and take a path on the right where a seat is set back from the lane.

Wait for a bright clear day. Don't forget the camera.

ASCENT FROM LOWESWATER
VIA THE TERRACE PATH
1100 feet of ascent : 2 miles

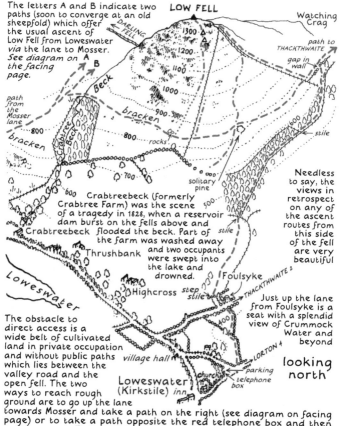

The letters A and B indicate two paths (soon to converge at an old sheepfold) which offer the usual ascent of Low Fell from Loweswater via the lane to Mosser. See diagram on the facing page.

LOW FELL

Watching Crag

DARLING FELL

1300

path to THACKTHWAITE

1200

gap in wall

1100

1000

path from the Mosser lane

Beck

900

bracken

800

Crabtree Beck

bracken

800

rocks

stile

700

600

solitary pine

Crabtreebeck (formerly Crabtree Farm) was the scene of a tragedy in 1828, when a reservoir dam burst on the fells above and Crabtreebeck flooded the beck. Part of the farm was washed away and two occupants were swept into the lake and drowned.

500

stile

Needless to say, the views in retrospect on any of the ascent routes from this side of the fell are very beautiful

Thrushbank

Loweswater

Foulsyke

Highcross step stile

THACKTHWAITE

Just up the lane from Foulsyke is a seat with a splendid view of Crummock Water and beyond

The obstacle to direct access is a wide belt of cultivated land in private occupation and without public paths which lies between the valley road and the open fell. The two ways to reach rough ground are to go up the lane

village hall

400

LORTON 4

looking north

Loweswater (Kirkstile) inn

church parking telephone box

towards Mosser and take a path on the right (see diagram on facing page) or to take a path opposite the red telephone box and then continue past Foulsyke and onto a pleasant woodland path.

Be warned, however, the way up beside the fence on the right-hand edge of this diagram is very steep. In descent, none of the routes shown are particularly pleasant.

From the valley below, the rugged southern flank of Low Fell seems to rule out a direct ascent; however, there are a number of ways up from the popular terrace path above the intake wall including one that visits an imposing pine tree. Now if only there was a path through the lower pastures...

ASCENT FROM THACKTHWAITE
1250 feet of ascent : 2 miles

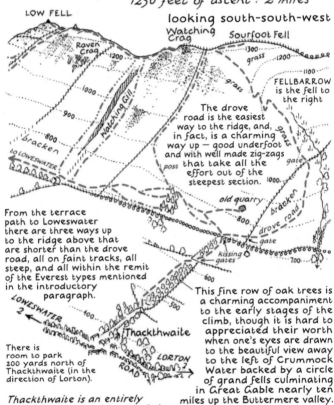

looking south-south-west

LOW FELL

Watching Crag

Sourfoot Fell

Raven Crag

1200

1300 grass

1200

1100

FELLBARROW
is the fell to
the right

1000

900

grass

gate

800 bracken

TO LOWESWATER

Matching Gill

post

1000

The drove road is the easiest way to the ridge, and, in fact, is a charming way up — good underfoot and with well made zig-zags that take all the effort out of the steepest section.

old quarry

800

bracken

drove road

gate

From the terrace path to Loweswater there are three ways up to the ridge above that are shorter than the drove road, all on faint tracks, all steep, and all within the remit of the Everest types mentioned in the introductory paragraph.

kissing gates

700

600

LOWESWATER 2

100

There is room to park 200 yards north of Thackthwaite (in the direction of Lorton).

Thackthwaite

500

LORTON ROAD

Thackthwaite is an entirely delightful little hamlet — wooded, tranquil, mercifully free of any significant traffic — which looks as if, sometime around the middle of the 1950s, it fell into a time warp from which it has no intention of escaping.

This fine row of oak trees is a charming accompaniment to the early stages of the climb, though it is hard to appreciated their worth when one's eyes are drawn to the beautiful view away to the left of Crummock Water backed by a circle of grand fells culminating in Great Gable nearly ten miles up the Buttermere valley.

The lane from the village becomes overgrown and impassable after 200 yards; here use a gate on the left and continue up the fields alongside to the gate in the intake wall.

When the doctor forbids climbing above 1500 feet, the future of his patient need not be entirely bleak. There is always Low Fell, and its ascent from Thackthwaite by way of Watching Crag is a very lovely epitome of the best of the days gone by. It is also a worthwhile little exercise for those perfect specimens with strength enough to tackle Everest.

THE SUMMIT

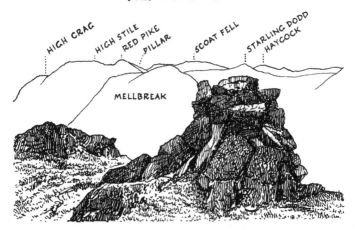

HIGH CRAG — HIGH STILE — RED PIKE — PILLAR — SCOAT FELL — STARLING DODD HAYCOCK

MELLBREAK

The biggest cairn is on the southern eminence, which is treated as the summit in this book, but the smooth north top appears to be slightly higher. This is confirmed by the O.S. Explorer map, which gives the altitudes as 1352' and 1388' respectively. This means that the column at 1363' on the more massive Fellbarrow is not the highest point on the range, as was once thought. Two cairns 100 and 120 yards south-east of the main cairn indicate better viewpoints for the Loweswater valley, Crummock Water and the Buttermere valley.

DESCENTS: For Foulsyke head north and follow the fence steeply down to a horizontal path leading to a stile in the intake wall. The steepness may be avoided by taking the longer route to Thackthwaite. For Crabtreebeck follow the ridge to the north and look for a path on the left leading to a fence. Follow the fence down to Crabtree Beck and turn left to a sheepfold. Beyond here the route can become confusing in mist, and it is easier to use the longer route over Darling How. The direct route on the western flank to Crabtree Beck (shown on *page 3*) is probably the best of all the ways down but may be difficult to follow in mist.

Cairn on the north top, now rather larger

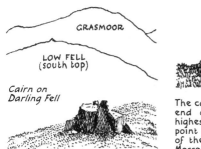

GRASMOOR

LOW FELL (south top)

Cairn on Darling Fell

The cairn on Darling Fell marks the end of the ridge and not the highest point on the fell. The highest point is situated forty yards east of the fence coming up from the Mosser lane.

THE VIEW

South-east the view is of classical beauty, an inspired and inspiring vision of loveliness that has escaped the publicity of picture postcards and poets' sonnets, a scene of lakes and mountains arranged to perfection. The grouping of fells above Mosedale is also attractively presented, with Pillar an unexpected absentee, only a small section of its western shoulder being seen behind Red Pike. Grasmoor is a tremendous object. Westwards is the sea.

Principal Fells

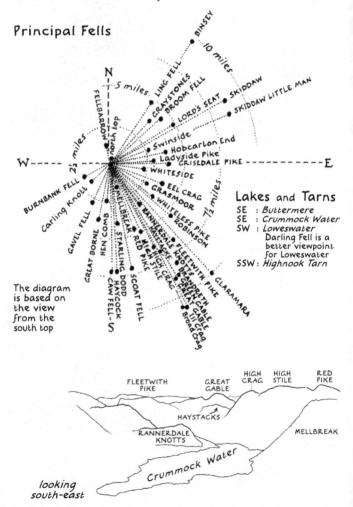

BINSEY

10 miles

N

5 miles · LING FELL
GRAYSTONES
BROOM FELL
LORD'S SEAT
SKIDDAW
SKIDDAW LITTLE MAN

FELLBARROW

2½ miles · Loweswater dog

Swinside
Hobcarton End
Ladyside Pike
GRISLEDALE PIKE

W
WHITESIDE
EEL CRAG

BURNBANK FELL
GRASMOOR
WHITELESS PIKE
ROBINSON

Corling Knott
MELLBREAK
1½ miles

GAVEL FELL
RANNERDALE
HIGH SNOCKRIGG
RED PIKE
HIGH STILE
FLEETWITH PIKE
CLARAMARA

GREAT BORNE
HEN COMB
STARLING DODD
HIGH CRAG
BRANDRETH
GREAT GABLE
Kirk Fell
Broad Crag

The diagram is based on the view from the south top

HAYCOCK
SCOAT FELL
CAW FELL

S

Lakes and Tarns

SE : Buttermere
SE : Crummock Water
SW : Loweswater
    Darling Fell is a
    better viewpoint
    for Loweswater
SSW : Highnook Tarn

FLEETWITH PIKE   GREAT GABLE   HIGH CRAG   HIGH STILE   RED PIKE

HAYSTACKS

RANNERDALE KNOTTS

MELLBREAK

Crummock Water

looking south-east

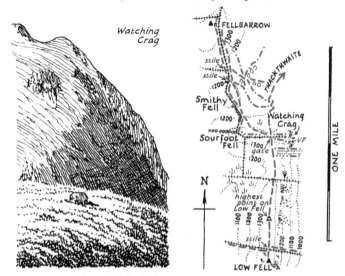

RIDGE ROUTE

To FELLBARROW, 1363' : 1½ miles : N
Several depressions : 400 feet of ascent

Watching Crag

FELLBARROW
stile
stile
THACKTHWAITE
Smithy Fell
Watching Crag
Sourfoot Fell
VP
gate
ONE MILE
N
highest point on Low Fell
LOW FELL

This simple walk is better enjoyed in reverse, from north to south, because when traversed in that direction the best views are always in front. Nevertheless, this is still a pleasant cross-country stroll on a good path with enough ups and downs to add interest. Note Low Fell's north top, which is actually the highest point on the fell and offers a fine view of Whiteside and Grasmoor. In good weather a detour to the top of Watching Crag is recommended — the bird's eye view of the Vale of Lorton far below is very beautiful. *Avoid this detour in mist* (there will be no view and there are crags which could pose a serious danger).

HOPEGILL HEAD   GRISEDALE PIKE   WHITESIDE   GRASMOOR

Gasgale Gill

Vale of Lorton

cairn

The view east from the cairn on Low Fell's north top (the highest point on the fell)

Mellbreak

1676'

OS grid ref: NY148186

from Kirkhead

In West Cumbria, where Mellbreak is a household word (largely through long association with the Melbreak Foxhounds (spelt with one 'l') the fell is highly esteemed, and there have always been people ready to assert that it is the finest of all. This is carrying local patriotism too far, but nevertheless it is a grand hill in a very beautiful situation with a character all its own and an arresting outline not repeated in the district.

There is only one Mellbreak.

Loweswater

BLAKE FELL ▲

GAVEL FELL ▲

MELLBREAK ▲

HEN COMB ▲

Buttermere

RED PIKE ▲

MILES

0 1 2 3 4

NATURAL FEATURES

There is, of course, a natural affinity between mountains and lakes; they have developed side by side in the making of the earth. Often there is a special association between a particular mountain and a particular lake, so that, in calling the one to mind the other comes inevitably to mind also: they belong together. The best example of this is provided by Wast Water and the Screes, and perhaps next best is the combination of Mellbreak and Crummock Water, essential partners in a successful scenery enterprise, depending on each other for effectiveness. Crummock Water's eastern shore, below Grasmoor, is gay with life and colour — trees, pastures, farms, cattle, traffic, tents and people — but it is the view across the lake, where the water laps the sterile base of Mellbreak far beneath the mountain's dark escarpment, where loneliness, solitude and silence prevail, that makes the scene unforgettable.

Mellbreak, seen thus, is a grim sight, the austere effect often heightened by shadow, and a much closer examination is needed to reveal the intimate detail of crag and gully and scree, the steep declivities cushioned in heather, the hidden corners and recesses, the soaring ravens of Raven Crag. From irkstile, at the northern foot, the gable of the fell assumes the arresting outline of a towering pyramid, suggesting a narrow crest, but the top widens into a considerable plateau having two summits of almost equal height separated by a broad saddle. Symmetry and simplicity are the architectural motifs, and the steep flank above Crummock Water has its counterpart to the west descending to the dreariest and wettest of Lakeland's many Mosedales. Thus the severance from other fells is complete. Mellbreak is isolated, independent of other high ground, aloof.

Its one allegiance is to Crummock Water.

from Scalehill Bridge

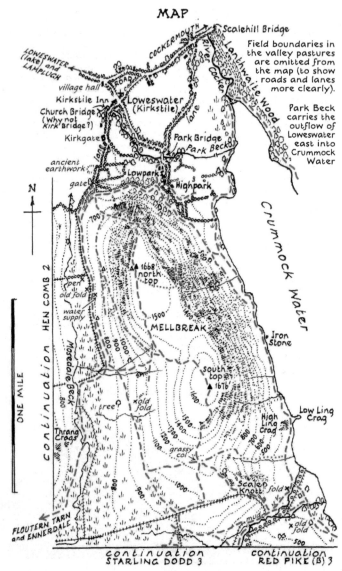

MAP

Field boundaries in the valley pastures are omitted from the map (to show roads and lanes more clearly).

Park Beck carries the outflow of Loweswater east into Crummock Water

The route that heads east from the 'grassy col' near Scale nott is good only between November and May (thick bracken otherwise).

'....a lovely peep around a corner....'
(direct ascent from Loweswater)

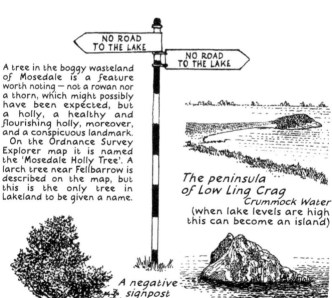

A tree in the boggy wasteland of Mosedale is a feature worth noting — not a rowan nor a thorn, which might possibly have been expected, but a holly, a healthy and flourishing holly, moreover, and a conspicuous landmark.

On the Ordnance Survey Explorer map it is named the 'Mosedale Holly Tree'. A larch tree near Fellbarrow is described on the map, but this is the only tree in Lakeland to be given a name.

The peninsula
of Low Ling Crag
Crummock Water
(when lake levels are high this can become an island)

A negative
signpost
irkstile Inn
road junction — one
of the signs has now
been removed

The
Mosedale Tree

Iron Stone
Crummock Water

ASCENT (to the north top) FROM LOWESWATER
1300 feet of ascent : 1¼ miles

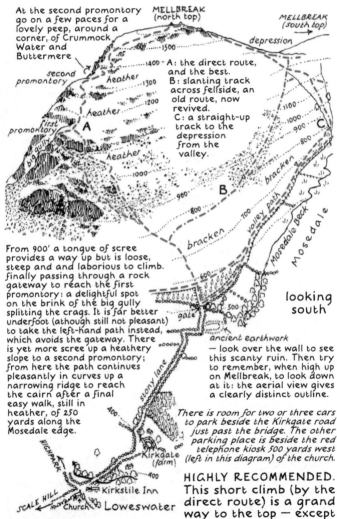

At the second promontory go on a few paces for a lovely peep, around a corner, of Crummock Water and Buttermere

MELLBREAK (north top)

MELLBREAK (south top)

depression

second promontory

first promontory

heather

A: the direct route, and the best.
B: slanting track across fellside, an old route, now revived.
C: a straight-up track to the depression from the valley.

big gully

heather

bracken

looking south

From 900' a tongue of scree provides a way up but is loose, steep and and laborious to climb. finally passing through a rock gateway to reach the first promontory: a delightful spot on the brink of the big gully splitting the crags. It is far better underfoot (although still not pleasant) to take the left-hand path instead, which avoids the gateway. There is yet more scree up a heathery slope to a second promontory; from here the path continues pleasantly in curves up a narrowing ridge to reach the cairn after a final easy walk, still in heather, of 250 yards along the Mosedale edge.

gate

valley path

Mosedale Beck

Mosedale

ancient earthwork
— look over the wall to see this scanty ruin. Then try to remember, when high up on Mellbreak, to look down at it: the aerial view gives a clearly distinct outline.

stony lane

There is room for two or three cars to park beside the Kirkgate road just past the bridge. The other parking place is beside the red telephone kiosk 500 yards west (left in this diagram) of the church.

HIGHPARK

Kirkgate (farm)

Kirkstile Inn

SCALE HILL

Church

Loweswater

HIGHLY RECOMMENDED. This short climb (by the direct route) is a grand way to the top — except for the initial scree. It is especially beautiful when the heather is in bloom. The upper part of the path is a joy to follow. Steep, but no difficulties.

ASCENT FROM CRUMMOCK WATER

1350 feet of ascent : ¾ mile (to the north top)
1450 feet of ascent : 1 mile
(to the south top)

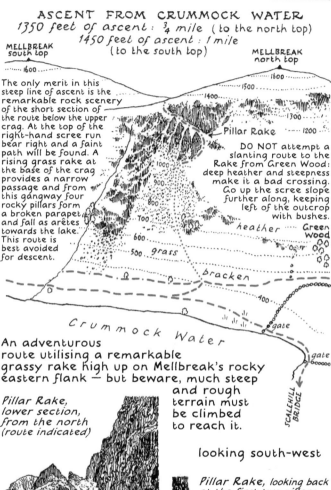

MELLBREAK
south top

.... 1600 ....

MELLBREAK
north top

.... 1600 ....
.... 1500 ....
.... 1400 ....
.... 1300 ....

← Pillar Rake   .... 1200 ....

The only merit in this steep line of ascent is the remarkable rock scenery of the short section of the route below the upper crag. At the top of the right-hand scree run bear right and a faint path will be found. A rising grass rake at the base of the crag provides a narrow passage and from this gangway four rocky pillars form a broken parapet and fall as arêtes towards the lake. This route is best avoided for descent.

DO NOT attempt a slanting route to the Rake from Green Wood: deep heather and steepness make it a bad crossing. Go up the scree slope further along, keeping left of the outcrop with bushes.

1000
900
800
700
600
500 grass
400

heather   Green Wood

bracken

gate

Crummock Water

gate

SCALEHILL BRIDGE →

An adventurous route utilising a remarkable grassy rake high up on Mellbreak's rocky eastern flank — but beware, much steep and rough terrain must be climbed to reach it.

Pillar Rake, lower section, from the north (route indicated)

looking south-west

Pillar Rake, looking back at the first two pillars (route indicated)

ASCENT (to the south top) FROM BUTTERMERE
1300 feet of ascent : 2½ miles

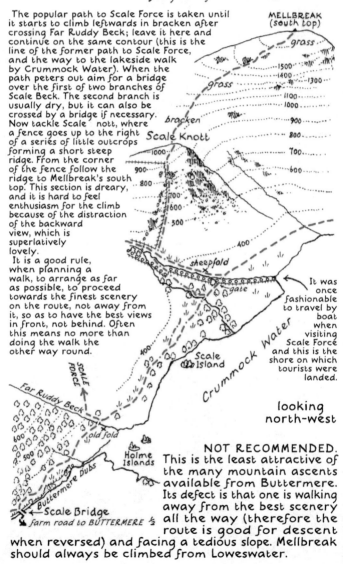

MELLBREAK
(south top)

grass

1500
1400
1300
1100
1000

grass

bracken 900
800
700
Scale Knott 600
1000
900
800
700
600
500

400

sheepfold

gate

400

SCALE
FORCE

Far Ruddy Beck

old fold

600
500

Buttermere Dubs

Scale Bridge
farm road to BUTTERMERE ½

Scale
Island

Holme
Islands

Crummock Water

looking
north-west

The popular path to Scale Force is taken until it starts to climb leftwards in bracken after crossing Far Ruddy Beck; leave it here and continue on the same contour (this is the line of the former path to Scale Force, and the way to the lakeside walk by Crummock Water). When the path peters out aim for a bridge over the first of two branches of Scale Beck. The second branch is usually dry, but it can also be crossed by a bridge if necessary. Now tackle Scale Knott, where a fence goes up to the right of a series of little outcrops forming a short steep ridge. From the corner of the fence follow the ridge to Mellbreak's south top. This section is dreary, and it is hard to feel enthusiasm for the climb because of the distraction of the backward view, which is superlatively lovely.

It is a good rule, when planning a walk, to arrange as far as possible, to proceed towards the finest scenery on the route, not away from it, so as to have the best views in front, not behind. Often this means no more than doing the walk the other way round.

It was once fashionable to travel by boat when visiting Scale Force and this is the shore on which tourists were landed.

NOT RECOMMENDED. This is the least attractive of the many mountain ascents available from Buttermere. Its defect is that one is walking away from the best scenery all the way (therefore the route is good for descent when reversed) and facing a tedious slope. Mellbreak should always be climbed from Loweswater.

THE SUMMIT

1: FLEETWITH PI E
2: GLARAMARA
3: GREY NOTTS
4: BRANDRETH
5: GREEN GABLE
6: GREAT GABLE
7: HAYSTAC S

south-east from the north top

Mellbreak has two distinct summits, two-thirds of a mile apart and separated by a pronounced depression. The more attractive of the two is the heathery north top, measured by the Ordnance Survey as 1668 feet above sea level; the duller grassy south top is credited with 1676 feet — here is a small rocky outcrop, sometimes with a cairn; there is higher ground 75 yards to the north-east. Nobody would have complained if the measurements had been reversed, by some rare error, for it is the lower north top, crowning a splendid tower of rock, that captures the fancy, not the other. The width and extent of the top of the fell between the two summits comes as a surprise — the narrow ridge promised by distant views of the fell is an illusion.

DESCENTS: It is usual to descend into Mosedale from the west edge of the depression. From the south top, for Buttermere, follow the ridge to the south until you come to a fence. Turn right to avoid the steep descent from Scale nott, or turn left to avoid the mud along Scale Beck. For Loweswater, from the north top, the route from the depression into Mosedale is safest unless the direct route is already familiar and the weather clear: *in mist, the head of the big gully where the path splits is a potentially dangerous place. On no account should a descent down the eastern flank to Crummock Water be attempted, except by Pillar Rake, and then only if the route is already known and the weather is clear. The start of the Rake, which is very difficult to find in descent, lies just north of a narrow promontory.*

RIDGE ROUTES

west from the south top

Mellbreak is itself a ridge, like the keel of an overturned boat (collapsed in the middle). It has no links with other fells.

Mellbreak 9

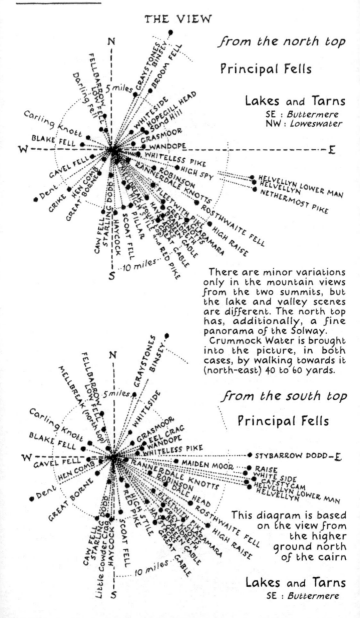

THE VIEW

from the north top

Principal Fells

Lakes and Tarns
SE : *Buttermere*
NW : *Loweswater*

N

5 miles

GRAYSTONES
BINSEY
BROOM FELL
WHITESIDE
HOPEGILL HEAD
Sand Hill
GRASMOOR
WANDOPE
WHITELESS PIKE
HIGH SPY
ROBINSON
RANNERDALE KNOTTS
FLEETWITH PIKE
ROSTHWAITE FELL
HIGH RAISE
FELLBARROW
LOW FELL
Darling Fell
Carling Knott
BLAKE FELL
GAVEL FELL
DENT
CRIKE
HEN COMB
GREAT BORNE
CAW FELL
STARLING DODD
HAYCOCK
SCOAT FELL
PILLAR
RED PIKE
GREAT GABLE
KIRK FELL
GREY KNOTTS
BRANDRETH
SCAFELL
GREAT END
W
E
HELVELLYN LOWER MAN
HELVELLYN
NETHERMOST PIKE
10 miles
S

There are minor variations
only in the mountain views
from the two summits, but
the lake and valley scenes
are different. The north top
has, additionally, a fine
panorama of the Solway.
Crummock Water is brought
into the picture, in both
cases, by walking towards it
(north-east) 40 to 60 yards.

from the south top

Principal Fells

N

5 miles

GRAYSTONES
BINSEY
WHITESIDE
GRASMOOR
EEL CRAG
WANDOPE
WHITELESS PIKE
MAIDEN MOOR
STYBARROW DODD
RAISE
WHITE SIDE
CATSTYCAM
HELVELLYN
HELVELLYN LOWER MAN
FELLBARROW
LOW FELL
MELLBREAK (north top)
Carling Knott
BLAKE FELL
GAVEL FELL
HEN COMB
DENT
GREAT BORNE
CAW FELL
STARLING DODD
Little Cowder Crag
SCOAT FELL
HAYCOCK
RED PIKE
HIGH STILE
RANNERDALE KNOTTS
ROBINSON
DALE HEAD
FLEETWITH PIKE
PILLAR
KIRK FELL
GREAT GABLE
GREEN GABLE
BRANDRETH
ROSTHWAITE FELL
HIGH RAISE
W
E
GAVEL FELL
10 miles
S

This diagram is based
on the view from
the higher ground north
of the cairn

Lakes and Tarns
SE : *Buttermere*

Grasmoor
from the
north top

Rannerdale from the south top
(Whiteless Pike, left background)

Middle Fell

1908'

OS grid ref: NY151072

Wasdale Head
▲ SEATALLAN ●
MIDDLE ▲ ● Bowderdale
FELL
▲ BUCKBARROW
● Greendale

● Strands
MILES
0 1 2 3 4

from Wast Water

NATURAL FEATURES

Many of the lesser fells of Lakeland make up for their lack of height by an aggressive fierceness of expression that seems more appropriate to greater mountains and by an intimidating ruggedness and wildness of terrain that makes their ascent rather more formidable than their size and altitude would suggest. Middle Fell, overlooking Wast Water, comes into this category. Tier above tier of hostile crags, steep slopes overrun by tumbled boulders, vegetation masking pitfalls and crevices: these are the features that rule out, at a glance, any possibility of a simple climb either from the lakeside or from Nether Beck at its eastern base, these being the two aspects that face the traveller along the valley. Nor, if one ventures up by Greendale Gill, on the west, does the scene relent, although a route here presents itself. It is only on the short side of the fell, where there is a high saddle connecting with Seatallan, that a weakness in the fell's armour becomes apparent and the climb to the cairn is comfortable. As a viewpoint for the Wasdale fells, the summit is magnificently placed, and it is fitting that a reward such as this should be earned only by effort.

Waterfalls, Nether Beck

*Middle Fell
from the headwaters
of Nether Beck*

MAP

continuation SEATALLAN 4

Rough Crag

It is worth noting that, in periods of wet weather, the crossing of Greendale Gill can be difficult.

N

Nether Beck

continuation RED PIKE (W) 3 and 4

Greendale Tarn

ONE MILE

▲ MIDDLE FELL 1908

Iron Crag

continuation SEATALLAN 4

Goat Crag

Netherbeck Bridge

WASDALE HEAD 2

Long Crag

Goat Gill

parking place

Wast Water

monument

car parks

GOSFORTH 5

Greendale

STRANDS (NETHER WASDALE) 2

Greendale Tarn

ASCENT FROM WASDALE
(GREENDALE)
1650 feet of ascent : 1½ miles

Watch for the bifurcation at 700': the uphill branch to the right (which is taken) is an offshoot of the original path for Greendale Tarn. The summit track ascends a green slope first, then a patch of boulders, and continues all the way to the summit. The gradient is now easy, all the rock outcrops are avoided, and after a simple climb that will seem longer than expected the summit cairn is reached on the Wasdale edge of a small plateau.

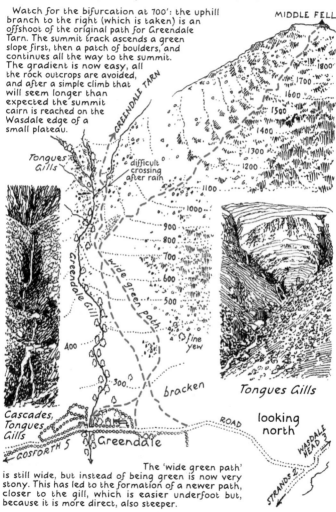

MIDDLE FELL

1800
1700
1600
1500
1400
1300
1200

GREENDALE TARN

Tongues Gills

difficult crossing after rain

1100

1000

900

800

700

600

500

Greendale Gill

wide green path

400

fine yew

300

bracken

Tongues Gills

Cascades, Tongues Gills

GOSFORTH 5

Greendale

ROAD

looking north

WASDALE HEAD 3

STRANDS 2

The 'wide green path' is still wide, but instead of being green is now very stony. This has led to the formation of a newer path, closer to the gill, which is easier underfoot but, because it is more direct, also steeper.

With free car parking on the roadside verges, Middle Fell is another 'motorists' mountain and a convenient objective for family parties, *but not in mist.*

THE SUMMIT

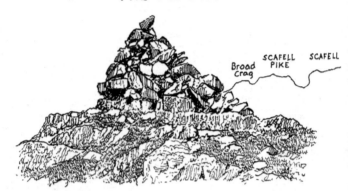

The summit cairn crowns a small rocky mound on the Wasdale edge of a grassy depression on the top of the fell, and although it is a splendid vantage point there is little in the immediate vicinity to suggest the rocky nature of the slopes just below.

DESCENTS: In clear weather, easy descents may be made to join the path going down to Greendale south-west, or north to the marshy flats above Greendale Tarn; in other directions lies trouble. eep to grass, skirting innumerable low crags. *In mist* use only the south-west route: the slope is gentle (bear right if steep ground is encountered) and longer than expected (nearly a mile) before the path on the east side of Greendale Gill is joined.

To SEATALLAN, 2266': 1½ miles
N, NNW and SW
Depression at 1550'
750 feet of ascent

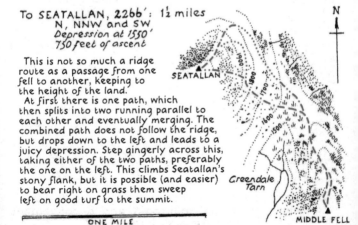

This is not so much a ridge route as a passage from one fell to another, keeping to the height of the land.

At first there is one path, which then splits into two running parallel to each other and eventually merging. The combined path does not follow the ridge, but drops down to the left and leads to a juicy depression. Step gingerly across this, taking either of the two paths, preferably the one on the left. This climbs Seatallan's stony flank, but it is possible (and easier) to bear right on grass them sweep left on good turf to the summit.

ONE MILE

THE VIEW

The most extensive views are not necessarily the finest, and here, from Middle Fell, is a charmer restricted in distance by the Wasdale mountains, which, however, compensate for the deficiency by their own striking appearance. Wast Water is seen full length, backed by the Screes, and, beyond, Black Combe fills up the horizon southward.

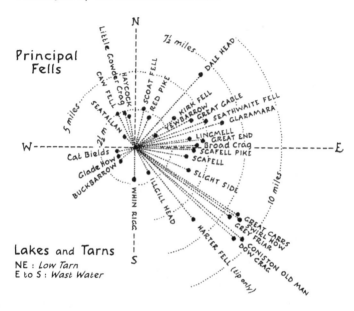

Principal Fells

N

7½ miles

5 miles

Little Cowder Crag
CAW FELL
HAYCOCK
SEATALLAN
SCOAT FELL
RED PIKE
DALE HEAD
KIRK FELL
YEWBARROW
GREAT GABLE
SEATHWAITE FELL
GLARAMARA
LINGMELL
GREAT END
Broad Crag
SCAFELL PIKE
SCAFELL
SLIGHT SIDE

W — — — E

Cat Bields
Glade How
BUCKBARROW
WHIN RIGG
ILLGILL HEAD
HARTER FELL (tip only)
GREAT CARRS
SWIRL HOW
GREY FRIAR
CONISTON OLD MAN
DOW CRAG

10 miles

S

Lakes and Tarns
NE : *Low Tarn*
E to S : *Wast Water*

*Wastwater Screes
from Middle Fell*

Pillar

2927'

OS grid ref: NY171121

from Brin Crag, Brandreth

NATURAL FEATURES

Great Gable, Pillar and Steeple are the three mountain names on Lakeland maps most likely to fire the imagination of youthful adventurers planning a first tour of the district, inspiring exciting visions of slim, near-vertical pinnacles towering grandly into the sky.

Great Gable lives up to its name, especially if climbed from Wasdale; Pillar has a fine bold outline but is nothing like a pillar; Steeple is closely overlooked by a higher flat-topped fell and not effectively seen.

Pillar, in fact, far from being a spire of slender proportions, is a rugged mass broadly based on half the length of Ennerdale, a series of craggy buttresses supporting the ridge high above this wild north face; and the summit itself, far from being pointed, is wide and flat.

The name of the fell therefore clearly derives from a conspicuous feature on the north face directly below the top, the most handsome crag in Lakeland, originally known as the Pillar Stone and now as Pillar Rock. The Rock, despite a remote and lonely situation, had a well established local notoriety and fame long before tourists called wider attention to it (in fact, the Rock was first scaled as long ago as 1826), and an object of such unique appearance simply had to be given a descriptive name, although, at the time, one was not yet needed to identify the mountain of which it formed part. *The Pillar* was an inspiration of shepherds. Men of letters could not have chosen better.

The north face of the fell has a formidable aspect. Crags and shadowed hollows, scree and tumbled boulders, form a wild, chaotic scene, a setting worthy of a fine mountain.

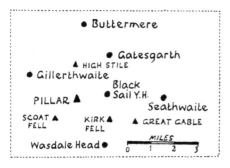

continued

NATURAL FEATURES

continued

Pillar is the highest mountain west of Great Gable, from which it is sufficiently removed in distance to exhibit distinctive slopes on all sides. It dominates the sunset area of Lakeland superbly, springing out of the valleys of Mosedale and Ennerdale, steeply on the one side and dramatically on the other, as befits the overlord of the western scene. A narrow neck of land connects with a chain of other grand fells to the south, and a depression forms the east boundary and is crossed by Black Sail Pass at 1800', but elsewhere the full height of the fell from valley level is displayed. Some of the streams flow west *via* Ennerdale Water and some south *via* Wast Water, but their fate, discharge into the Irish Sea from the coast near Seascale, is the same, only a few miles separating the two outlets.

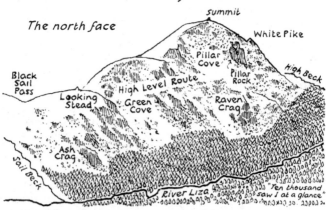

The north face

summit · White Pike · Black Sail Pass · Looking Stead · High Level Route · Green Cove · Pillar Cove · Pillar Rock · High Beck · Raven Crag · Ash Crag · Sail Beck · River Liza · "ten thousand saw I at a glance"

Afforestation in Ennerdale has cloaked the lower slopes on this side in a dark and funereal shroud of foreign trees, an intrusion that nobody who knew Ennerdale of old can ever forgive, the former charm of the valley having been destroyed thereby. We condemn vandalism and sanction this mess! Far better the old desolation of boulder and bog when a man could see the sky, than this new desolation of regimented timber shutting out the light of day. It is an offence to the eyes to see Pillar's once-colourful fellside now hobbled in such a dowdy and ill suited skirt, just as it is to see a noble animal caught in a trap. Yet, such is the majesty and power of this fine mountain that it can shrug off the insults and indignities, and its summit soars no less proudly above. It is the admirers of this grand pile who feel the hurt.

A Pillar Rock portfolio

from the east

Pillar 5

Pisgah   High Man

Low Man

Shamrock

Green Ledge

Savage Gully

Walkers Gully

Jordan Gap

Pisgah   High Man   top of Great Chimney

above: Principal features of the drawing at the foot of the page. The start of the Slab and Notch route is indicated.

left: Principal features of the drawing on the previous page. The blacked-out portion is the area covered by the drawing at the foot of this page and gives some impression of the scale of the whole (about 500 feet high)

To walkers whose experience is limited to easy scrambling on rough ground, Pillar Rock is positively out of bounds. Don't even try to get a foothold on it. The climbing guides mention easy routes (the Old West and the Slab and Notch) but these are NOT easy for a walker who is not a climber, and lead into dangerous situations. Walker's Gully is named after a man who fell to his death there.
There used to be a stretcher box here ...

below:
East face of High Man

as seen from Shamrock Traverse

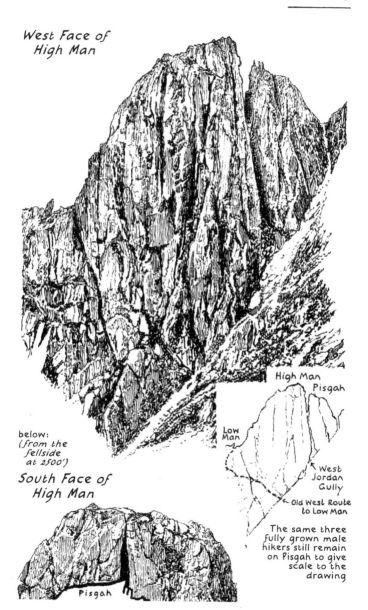

West Face of
High Man

below:
(from the
fellside
at 2500')

South Face of
High Man

Pisgah

High Man
Pisgah
Low
Man
West
Jordan
Gully
Old West Route
to Low Man

The same three
fully grown male
hikers still remain
on Pisgah to give
scale to the
drawing

MAP

The map has been extended to the west to show the approach from Irish Bridge

BOWNESS 1½

forest road

Irish Bridge

1400

Low Gillerthwaite

Y.H. High Gillerthwaite

River Liza

continuation left

forest road

Moss Dub

500

Low Beck

continuation right

500

Ennerdale

River Liza

felled area

1000

SCARTH CAP

felled

felled area

felled

1000
1100

1200

1200

1300

1500

High Beck

1900

White Pike

Pillar Rock

Hind Cove

continuation SCOAT FELL 4

Windgap Cove

2500

PILLAR
2927

2800

2700

2600

2500

2400

2300

2200

2000

1500

Wind Gap

1000
900
800

Mosedale Beck

fold

continuation RED PIKE (W) 4

continuation on opposite page

The Bridges over the River Liza

It is important for those who climb Pillar from Ennerdale, or descend to this valley, to know exactly where the footways are in relation to the bridges over the Liza, which cannot easily be waded or forded. A former footbridge 300 yards upstream from High Beck has gone, but there are others along the base of the mountain. Irish Bridge near the head of Ennerdale Water is nearly always crossable, but, if it is not, there is a footbridge only a quarter of a mile upstream. A further two miles up the valley is a concrete road bridge, and this is useful for the direct ascent *via* Pillar Cove. Next, two-thirds of a mile further, is the memorial footbridge, provided mainly to facilitate the approach to Pillar Rock from Buttermere. The last, in open country beyond the plantations, is the much used footbridge at the foot of Black Sail Pass.

MAP

Black Sail is the most remote youth hostel in the Lake District, being 6 miles along the valley from the public car park at Bowness Point. The hostel is open to all but it is advisable to book well in advance.

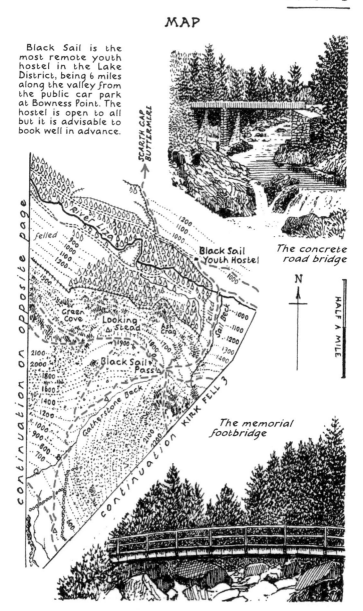

The concrete road bridge

The memorial footbridge

ASCENT FROM WASDALE HEAD

2700 feet of ascent
4½ miles via Black Sail Pass
3¼ miles via Wind Gap

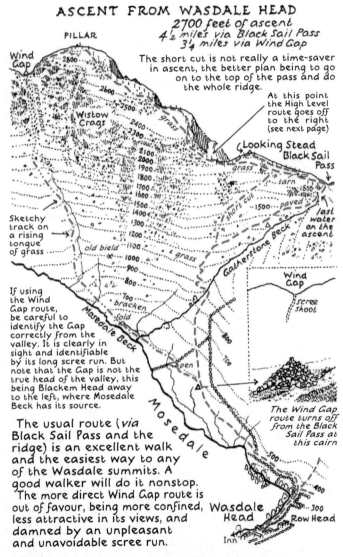

PILLAR

Wind Gap

2800

Wistow Crags

2600

2500

2400

2300

2200

2100

2000

1900

1800

1700

1600

1500

1400

1300

1200

1100

1000

900

800

700

grass

The short cut is not really a time-saver in ascent, the better plan being to go on to the top of the pass and do the whole ridge.

At this point the High Level route goes off to the right (see next page)

Looking Stead

Black Sail Pass

grass

tarn

short cut

paved

last water on the ascent

Gatherstone Beck

Wind Gap

scree shoot

Sketchy track on a rising tongue of grass

old bield

bracken

fold

pen

Mosedale Beck

If using the Wind Gap route, be careful to identify the Gap correctly from the valley. It is clearly in sight and identifiable by its long scree run. But note that the Gap is not the true head of the valley, this being Blackem Head away to the left, where Mosedale Beck has its source.

Mosedale

The usual route (via Black Sail Pass and the ridge) is an excellent walk and the easiest way to any of the Wasdale summits. A good walker will do it nonstop. The more direct Wind Gap route is out of favour, being more confined, less attractive in its views, and damned by an unpleasant and unavoidable scree run.

The Wind Gap route turns off from the Black Sail Pass at this cairn

500

400

300

Wasdale Head

Row Head

Inn

Don't go wrong at the very start! The way lies NOT over the bridge but along the bank of the stream, passing behind the farmhouse of Row Head.

looking north

ASCENT FROM ENNERDALE
(BLACK SAIL YOUTH HOSTEL)

2000 feet of ascent : 2¾ miles
(2100 feet, 3 miles
by High Level Route)

The main ridge, from Black Sail Pass to the summit, is a pleasant walk without difficulty, three stony rises being succeeded by splendid turf. A line of iron posts accompanies the ridge but the path, in many places, deviates to the left.

The High Level route is a traverse across the fellside (aiming for Pillar Rock), not a way to the summit, although the two can be connected (see next page). This is a fine pedestrian way, highly recommended, rough but not difficult.

Originally the High Level Route had an awkward start. A new variation avoids the difficulty.

PILLAR

Great Doup

Hind Cove

Green Cove

Pillar Rock

Robinson's Cairn

High Level Route

← detail →

Looking Stead

WASDALE HEAD direct route

tarn

WASDALE HEAD

Black Sail Pass

Main ridge:
1: zigzag path
2: direct path
High Level route:
3: original start
4: new variation
Main ridge:
5: from Black Sail

The main path avoids the actual top of Looking Stead, but walkers should not. It is an excellent viewpoint for a survey, both of the High Level route and of Ennerdale.

Black Sail was always known for having a gate at the top of the pass, which prompted the author to write
...but only a fanatical purist would think of using it.

Ash Crag

River Liza

felled

Sail beck

Black Sail Y.H.

moraines

Sojourners at the hostel are fortunate in having Pillar on their doorstep, and can enjoy one of the best days of their young lives by climbing it.

looking west

Pillar 11

Robinson's Cairn to the summit

The end of the Traverse with stretcher box (now gone)

Pisgah

summit

High Man

Pillar Rock

Low Man

Shamrock

Great Doup

2800
2700
2600
2500

steep loose scree slope

Pisgah

Shamrock Traverse
2400
2300

start of Traverse
2200

scree slope

2100

low rock ridge

slight descent across a bouldery hollow

High Level Route

Robinson's Cairn

There are no difficulties or dangers on this route *provided the path is kept underfoot.* There ARE difficulties and dangers if exploratory deviations are attempted, especially on the Traverse; here, care is needed on a tilted rock slab if it is icy. The walking is rough, but not steep; the track is loose and stony, but safe. The rock scenery is magnificent.

The start of the Traverse (a wide, tilted shelf or rake)

Robinson's Cairn

— a memorial to JOHN WILSON ROBINSON, a pioneer fellwalker and rock climber; a man sincerely devoted to the fells. A tablet, beautifully worded, is affixed to a nearby rock.

ASCENT FROM ENNERDALE
(IRISH BRIDGE)
2500 feet of ascent
3 miles (A) : 2½ miles (B)

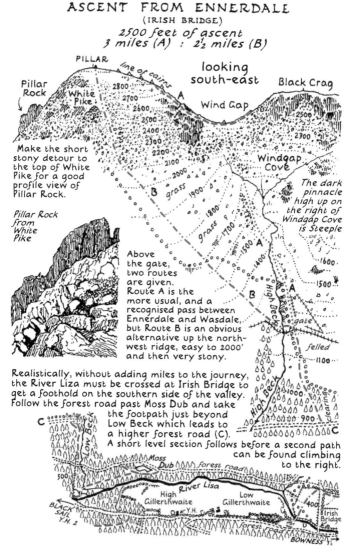

looking
south-east

PILLAR

line of cairns

Pillar
Rock

White
Pike

2800
2700
2600
2500
2400
2300
2200
2100
2000
1900
1800
1700

A

Wind Gap

Black Crag

2500

2300

Windgap
Cove

Make the short
stony detour to
the top of White
Pike for a good
profile view of
Pillar Rock.

*Pillar Rock
from White
Pike*

B   grass

grass

The dark
pinnacle
high up on
the right of
Windgap Cove
is Steeple

1600

1500

A

B   A

High Beck

gate

felled

1100

Above
the gate,
two routes
are given.
Route A is the
more usual, and a
recognised pass between
Ennerdale and Wasdale,
but Route B is an obvious
alternative up the north-
west ridge, easy to 2000'
and then very stony.

Realistically, without adding miles to the journey,
the River Liza must be crossed at Irish Bridge to
get a foothold on the southern side of the valley.
Follow the forest road past Moss Dub and take
the footpath just beyond
Low Beck which leads to
a higher forest road (C).
A short level section follows before a second path
can be found climbing
to the right.

High Beck

1000

900

C   Low Beck

500

Moss
Dub   forest road

River Lisa

High
Gillerthwaite   Low
Gillerthwaite

BLACK
SAIL
Y.H. 2

Y.H.

forest road

BOWNESS

400

Irish
Bridge

C

The disadvantage of this route is the long approach
before any climbing; but thereafter some grand and
rugged scenery makes this a splendid expedition.

ASCENT FROM ENNERDALE
(direct from THE MEMORIAL FOOTBRIDGE)

2250 feet of ascent
1¼ miles

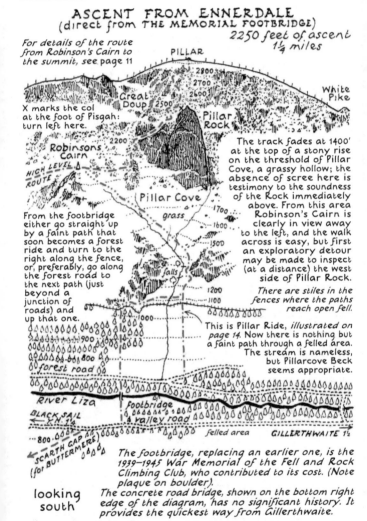

For details of the route from Robinson's Cairn to the summit, see page 11

PILLAR

2900
2700
2600

White Pike

Great Doup 2500

Pillar Rock

X marks the col at the foot of Pisgah: turn left here.

2200

Robinsons Cairn

HIGH LEVEL ROUTE

Pillar Cove

grass

The track fades at 1400' at the top of a stony rise on the threshold of Pillar Cove, a grassy hollow; the absence of scree here is testimony to the soundness of the Rock immediately above. From this area Robinson's Cairn is clearly in view away to the left, and the walk across is easy, but first an exploratory detour may be made to inspect (at a distance) the west side of Pillar Rock.

1700
1600
1500

From the footbridge either go straight up by a faint path that soon becomes a forest ride and turn to the right along the fence, or, preferably, go along the forest road to the next path (just beyond a junction of roads) and up that one.

falls

1200
1100

There are stiles in the fences where the paths reach open fell.

1000

900

800

forest road

This is Pillar Ride, *illustrated on page 14.* Now there is nothing but a faint path through a felled area. The stream is nameless, but Pillarcove Beck seems appropriate.

River Liza

Footbridge

BLACK SAIL YH 1½

a valley road

felled area

GILLERTHWAITE 1½

800

SCARTH GAP
(for BUTTERMERE)

looking south

The footbridge, replacing an earlier one, is the 1939–1945 War Memorial of the Fell and Rock Climbing Club, who contributed to its cost. (Note plaque on boulder).

The concrete road bridge, shown on the bottom right edge of the diagram, has no significant history. It provides the quickest way from Gillerthwaite.

A steep and rough, but romantic and adventurous climb in magnificent surroundings: the finest way up the mountain. Pillar Rock grips the attention throughout. Unfortunately the route is somewhat remote from tourist centres, but strong walkers can do it from Buttermere *via* Scarth Gap.

ASCENT FROM BUTTERMERE

Via the footbridge : 3550 feet of ascent : 5¼ miles
Via Black Sail Pass : 3250 feet of ascent : 6¼ miles

Most walkers when planning to climb a mountain aim to avoid any downhill section between their starting point and the summit, and if the intermediate descent is considerable the extra effort of regaining lost height may rule out the attempt altogether. A good example is Great Gable from Langdale, where the descent from Esk Hause to Sty Head is a loss of height of 700 feet and a double loss of this amount if returning to Langdale. Plus the 3000' of effective ascent, this is too much for the average walker. Distance is of less consequence. The same applies to ascent of Pillar from Buttermere. This is a glorious walk, full of interest, but it cannot be done without first climbing the High Stile range (at Scarth Gap) and then descending into Ennerdale before setting foot on Pillar. If returning to Buttermere, Ennerdale and the High Stile range will have to be crossed again towards the end of an exhausting day. There is no sadder sight than a Buttermere-bound pedestrian crossing Scarth Gap on his hands and knees as the shadows of evening steal o'er the scene. *The route is therefore recommended for strong walkers only.*

The most thrilling line of ascent of Pillar is by way of the memorial footbridge, this being very conveniently situated for the Buttermere approach (the bridge was, in fact, provided to give access to Pillar from this direction). A slanting route down to the footbridge leaves the Scarth Gap path some 150 yards on the Ennerdale side of the pass. The bifurcation is not clear, but the track goes off to the right above the plantation, becoming distinct and crossing the fences by three stiles. The climb from the bridge is described on the opposite page. A less arduous route of ascent is to keep to the Scarth Gap path into Ennerdale and climb out of the valley by Black Sail Pass to its top, where follow the ridge on the right — but this easier way had better be reserved for the return when energy is flagging.

To find the slanting path from Scarth Gap look for the rocky knoll, with tree (illustrated) and turn right on grass above it

Pillar Rock from the north

The Pillar Ride

THE SUMMIT

shelter

north shelter

As in the case of many fells of rugged appearance, the summit is one of the smoothest places on Pillar, and one may perambulate within a 50-yard radius of the cairn without being aware of the declivities on all sides. There are stones, but grass predominates. The number of erections, including two wind shelters and a survey column, testifies to the importance of the summit in the esteem of fellwalkers and map makers.

DESCENTS:

To Wasdale Head: In fair weather or foul, there is one royal road down to Wasdale Head, and that is by the eastern ridge to join Black Sail Pass on its journey thereto. The views are superb, and the walking is so easy for the most part that they can be enjoyed while on the move. There should be no difficulty in following the path in mist — only in one cairned section is it indistinct — but the fence posts are there in any event as a guide to the top of the Pass. The improved path from Black Sail Pass is preferable to the short cut from Looking Stead. The route into Mosedale *via* Wind Gap is much less satisfactory, and no quicker although shorter. Another way into Mosedale sometimes used is the obvious scree gully opening off the ridge opposite the head of Great Doup, but why suffer the torture of a half-mile of loose stones when the ridge is so much easier and pleasanter?

To Ennerdale: If bound for Black Sail Hostel, follow the eastern ridge to the pass, and there turn left on a clear path. If bound for Ennerdale Youth Hostel (High Gillerthwaite) or places west, head north-west up White Pike and its ridge, which has a rough section of boulders below the Pike; but in stormy weather prefer the route joining High Beck from Wind Gap.

To Buttermere: In clear weather, the direct route climbing up out of Ennerdale may be reversed; at the forest road beyond the memorial footbridge walk up the valley for 120 yards, then taking a slanting path through the plantation on the left to Scarth Gap. In bad conditions, it is safer to go round by Black Sail Pass.

To any of the above destinations via Robinson's Cairn

Leave the summit at the north wind shelter. Pillar Rock comes into view at once, and a path with many bends leads down to the point where the first of its buttresses (Pisgah) rises from the fellside. Here turn right (where once there was a stretcher box) and down Shamrock Traverse to easy ground and the Cairn. On no account descend the hollow to the right of Pisgah: this narrows to a dangerous funnel of stones and a sheer drop into a gully. (This is known as Walker's Gully, NOT because it is a gully for walkers, but because a man of this name fell to his death here).

PLAN OF THE SUMMIT

100 YARDS

WHITE PIKE · PILLAR ROCK · shelter · Great Doup · shelter · 2900 · WIND GAP · 2900 · BLACK SAIL PASS

Pillar Rock as seen from the north shelter

RIDGE ROUTES

TO SCOAT FELL, 2760': 1¼ miles : WSW
Depression at 2480' (Wind Gap) : 300 feet of ascent

A fine little journey in spectacular scenery.

After an indefinite start, a line of cairns leads down to Wind Gap, the last stage of the descent being steep and rough, but not difficult. Beyond the Gap a clear path goes up the facing slope into the boulders preceding the easy grassy promenade along the top above Black Crag. Then follows a slight loss of height before the final rise to Scoat Fell, the summit wall of which is joined in a chaotic pile of boulders.

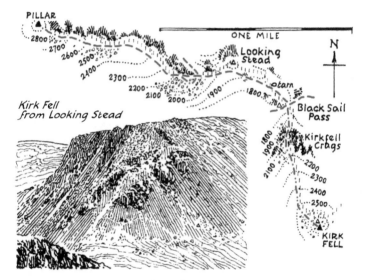

*Kirk Fell
from Looking Stead*

TO KIRK FELL, 2630': 2½ miles : ESE, then S
Depression at 1800' (Black Sail Pass) : 850 feet of ascent

Excellent views, both near and far; a good walk.

The Ennerdale fence (what is left of it) links the two tops, and the route never ventures far from it. The eastern ridge of Pillar offers a speedy descent, the path being clear except on one grassy section, which is, however, well cairned. At Black Sail Pass, the crags of irk Fell look ferocious and hostile, but a thin track goes off bravely to tackle them and can be relied upon to lead to the dull top of irk Fell after providing a minor excitement where a high rock step needs to be surmounted.

THE VIEW

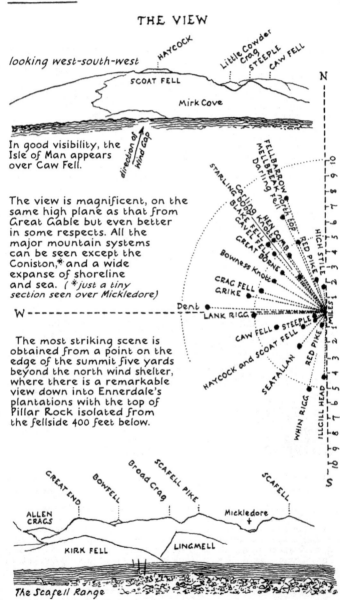

looking west-south-west

HAYCOCK

Little Cowder Crag

STEEPLE

CAW FELL

SCOAT FELL

Mirk Cove

N

In good visibility, the Isle of Man appears over Caw Fell.

direction of Wind Gap

The view is magnificent, on the same high plane as that from Great Gable but even better in some respects. All the major mountain systems can be seen except the Coniston,* and a wide expanse of shoreline and sea. (*just a tiny section seen over Mickledore)

FELLBARROW
MELLBREAK north top
Darling Fell

STARLING DODD
Carling Knott
HEN COMB
BLAKE FELL
GAVEL FELL
GREAT BORNE

RED PIKE

HIGH STILE

Bowness Knotts

CRAG FELL
GRIKE

W - - - - - - - - Dent

LANK RIGG

CAW FELL STEEPLE

RED PIKE

HAYCOCK and SCOAT FELL

SEATALLAN

The most striking scene is obtained from a point on the edge of the summit five yards beyond the north wind shelter, where there is a remarkable view down into Ennerdale's plantations with the top of Pillar Rock isolated from the fellside 400 feet below.

WHIN RIGG

ILLGILL HEAD

S

GREAT END

BOWFELL

Broad Crag

SCAFELL PIKE

SCAFELL

ALLEN CRAGS

Mickledore

KIRK FELL

LINGMELL

The Scafell Range

THE VIEW

Principal Fells

Lakes and Tarns

SSE : *Eel Tarn*
SSE : *Burnmoor Tarn*
WNW : *Ennerdale Water*
NNW : *Loweswater*

Innominate Tarn on Haystacks, ENE, is brought in the view by walking 10 yards from the column eastwards

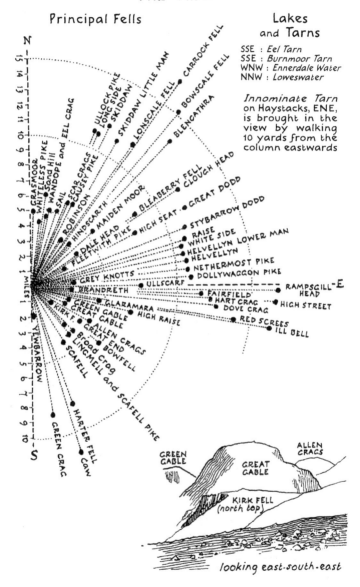

looking east-south-east

Red Pike

(Buttermere)

2479'

OS grid ref: NY161155

from Crummock Water

The duplication of place names is a source of confusion and error. In the Lake District there are dozens of Raven Crags and Black Crags, many Dodds, six Mosedales, two Seathwaites, three Sourmilk Gills, and several other instances of name repetition in different areas. Amongst the major fells, there are two High Raises, two High Pikes and two Harter Fells — all sufficiently well dispersed in widely separated localities to mitigate any confusion. But two Red Pikes, only three miles apart, require distinct identification. It is usual to refer to the one dealt with in this chapter, which the name aptly fits, as the Buttermere Red Pike, and the other, which is higher and bulkier, but for which the name is less suited, as the Wasdale Red Pike.

Buttermere ●

STARLING
DODD ▲

Gatesgarth
●

▲ RED PIKE

▲ HIGH STILE

Gillerthwaite ●

▲ HIGH
CRAG

MILES

0   1   2   3

NATURAL FEATURES

The most trodden mountain track out of Buttermere, a ladder of stones, leads to the summit of Red Pike (which itself cannot be seen from the village), and indeed this is the only tourist path permitted by the extremely steep and rough fellside on the south, overlooking the valley. Red Pike is deservedly a popular climb: the way to it is both interesting and beautiful, the summit is a graceful cone without complications, the cairn being set exactly at the head of the path; and the view is excellent. Less imposing than its near neighbour, High Stile, Red Pike is nevertheless a greater favourite with visitors (which is unjustifiable on merit).

Following the general pattern of the mountains in the High Stile range, Red Pike sends out a stony buttress to the north-east, but unlike its fellows this one succeeds a depression, the Saddle, and then rises to a subsidiary, Dodd, before plunging down to the valley, the final slope being pleasantly wooded and featuring the attraction everybody remembers Buttermere by — the long cascade of Sourmilk Gill. Westwards, Red Pike extends a curving arm trending north to Crummock, and within it nestles the heathery hollow of Ling Comb; outside its curve the fell creases into a watercourse, and here is another of Red Pike's star attractions, Lakeland's highest waterfall, Scale Force. East of the buttress, shared with High Stile, is the hanging valley of Bleaberry Comb and secluded Bleaberry Tarn, thought to occupy the crater of a dead volcano. To the south the fell slopes steeply down, without incident, to Ennerdale.

1 : *The summit*	7 : *Ling Comb*	13 : *Far Ruddy Beck*
2 : *High Stile*	8 : *Lingcomb Edge*	14 : *Scale Beck*
3 : *Dodd*	9 : *Gate Fell*	15 : *Scale Force*
4 : *The Saddle*	10 : *Blea Crag*	16 : *Buttermere*
5 : *Bleaberry Comb*	11 : *Sourmilk Gill*	17 : *Buttermere Dubs*
6 : *Bleaberry Tarn*	12 : *Near Ruddy Beck*	18 : *Crummock Water*

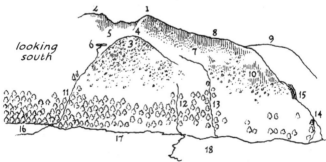

looking south

Syenite in the rock and subsoil of the fell produces the rich red colouring that has given Red Pike its name and this is particularly marked in places where surface disturbance has occurred (the stony track by the side of Scale Force is a good example), remaining brilliant until weathering results in a more sombre ruddiness.

MAP

Scale ('a rough hut or shelter on a hillside') is a word that
occurs often in place names in Lakeland,
e.g. Portinscale, Bowscale, Lonscale,
Warnscale, Scale Hill and
many others.

*Visitors to
Scale Force
please note —*

The best route to Scale
Force from Buttermere
bears left after crossing
Far Ruddy Beck. It is
cairned, and easy enough
to follow. The original
route crossed the two
branches of Scale Beck,
but it is not recommended
because it is one of the
wettest paths in the
district and because of
the mud on the far side
of Scale Beck. *It is
a mistake to imagine
(as many do) that the
force may be reached
by this route in fancy
shoes — thigh-length
gum boots are the
ideal wear.*

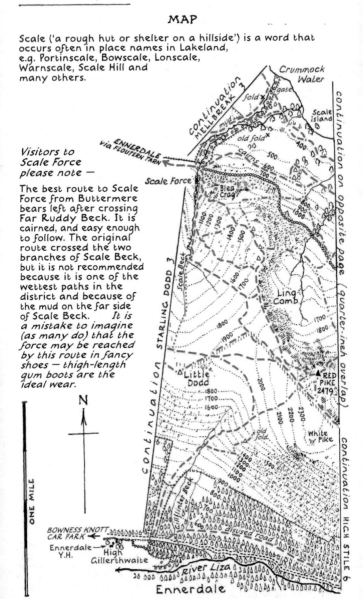

MAP

If the lie of the ground is favourable, a mountain stream needs little persuasion to change its course a few boulders washed down in time of flood, landslides or erosion are common causes. Examples are many.

Note that Scale Beck reaches Crummock Water at two places 400 yards apart. The bifurcation upstream was due to storm, but in this case there has been a partial recovery and both branches carry water to the lake when the water level is high.

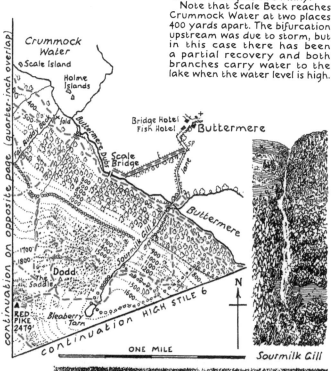

Sourmilk Gill

Scale Bridge

ASCENT FROM BUTTERMERE
via BLEABERRY TARN

2150 feet of ascent : 1¼ miles

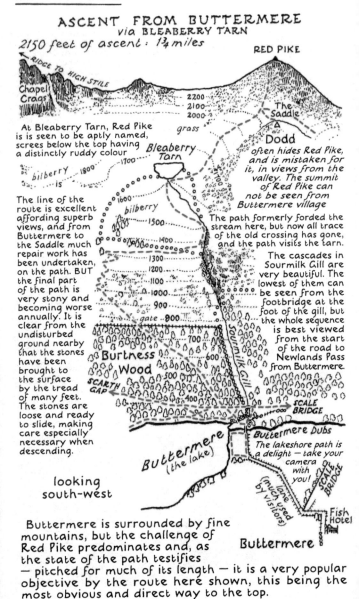

RED PIKE

RIDGE TO HIGH STILE

Chapel Crags

2200
2100
2000

The Saddle

grass

Dodd

Bleaberry Tarn

1700

bilberry is

1800

At Bleaberry Tarn, Red Pike is is seen to be aptly named, screes below the top having a distinctly ruddy colour

often hides Red Pike, and is mistaken for it, in views from the valley. The summit of Red Pike can not be seen from Buttermere village

The line of the route is excellent affording superb views, and from Buttermere to the Saddle much repair work has been undertaken, on the path. BUT the final part of the path is very stony and becoming worse annually. It is clear from the undisturbed ground nearby that the stones have been brought to the surface by the tread of many feet. The stones are loose and ready to slide, making care especially necessary when descending.

1600
bilberry
1500
1400
1300
1200
1100
1000
900
gate 900
700
600
500
400

Burtness Wood

SCARTH GAP

Sourmilk Gill

The path formerly forded the stream here, but now all trace of the old crossing has gone, and the path visits the tarn.

The cascades in Sourmilk Gill are very beautiful. The lowest of them can be seen from the footbridge at the foot of the gill, but the whole sequence is best viewed from the start of the road to Newlands Pass from Buttermere.

SCALE BRIDGE

Buttermere Dubs

The lakeshore path is a delight — take your camera with you!

Buttermere (the lake)

looking south-west

lane (much used by visitors)

SCALE BRIDGE

Fish Hotel

Buttermere

Buttermere is surrounded by fine mountains, but the challenge of Red Pike predominates and, as the state of the path testifies — pitched for much of its length — it is a very popular objective by the route here shown, this being the most obvious and direct way to the top.

ASCENT FROM BUTTERMERE
2150 feet of ascent 2¼ miles

looking south-west

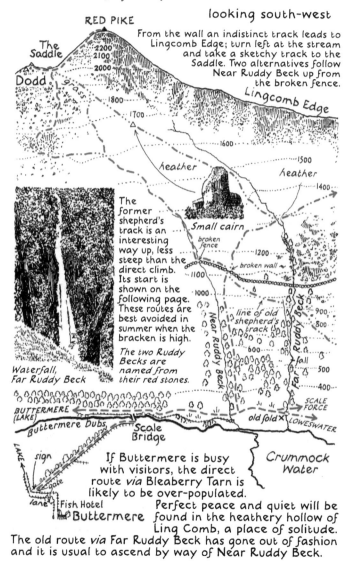

RED PIKE

The Saddle

Dodd

From the wall an indistinct track leads to Lingcomb Edge; turn left at the stream and take a sketchy track to the Saddle. Two alternatives follow Near Ruddy Beck up from the broken fence.

Lingcomb Edge

heather

heather

Small cairn

broken fence

broken wall

The former shepherd's track is an interesting way up, less steep than the direct climb. Its start is shown on the following page. These routes are best avoided in summer when the bracken is high.

line of old shepherd's track

Near Ruddy Beck

Far Ruddy Beck

fall

The two Ruddy Becks are named from their red stones.

Waterfall, Far Ruddy Beck

SCALE FORCE

old fold ✕

LOWESWATER

BUTTERMERE (LAKE)

Buttermere Dubs

Scale Bridge

Crummock Water

LAKE

sign

gate

lane Fish Hotel

Buttermere

If Buttermere is busy with visitors, the direct route *via* Bleaberry Tarn is likely to be over-populated.

Perfect peace and quiet will be found in the heathery hollow of Ling Comb, a place of solitude.

The old route *via* Far Ruddy Beck has gone out of fashion and it is usual to ascend by way of Near Ruddy Beck.

ASCENT FROM BUTTERMERE
via LINGCOMB EDGE
2150 feet of ascent : 2¾ miles

RED PIKE

The Saddle

2200
2100

1900

1800

looking south-south-west

Lingcomb Edge

grass

cairn on Lingcomb Edge

Lingcomb Edge, looking to Red Pike

Ling Comb

path from Far Ruddy Beck

1600

1500

1300

1200

Turn up steep slope

old shepherd's track

Far Ruddy Beck

700

600

SCALE FORCE

Scale Bridge

old fold ✕

grass

bracken

three holly trees

500

400

Scale Island

LOWESWATER

Crummock Water

The old shepherd's track, although very sketchy underfoot, offers a route into Ling Comb that may be considered — its latter stages are indicated on the previous page, as is the route of the path from Far Ruddy Beck which joins Lingcomb Edge at its lower stages.

If Scale Force has not already been visited, the route on the next page should be taken in preference to the one here shown.

This direct route has some steep scrambling in lush heather above the wall, and there is not a clear path underfoot for much of the way thus entailing some route finding; otherwise it is pleasant and quiet and has superb views of the Crummock district.

ASCENT FROM BUTTERMERE
VIA SCALE FORCE
2200 feet of ascent
4 miles

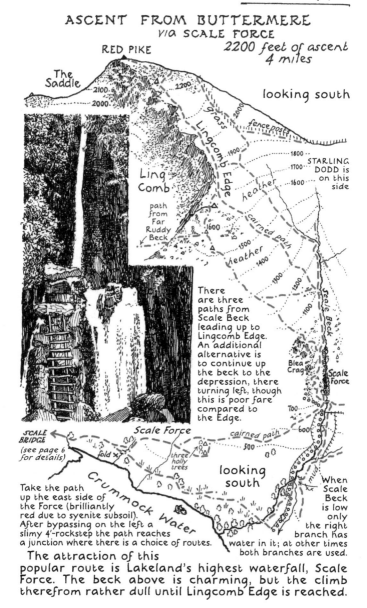

RED PIKE

The Saddle

looking south

2100
2000
2200
2000

grass

Lingcomb Edge

fence posts

1900

1800
1700
1600

STARLING DODD is on this side

Ling Comb

heather

path from Far Ruddy Beck

1600

cairned path

1500
1400

heather

1300
1200
1100

Scale Beck

Blea Crag

Scale Force

There are three paths from Scale Beck leading up to Lingcomb Edge. An additional alternative is to continue up the beck to the depression, there turning left, though this is poor fare compared to the Edge.

700

600

SCALE BRIDGE (see page 6 for details)

Scale Force

fold ✕

three holly trees

cairned path

500

looking south

Crummock Water

When Scale Beck is low only the right branch has water in it; at other times both branches are used.

mud

Take the path up the east side of the Force (brilliantly red due to syenite subsoil). After bypassing on the left a slimy 4'-rockstep the path reaches a junction where there is a choice of routes.

The attraction of this popular route is Lakeland's highest waterfall, Scale Force. The beck above is charming, but the climb therefrom rather dull until Lingcomb Edge is reached.

ASCENT FROM ENNERDALE
(HIGH GILLERTHWAITE)

2000 feet of ascent
1¼ miles

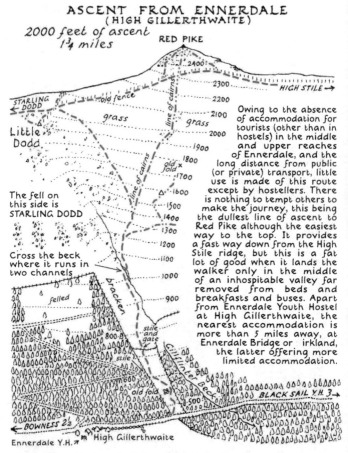

RED PIKE

2400

HIGH STILE →

2300

STARLING DODD ←

old fence

2200

grass

2100

grass

2000

Little Dodd

line of cairns

1900

old fold x

1800

1700

line of cairns

△ 1600

1500

The fell on this side is STARLING DODD

1400

1300

1200

1100

1000

Cross the beck where it runs in two channels

bracken

900

felled

stile and gate

800

stile

Gillflinter Beck

700

600

old fold

500

BLACK SAIL Y.H. 3 →

← BOWNESS 2½

High Gillerthwaite

Ennerdale Y.H. ↗

looking north-west

Owing to the absence of accommodation for tourists (other than in hostels) in the middle and upper reaches of Ennerdale, and the long distance from public (or private) transport, little use is made of this route except by hostellers. There is nothing to tempt others to make the journey, this being the dullest line of ascent to Red Pike although the easiest way to the top. It provides a fast way down from the High Stile ridge, but this is a fat lot of good when it lands the walker only in the middle of an inhospitable valley far removed from beds and breakfasts and buses. Apart from Ennerdale Youth Hostel at High Gillerthwaite, the nearest accommodation is more than 5 miles away, at Ennerdale Bridge or Kirkland, the latter offering more limited accommodation.

In the six-mile length of Ennerdale between Bowness and Black Sail Youth Hostel there is only one break in the dense plantations on the north side of the rough valley road. This is a narrow strip of unplanted ground between fences rising from the road 350 yards east of High Gillerthwaite. It is the only avenue by which sheep may be brought down from the fells and may be used for the ascent of Red Pike.

The path is cairned above Gillflinter Beck and easy to follow, mainly on grass, but tedious and unexciting, interest being restricted to the retrospective view of the Pillar Group across the valley.

THE SUMMIT

The summit projects from the main mass of the fell, boldly, like a promontory from a cliff face, having a steep fall on three sides, a flat top, and a gentle decline to a grassy plateau southwards, which is crossed by a boundary fence above the Ennerdale slope. A wind shelter and a large cairn occupy the abrupt corner of the promontory directly at the head of the Buttermere path. The top is grassy, with an intermingling of small outcrops and stony patches.

The summit, from Bleaberry Tarn

DESCENTS: The top is well trodden but not formed into definite tracks. Two lines of guide cairns lead away southwards, to Gillerthwaite and to High Stile; if, in mist, doubt arises in selection, error will be revealed when the fence is reached, the High Stile route turning left in company with it, the Gillerthwaite crossing it. The Scale Force line of descent is marked by a cairn that comes into view a few yards from the summit cairn. In mist it is best to leave this route alone. The direct route down to Buttermere by way of Bleaberry Tarn is marked by a well situated cairn. In a few yards the path splits into two, both branches being very difficult to negotiate because of loose stones. Once the Saddle is reached, there is a choice of going right (the usual route *via* Bleaberry Tarn, awkward in places with some poor pitching) or left (*via* Near Ruddy Beck).

High Stile in the background.
The large cairn has been replaced by a cairn and a shelter

THE VIEW

Lakes and Tarns

NE : Derwent Water
E : Buttermere
E : Bleaberry Tarn (seen a few paces east of the cairn)
W : Ennerdale Water
W : Reservoir near Dent
NW: Loweswater
N : Crummock Water

Red Pike's view is notable for the number of lakes that can be seen, really seen and not merely glimpsed; their prominence adds an unusual beauty to the scene.

Despite High Stile's impending bulk the mountain view is quite satisfying, the Grasmoor group, seen from tip to toe, being very conspicuous.

Many detailed descriptions of this view have appeared in print, not always completely in accordance with the facts.

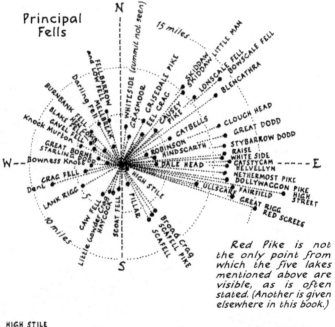

Principal Fells

Red Pike is not the only point from which the five lakes mentioned above are visible, as is often stated. (Another is given elsewhere in this book.)

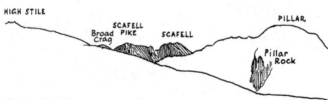

looking south-east

RIDGE ROUTES

To HIGH STILE. 2644': ¾ mile: S, then SE and E.
Depression at 2300'
350 feet of ascent
Very easy, becoming rough finally.

A line of marker cairns heads
south to the old fence, which
may be followed across excellent
turf to the stony rise of High Stile,
but in clear weather keep to the edge
of the escarpment to get the best
views; watch in particular for the
striking aspect of Chapel Crags from
the head of the scree gully alongside.

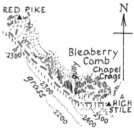

ONE MILE

The ridge to High Stile

Chapel Crags

head of Chapel Crags gully

To STARLING DODD, 2077': 1¼ miles: W, then WNW.
Depressions at 1880' and 1850'
240 feet of ascent
Little of interest.

ONE MILE

Surveyed from
Red Pike, this
route obviously
is a long trudge
over grass with
no excitements.
So it proves. As the
start of a high-level
way down to Ennerdale, continuing over Great Borne, it is better.

Red Pike

(Wasdale)

2707'

OS grid ref: NY165106

from Over Beck

▲ PILLAR
▲ SCOAT FELL
HAYCOCK ▲ ▲ RED PIKE

Wasdale
● Head

YEWBARROW ▲

● Overbeck Bridge

MILES

0   1   2   3   4

from Black Crag

NATURAL FEATURES

There are several Mosedales, and the best known of them, and the best, is the one branching from Wasdale Head. The circuit of the ridges around this side valley is a succession of exciting situations and fine vantage points in rugged surroundings, and a highlight greatly enjoyed on this splendid expedition is the traverse along the crest of the mile-long escarpment of Red Pike, its top cairn dramatically poised on the brink of a wild cataract of crags forming the eastern face: this is a grim declivity falling 2000 feet to the valley, a place for adventurers or explorers perhaps but it carries no walkers' paths. In contrast the western slopes decline more gradually over an extensive area jewelled by Scoat Tarn and Low Tarn, before coming down roughly to Nether Beck. North, Red Pike abuts closely against Scoat Fell, and the southern boundary is formed by Over Beck. Red Pike claims a short water frontage on Wast Water in the narrow strip of cultivated land lying between the outlets of Nether Beck and Over Beck, and only here, in the pastures and trees of Bowderdale, does the fell's fierce expression relent a little; only here does its dourness break into a pleasant smile. Just here, by the water's edge, is an oasis of sylvan beauty quite uncharacteristic of the fell towering behind, which, everywhere else, exemplifies the utter wildness and desolation of true mountain country.

looking
north-west

1 : The summit	11 : Wast Water
2 : Scoat Fell	12 : Nether Beck
3 : Haycock	13 : Over Beck
4 : Black Crag	14 : Brimfull Beck
5 : Wind Gap	15 : Black Beck
6 : Pillar	16 : Mosedale Beck
7 : Yewbarrow	17 : Gosforth Crag
8 : Dore Head	18 : Blackbeck Knotts
9 : Scoat Tarn	19 : Knott Ends
10 : Low Tarn	

For a century there has been confusion between this Red Pike and its namesake overlooking Buttermere. Confusion is worse confounded by their proximity, the summits being only three miles apart. To make a distinction, it is usual to refer to the subject of this chapter as the Wasdale Red Pike.

MAP

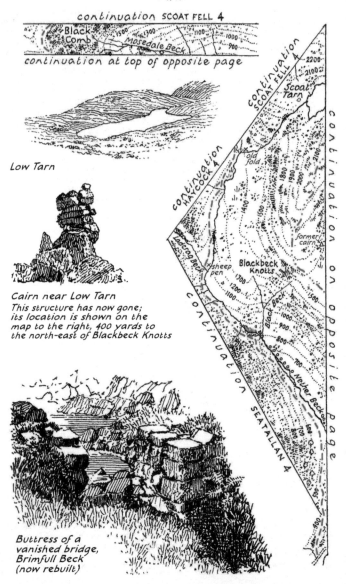

continuation SCOAT FELL 4

Black Comb

Mosedale Beck

continuation at top of opposite page

Low Tarn

Cairn near Low Tarn
This structure has now gone;
its location is shown on the
map to the right, 400 yards to
the north-east of Blackbeck Knotts

continuation SCOAT FELL 4

Scoat Tarn

old fold

continuation HAYCOCK 4

Lingcomb Beck

sheep pen

former cairn

Blackbeck Knotts

Black Beck

continuation SEATALLAN 4

Nether Beck

continuation on opposite page

Buttress of a
vanished bridge,
Brimfull Beck
(now rebuilt)

MAP

continuation at top of opposite page

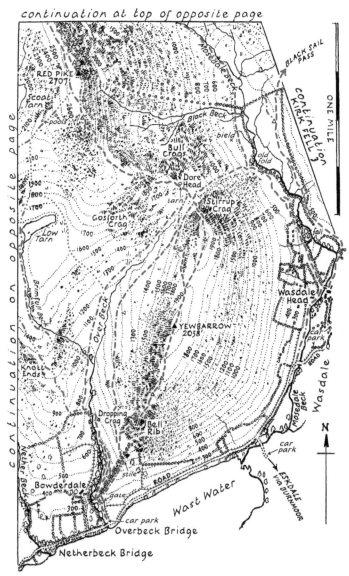

ASCENT FROM WASDALE
(OVERBECK BRIDGE)
2500 feet of ascent · 3 miles

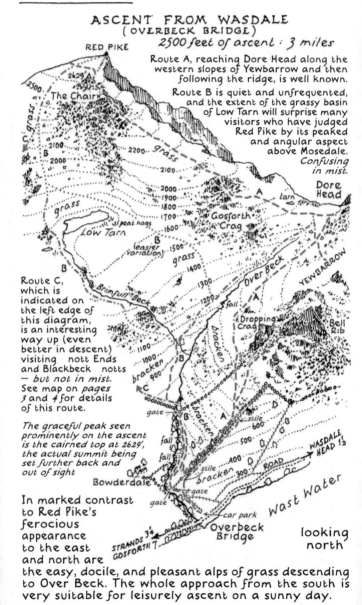

RED PIKE

2629

The Chair

2500

C grass

B

2100

2000

grass

Low Tarn

peat hags

Brimfull Beck

1100

1000

900

bracken

gate

fall

fall

Bowderdale

gate

grass

2200

2100

2000
1900
1800
1700
1600

lesser variation

1500

grass

1400

1300

1200

fall

bracken

B

bracken

A

stile

600

500

stile

400

bracken

stile

300

gate

gate

car park

STRANDS 3¾
GOSFORTH 7

Overbeck
Bridge

tarn

Dore
Head

Gosforth
Crag

Over Beck

YEWBARROW

Dropping
Crag

Bell
Rib

ROAD

WASDALE
HEAD 1½

Wast Water

looking
north

Route A, reaching Dore Head along the western slopes of Yewbarrow and then following the ridge, is well known.

Route B is quiet and unfrequented, and the extent of the grassy basin of Low Tarn will surprise many visitors who have judged Red Pike by its peaked and angular aspect above Mosedale. *Confusing in mist.*

Route C, which is indicated on the left edge of this diagram, is an interesting way up (even better in descent) visiting nott Ends and Blackbeck notts — *but not in mist.* See map on *pages 3 and 4* for details of this route.

The graceful peak seen prominently on the ascent is the cairned top at 2629', the actual summit being set further back and out of sight

In marked contrast to Red Pike's ferocious appearance to the east and north are the easy, docile, and pleasant alps of grass descending to Over Beck. The whole approach from the south is very suitable for leisurely ascent on a sunny day.

ASCENT FROM WASDALE HEAD
2450 feet of ascent : 2½ miles

Although this walk is commonly undertaken as part of a splendid ridge route — the Mosedale Horseshoe — continuing over Scoat Fell and Pillar, it is a fine expedition even if Red Pike is the only objective, for this is a fell deserving a leisurely and detailed exploration; in which event the descent by way of Low Tarn and Over Beck is recommended.

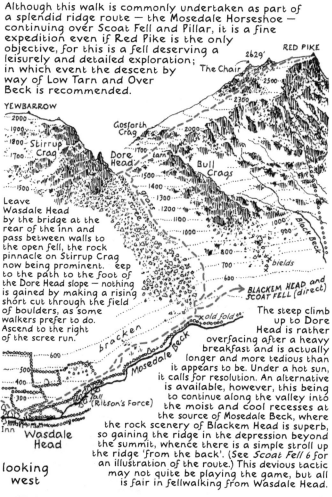

Leave Wasdale Head by the bridge at the rear of the inn and pass between walls to the open fell, the rock pinnacle of Stirrup Crag now being prominent. Keep to the path to the foot of the Dore Head slope — nothing is gained by making a rising short cut through the field of boulders, as some walkers prefer to do. Ascend to the right of the scree run.

The steep climb up to Dore Head is rather overfacing after a heavy breakfast and is actually longer and more tedious than it appears to be. Under a hot sun, it calls for resolution. An alternative is available, however, this being to continue along the valley into the moist and cool recesses at the source of Mosedale Beck, where the rock scenery of Blackem Head is superb, so gaining the ridge in the depression beyond the summit, whence there is a simple stroll up the ridge 'from the back'. (See *Scoat Fell 6* for an illustration of the route.) This devious tactic may not quite be playing the game, but all is fair in fellwalking from Wasdale Head.

This route serves to prove that the Scafells and Great Gable have not a monopoly of the best walks around Wasdale Head. The ridge of Red Pike is excellent, lovely turf alternating with a few simple scrambles on pleasant rock.

THE SUMMIT

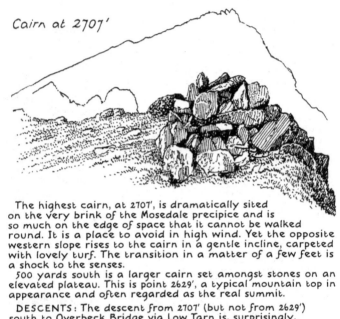

Cairn at 2707'

The highest cairn, at 2707', is dramatically sited on the very brink of the Mosedale precipice and is so much on the edge of space that it cannot be walked round. It is a place to avoid in high wind. Yet the opposite western slope rises to the cairn in a gentle incline, carpeted with lovely turf. The transition in a matter of a few feet is a shock to the senses.

500 yards south is a larger cairn set amongst stones on an elevated plateau. This is point 2629', a typical mountain top in appearance and often regarded as the real summit.

DESCENTS: The descent from 2707' (but not from 2629') south to Overbeck Bridge via Low Tarn is, surprisingly, one of the easiest in the district, on grass throughout and gently graded, but there are only faint traces of paths; similarly, the descent via Blackbeck notts and nott Ends is largely pathless.

Cairn at 2629'

In mist, aim for Dore Head, keeping the escarpment on the left, and the start of the path will be found twenty yards east of the 2629' top; at Dore Head go left down the scree or the grass bank alongside, for Wasdale Head, or turn right for Overbeck Bridge. An interesting but rather longer alternative is to descend from the col northwards to Scoat Tarn and Nether Beck. *Do not attempt the Blackem Head route into Mosedale unless it has been prospected in ascent.*

THE SUMMIT

continued

The Chair

A summit feature that often escapes attention nowadays is an outcrop of rock that has been converted into a comfortable seat by the erection of a back rest and side arms of stones. This is The Chair, and a century ago was so well known that people spoke of climbing The Chair as today they speak of climbing Red Pike. It occupies a vantage point on the edge of the stony plateau of the south summit, overlooking Wast Water, and is 120 yards south of the 2629' cairn. It is within 100 yards of the Dore Head track and prominently in view therefrom but may be mistaken at a glance for a cairn. It has survived the storms of many years remarkably well, but is not proof against vandals. Please respect it.

On the ascent from Overbeck Bridge it is The Chair that is so conspicuously in view, apparently on the highest point, and not the summit cairn as may be thought.

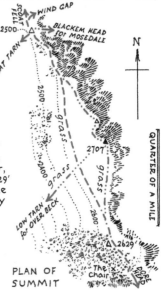

PLAN OF SUMMIT

Quite unaccountably, the ridge path prefers to skirt the highest cairn instead of visiting it.

THE VIEW

The view is good only in parts. Scoat Fell and Pillar, nearby and higher, shut out the distance northwards and have little attraction. The Scafell range, seen full length and in true perspective, is the best feature. There is a striking aerial view of Black Comb, which will impress those who have come up by this route.

Principal Fells

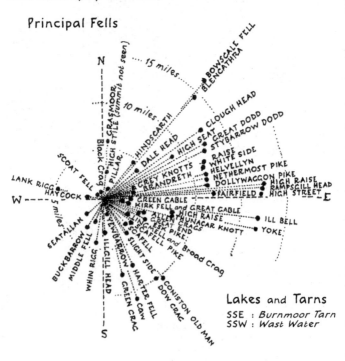

Lakes and Tarns

SSE : *Burnmoor Tarn*
SSW : *Wast Water*

GREEN GABLE · GREAT GABLE · KIRK FELL · GREAT END · ESK PIKE

looking
east

RIDGE ROUTES

To SCOAT FELL, 2760': ¾ mile: NNW
Depression at 2500': 270 feet of ascent

A dull climb, but brief.

Follow the escarpment north to the depression, then go straight up the opposite slope, ignoring paths trending to the right. Bear left to avoid a rough area of boulders at the east end of the summit wall. Cross the wall (on which the cairn stands) to obtain fine views of Steeple across Mirk Cove.

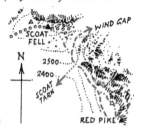

ONE MILE

To YEWBARROW, 2058': 1¾ miles: S, SE and SSW
Depression at 1520': 680 feet of ascent

A pleasant descent followed by an arduous scramble.

Down to Dore Head at 1520' everything is just fine. The south summit will have been crossed, the Chair will have been found and sat upon, two rough rocky declivities will have been negotiated without much difficulty and a good speed maintained down the easy grass slopes. But, at Dore Head, Yewbarrow looks really hostile. Steep scree and grass lead up to a barrier of rock (Stirrup Crag) that looks impassable, but grimly determined pedestrians can force a way up a series of cracks following evidences of the sufferings of those who have gone before. After 40 yards of toil there is sudden relief as grass is met again, and easy walking across a wide depression and up the opposite slope leads to the summit. Anxiety then shifts to the job of getting off safely... which is another story in another chapter.

If there are no witnesses about to tell of their shame, timid walkers may avoid Stirrup Crag entirely by taking the Overbeck path from Dore Head then turning off left on a thin path which — via a stony zigzag beneath a line of low cliffs — slants up to the depression on Yewbarrow (route indicated on map above).

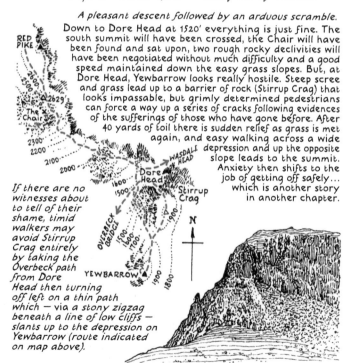

Stirrup Crag and Dore Head, as seen from the slopes of Red Pike

Scoat Fell

2760'

OS grid ref: NY159114

- Gillerthwaite
- ▲ PILLAR
- ▲ SCOAT FELL
- ▲ HAYCOCK
- ▲ RED PIKE
- Wasdale
  Head
- Netherbeck Bridge

MILES

0 1 2 3 4

from Kirk Fell

NATURAL FEATURES

Although often climbed from Wasdale as a part of the 'Mosedale Horseshoe', Scoat Fell has no fan club and few devotees, for the long plateau forming the top compares unfavourably with the more shapely summits of other fells even easier of access from Wasdale Head; and, moreover, a massive stone wall following the watershed impedes freedom of view and freedom of movement: the top of a mountain is never improved by man's handiwork, only a simple cairn being acceptable.

Yet Scoat Fell triumphs over its disabilities, and provides magnificent mountain scenery on all sides. The mile-long escarpment facing Ennerdale, between Wind Gap and Mirklin Cove, is tremendously exciting, wild and desolate terrain, interrupted only by a thin arête linking with Steeple, a subsidiary pinnacle of remarkable proportions towering gracefully across the void. All along here is scenery of high quality.

The fell descends broadly to Ennerdale in grass and heather slopes between Deep Gill and High Beck, and is afforested below 1200 feet; on the Wasdale side, where Red Pike soon obstructs the descent, the upper reaches of Nether Beck and Mosedale Beck form the boundaries.

Scoat Tarn is shared with Red Pike, but two lesser sheets of water, Tewit Tarn (which is now completely covered in vegetation) and Moss Dub, a valley pool in the Ennerdale forest, are within the territory of Scoat Fell exclusively.

Steeple (left) and Scoat Fell,
looking across Mirklin Cove

Scoat Fell 3

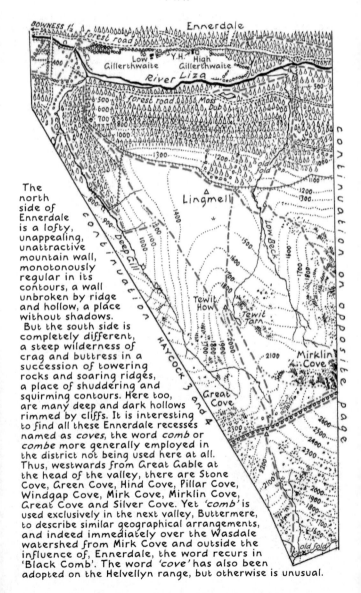

MAP

The north side of Ennerdale is a lofty, unappealing, unattractive mountain wall, monotonously regular in its contours, a wall unbroken by ridge and hollow, a place without shadows.

But the south side is completely different, a steep wilderness of crag and buttress in a succession of towering rocks and soaring ridges, a place of shuddering and squirming contours. Here too, are many deep and dark hollows rimmed by cliffs. It is interesting to find all these Ennerdale recesses named as *coves*, the word *comb* or *combe* more generally employed in the district not being used here at all. Thus, westwards from Great Gable at the head of the valley, there are Stone Cove, Green Cove, Hind Cove, Pillar Cove, Windgap Cove, Mirk Cove, Mirklin Cove, Great Cove and Silver Cove. Yet *'comb'* is used exclusively in the next valley, Buttermere, to describe similar geographical arrangements, and indeed immediately over the Wasdale watershed from Mirk Cove and outside the influence of, Ennerdale, the word recurs in 'Black Comb'. The word *'cove'* has also been adopted on the Helvellyn range, but otherwise is unusual.

MAP

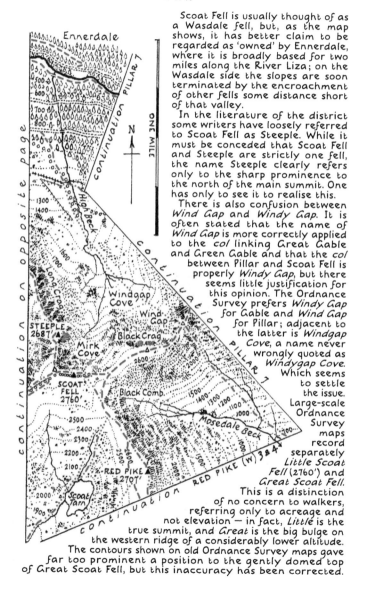

Scoat Fell is usually thought of as a Wasdale fell, but, as the map shows, it has better claim to be regarded as 'owned' by Ennerdale, where it is broadly based for two miles along the River Liza; on the Wasdale side the slopes are soon terminated by the encroachment of other fells some distance short of that valley.

In the literature of the district some writers have loosely referred to Scoat Fell as Steeple. While it must be conceded that Scoat Fell and Steeple are strictly one fell, the name Steeple clearly refers only to the sharp prominence to the north of the main summit. One has only to see it to realise this.

There is also confusion between *Wind Gap* and *Windy Gap*. It is often stated that the name of *Wind Gap* is more correctly applied to the *col* linking Great Gable and Green Gable and that the *col* between Pillar and Scoat Fell is properly *Windy Gap*, but there seems little justification for this opinion. The Ordnance Survey prefers *Windy Gap* for Gable and *Wind Gap* for Pillar; adjacent to the latter is *Windgap Cove*, a name never wrongly quoted as *Windygap Cove*. Which seems to settle the issue. Large-scale Ordnance Survey maps record separately *Little Scoat Fell* (2760') and *Great Scoat Fell*. This is a distinction of no concern to walkers, referring only to acreage and not elevation — in fact, *Little* is the true summit, and *Great* is the big bulge on the western ridge of a considerably lower altitude. The contours shown on old Ordnance Survey maps gave far too prominent a position to the gently domed top of Great Scoat Fell, but this inaccuracy has been corrected.

ASCENT FROM WASDALE
(NETHERBECK BRIDGE)
2550 feet of ascent : 4¼ miles

HAYCOCK   looking north   SCOAT FELL

Route A is
normally used
in the ascent of
Haycock, but is
also convenient
for Scoat Fell
(best views on
the far side
of the wall).
But Route
B is better
because of the
visit to Scoat
Tarn, a gem in
a wild setting.

2600
2500
2400
2300
2200
2000
1900

Scoat
Tarn

RED
PIKE

old fold

Beyond
Scoat Tarn a
thin path to the right of
the beck is easiest

split boulder,
Scoat Tarn

Ladding Beck
sheep
pen

1400
1300
1200
1100
1000

Nether Beck

900
800

falls

A good
path
proceeds
along the
west side
of Nether
Beck to
1400' where
the routes
diverge. This
path leaves the
road a quarter-
mile from
Netherbeck
Bridge. Its
start is
indicated
by a sign
post.

On Route B: looking back to Scoat Tarn from 2400'

Cutting across from the bridge
is not recommended because
of thick bracken and
marshy ground.

500
400
300
300

parking
place

WASDALE
HEAD 2

Netherbeck
Bridge

STRANDS 2¼
GOSFORTH 6½

ROAD

Wast Water

This is the easiest line
of approach to Scoat
Fell from any direction,
there being no steep
gradients. The biggest
attraction en route is
Scoat Tarn, the grandest of the western tarns,
and itself sufficient to justify the walk.

ASCENT FROM WASDALE HEAD
2500 feet of ascent : 3 miles

The gradual climb alongside Mosedale Beck (pathless, on grass) is very pleasant, and eagerness is added to the march by the promise of exciting ground ahead manifested by the beetling crags of Red Pike, which grow more impressive with every step. When the rowan-bedecked gorge and upper waterfall are passed, these crags are in full view and present a remarkable sight, falling in bewildering confusion from the summit ridge.

The stream bifurcates in a grassy hollow and further progress appears barred by a long low wall of rock beyond, but note on the left of this a straight boulder-strewn rake leading directly to the skyline and flanked by a succession of cliffs on both sides. Go up this, keeping to the right to avoid the worst of the boulders (two detours on grass are possible), finally passing through a narrow rock gateway to emerge on the ridge exactly in the depression between Red Pike and Scoat Fell, the summit of the latter being only ten minutes distant on the right.

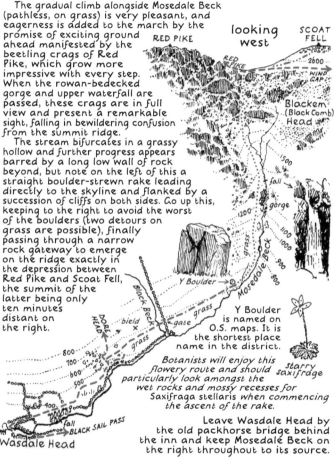

looking west

RED PIKE   SCOAT FELL

2600

WIND GAP

Blackem (Black Comb) Head

1500

fall

gorge

1200

1100
1000
900

grass

Mosedale Beck

800

Y Boulder

Black Beck

DORE HEAD

bield X

gate

grass

grass

800
700
600
500
400

fall
BLACK SAIL PASS

Wasdale Head

Y Boulder is named on O.S. maps. It is the shortest place name in the district.

Botanists will enjoy this flowery route and should particularly look amongst the wet rocks and mossy recesses for Saxifraga stellaris when commencing the ascent of the rake.

starry saxifrage

Leave Wasdale Head by the old packhorse bridge behind the inn and keep Mosedale Beck on the right throughout to its source.

Scoat Fell is usually reached from Wasdale Head *via* Dore Head and Red Pike, or *via* Pillar, *i.e.* as part of a ridge walk, but illustrated here is a direct way, little known and unfrequented, that climbs out of Mosedale through the magnificent rock scenery of Blackem Head and provides a route onto the ridge much more exciting than the usual tedious ascents of Dore Head and Wind Gap.

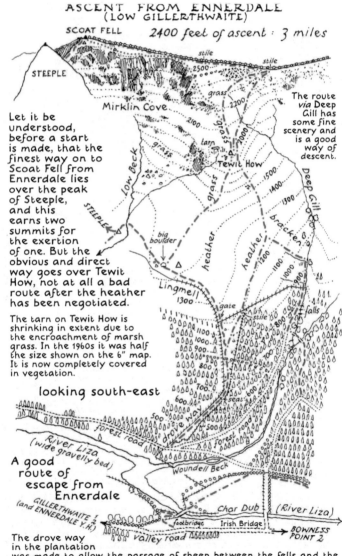

ASCENT FROM ENNERDALE
(LOW GILLERTHWAITE)

2400 feet of ascent : 3 miles

SCOAT FELL

STEEPLE

stile 2500

stile

grass 2200

The route *via* Deep Gill has some fine scenery and is a good way of descent.

Mirklin Cove

2100

grass

grass

tarn

Tewit How

2000

1600

1500

1400

1300

Deep Gill

Let it be understood, before a start is made, that the finest way on to Scoat Fell from Ennerdale lies over the peak of Steeple, and this earns two summits for the exertion of one. But the obvious and direct way goes over Tewit How, not at all a bad route after the heather has been negotiated.

STEEPLE

Low Beck

heather

bracken

1200

1100

1100

1000

big boulder

Lingmell 1300

heather

gate

stile

falls

The tarn on Tewit How is shrinking in extent due to the encroachment of marsh grass. In the 1960s it was half the size shown on the 6" map. It is now completely covered in vegetation.

1100
1000
900
800
700
600
500

seat

looking south-east

forest road

drove way

River Liza (wide gravelly bed)

A good route of escape from Ennerdale

forest road

Woundell Beck

Char Dub

(River Liza)

GILLERTHWAITE 1
(and ENNERDALE Y.H.)

footbridge Irish Bridge

BOWNESS POINT 2

valley road

The drove way in the plantation was made to allow the passage of sheep between the fells and the valley. It is a permitted access to the fells and may be approached by the forest road that crosses Woundell Beck from Irish Bridge. When the bridge is flooded use the footbridge further upstream.

THE SUMMIT

Summit cairn

Walkers who insist on summit cairns being sited precisely on the highest part of a summit have suffered a frustration here, for the exact spot representing the maximum altitude of Scoat Fell is fully occupied by a solid bit of wall. Not to be thwarted, however, our purists have had the enterprise to build a cairn on the top of the wall at this point, and so erected an edifice unique in Lakeland. But less meticulous visitors will generally accept as the summit the prominent cairn on open ground near the angle of the wall, where the cliffs of Mirk Cove terminate in a gentle slope leading to the Steeple arête: this is a few feet lower.

HAYCOCK

Great Scoat Fell

wall

Cairn near the wall

The top of the fell, stony in places, is an easy parade in the proximity of the wall but one is always conscious of the profound abyss of the northern coves close at hand and the gullies biting deeply into the edge of the plateau. Striking views are obtained by keeping along the rim of the cliffs and by following some of the headlands until they drop into space.

DESCENTS: *For Ennerdale*, in clear weather, the Steeple ridge is best, followed by the beautiful woodland path that accompanies Low Beck. An interesting alternative route (there is no path) is over Tewit How or by Deep Gill, turning down the easy slope beyond Mirklin Cove. *In mist*, the safest way down is *via* Tewit How or Deep Gill from the stile at the *col* between Scoat Fell and Haycock.

For Wasdale, the Red Pike ridge is the finest route if it can be seen, but *in mist* accompany the wall WSW to the Haycock *col*, where a

PLAN OF THE SUMMIT

Direct descents into Mirk and Mirklin Coves are dangerous

ENNERDALE

STEEPLE

quarter-mile

Mirklin Cove

Mirk Cove

PILLAR and WIND GAP

A

N

SCOAT TARN direct

RED PIKE and WASDALE

B

HAYCOCK

C

A : Tewit How and Deep Gill (direct)
B : Tewit How and Deep Gill (via col)
C : Netherbeck Bridge (via col)

good path on a grass slope, left, descends following the west bank of Nether Beck down to the road at Netherbeck Bridge.

THE VIEW

Only Pillar of the nearer fells overtops Scoat Fell and although it takes a big slice out of the distance there is enough left to see to occupy the attention for a long time on a clear day. The summit wall is an obstruction, preventing a comprehensive view in all directions.

Principal Fells

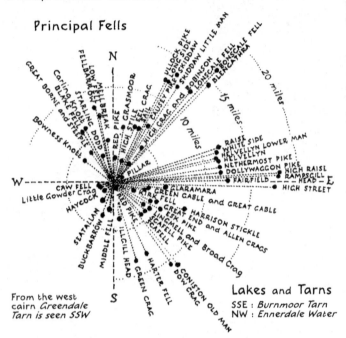

From the west cairn *Greendale Tarn* is seen SSW

Lakes and Tarns

SSE : Burnmoor Tarn
NW : Ennerdale Water

Some readers have written to claim that they have identified fells additional to those named on the diagrams of views in these books. This may well be so. The diagrams, as stated, show only the principal fells in view. Generally, in the case of a summit of low altitude, the list will be complete, but where a view is extensive, or where several fells appear in a tight group, it becomes impossible to indicate every one in the limited space available and a selection must be made: in such circumstances lower intermediate heights may be excluded to give preference to those forming the skyline; or again, where only a very small section of a fell can be seen, and then only in favourable conditions, it may be omitted rather than cause confusion, possibly, by including it. With regard to tarns, often these are indistinguishable from their surroundings, especially when of only slightly less elevation, and in many cases will be noticed only when illuminated by sunlight. (Which will account for any omissions of tarns in these views, for the author's wanderings have not always been accompanied by sunshine!)

RIDGE ROUTES

A prerequisite of a good mountain, from a walker's point of view, is that its summit should be the place of convergence of ridges from all directions, and Scoat Fell, which certainly *is* a good mountain, measures up to this requirement. Its four ridges all lead to the tops of other fells and provide splendid walks in exciting surroundings.

To STEEPLE, 2687´ : ¼ mile : N
Depression at 2620´
70 feet of ascent
Ten enjoyable minutes.

Unless time is pressing, this short walk should not be omitted even if it is intended to leave Scoat Fell by another route. Easy ground north of the cairn at the angle of the wall leads in a hundred yards to the top of the arête and the start of a distinct track. If, *in mist*, this cannot be found, do not proceed. Normally the way is clear and without difficulty.

looking to Steeple

To HAYCOCK, 2618´ : 1 mile : WSW : Depression at 2315´
330 feet of ascent
Just a matter of following the wall.

Preferably keep to the north side of the wall and fence as far as the depression, to get the views down into Mirklin Cove and across to Steeple, but on the stony climb up to Haycock the south side is just a little grassier and pleasanter for the feet. Along the route there are a number of stiles.

To RED PIKE, 2707´
¾ mile : SSE
Depression at 2500´
210 feet of ascent

Fine cliff scenery.

Cross the broken wall and head down the slope towards the serrated escarpment of Red Pike. A path will be picked up but when it trends right keep straight on or the top cairn will be bypassed.

To PILLAR, 2927´
1¼ miles : ENE
Depression at 2480´ (Wind Gap)
500 feet of ascent
Grand, just grand.

Big boulders make hard going at first, but then follows a grassy traverse to the fine cairn above Black Crag. More boulders must be crossed on the descent to Wind Gap. The facing slope is very rough but soon eases. Cairns lead to the flat top.

Seatallan 2266'

OS grid ref: NY140084

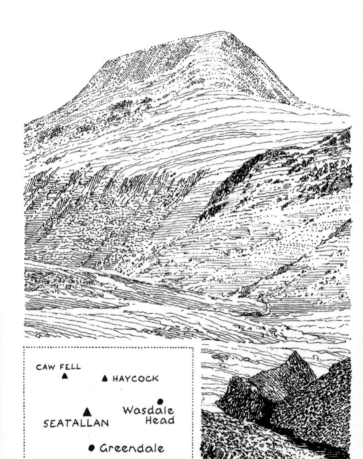

CAW FELL ▲

▲ HAYCOCK

▲ SEATALLAN

● Wasdale Head

● Greendale

● Strands

MILES
0 1 2 3 4

from below
Scoat Tarn

NATURAL FEATURES

When the organisers of a local mountain race selected the top of Seatallan as a checkpoint, some of the contestants confessed that they had never before heard of the fell, and it is probably true to say that the name is not generally known to walkers who have not yet based their activities on Wasdale Head.

Seatallan, formerly known as Seat Allan, forms a steep western wall to the quiet valley of Nether Beck for much of its length, exhibiting thereto a rocky slope above which the summit rises in easier gradients to a graceful cone. Northwards, the curve of the skyline, after a sharp initial fall, sweeps up to the more bulky Haycock; southwards are the two subsidiary heights of Middle Fell and Buckbarrow, both craggy, arresting the decline of the ground to Wast Water. In line with Middle Fell from the summit, hidden in an upland combe, is Greendale Tarn. It is to west and south-west, in the territory of Copeland Forest, that Seatallan shows its most innocuous slopes, extensive grass sheepwalks that descend gradually to Nether Wasdale and Gosforth, where the River Bleng, by a remarkable change of course, defines the boundaries of the fell on three sides. In this area, a wealth of timber old and new is provided by woodlands and plantations in a pleasant rural setting.

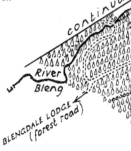

MAP

continuation CAW FELL 5

continuation on following page

felled
100
young trees
800
felled
gate
900
River Bleng
BLENGDALE LODGE (forest road)
Hollow Moor

N

The grass lane here shown is the best way to reach the open fell of Seatallan from Gosforth: it is direct and quiet. It leaves the road to Wasdale at the top of Wellington Brow.

GOSFORTH 22

grass lane

ONE MILE

MAP

continuation HAYCOCK 4

As in other areas lacking in prominent natural features, quite unremarkable objects on Seatallan are given names: Tod Hole, Buck Stone, Gray Crag, etc., These would not get a mention where detail is more crowded, as on Scafell.

continuation CAW FELL 6

continuation on opposite page

continuation on previous page

River Bleng

Raven Crag

old fold

bield

900

1100
1200
1300
1400
1600
1700

Stare Beck

Spinnel Beck

old fold

800
old cairns

folds

900

×fold

Tod Hole

1200

shelter ×

Cat Bields

1700

old ×bield

drove road

Buck Stone

1500

1600

1400

Glade How

900

Kil Beck

×fold

Gray Borran

1300

Gray Crag

1100

fold ×

1000
900
700

Hollow Moor

100

Wash Dub

Windsor Farm

farm road

700

GOSFORTH 4

Harrow Head

ROAD

In the Blengdale area the Ordnance Survey use the name 'Sheep Shelter' instead of 'Bield' on their 6" maps, this preference being unusual.

There is a small parking space for a couple of cars just to the east of Harrow Head

MAP

The 'column' half a mile north-east of Buckbarrow's summit is better known as 'Joss Naylor's cairn'. The legendary fellrunner and shepherd is said to have completed its construction on March 30th, 2002, the day the Queen Mother died.

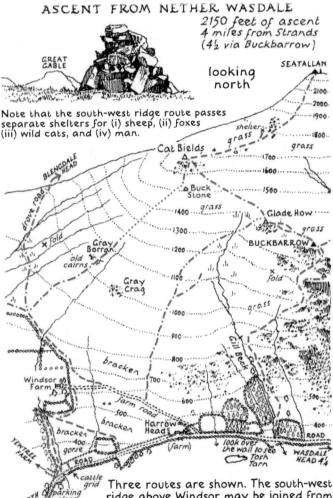

ASCENT FROM NETHER WASDALE
2150 feet of ascent
4 miles from Strands
(4½ via Buckbarrow)

GREAT GABLE

looking north

SEATALLAN

Note that the south-west ridge route passes
separate shelters for (i) sheep, (ii) foxes
(iii) wild cats, and (iv) man.

Cat Bields

Buck Stone

Glade How

BUCKBARROW

Gray Borran

Gray Crag

BLENCDALE HEAD

drove road

× fold

old cairns

Gill Beck

grass

bracken

Windsor Farm

farm road

bracken

Harrow Head

bracken

gorse

YEWTREE FARM

ROAD

cattle grid

parking place

GOSFORTH

STRANDS

(farm)

look over the wall to see Tosh Tarn

ROAD

WASDALE HEAD 4¼

Three routes are shown. The south-west
ridge above Windsor may be joined from
the drove road, but is wide and indefinite
and dreary in its lower parts. The best of
the alternatives is to include a visit to the
rocky top of Buckbarrow, which has better views.
The Glade How route from the farm road is good in descent.

For routes of ascent from the drove road (left edge of diagram)
see maps on *page 3* (*via Ill Gill*) and *Haycock 4* (*via Rossy Gill*).

ASCENT FROM WASDALE

(GREENDALE)
2050' of ascent : 2 miles

(NETHERBECK BRIDGE)
2100' of ascent : 3 miles

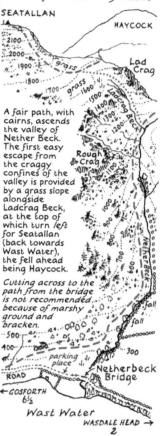

SEATALLAN

HAYCOCK

Lad Crag

2100
2000
1900
1800
1700
1600
1500
1400
1300
1200
1100

grass

Ladcrag Beck

Rough Crag

A fair path, with cairns, ascends the valley of Nether Beck. The first easy escape from the craggy confines of the valley is provided by a grass slope alongside Ladcrag Beck, at the top of which turn *left* for Seatallan (back towards Wast Water), the fell ahead being Haycock.

Cutting across to the path from the bridge is not recommended because of marshy ground and bracken.

Nether Beck

fall

fall

500
400
300

parking place

ROAD

Netherbeck Bridge

← GOSFORTH 6½

Wast Water

WASDALE HEAD → 2

SEATALLAN

2100
2000
1900
1800
1700
1500
1400
1300
1200
1100

Greendale Tarn

It is difficult to cross the gill here after rain.

Greendale Gill

MIDDLE FELL

800
700
600
500

Tongues Gills

Tongues Gills is a double plural: there are several tongues and gills forming magnificent ravine scenery.

300

grass path

fine yew

bracken

ROAD

Greendale

← GOSFORTH 5¼

WASDALE HEAD → 3½

looking north

Instead of proceeding thence as far as Greendale Tarn, which is unattractive, avoid its marshy surroundings by turning up the slope of Seatallan, keeping left to avoid the summit screes.

The walk up the fell to Tongues Gills is delightful, and the grim scenery of the gills (unseen from the road) is a great surprise.

looking north-west

Nether Beck occupies a quiet valley with pretty waterfalls, and the walk alongside is easy and pleasant. In contrast, the climb out of the valley to the top of Seatallan, on grass, will be found tedious.

THE SUMMIT

Different versions of Ordnance Survey maps describe the heap of stones variously as an 'ancient cairn' and a 'tumulus.'

Local archaeologists prefer to describe it as a large tumulus sixty-seven yards in circumference.

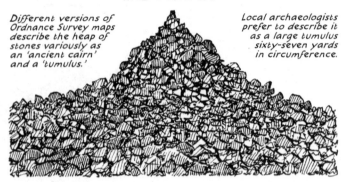

Stones galore, all in a great heap on a felltop predominantly of soft turf, is an unnatural phenomenon that greets all visitors to Seatallan's summit. Cairns are not a fashion introduced by walkers. Shepherds built cairns as landmarks for their own guidance in bad weather long before people climbed hills for pleasure. And long before the shepherds the first primitive dwellers in the district built cairns in and around their settlements and over their burial places. The big cairn on Seatallan is attributed to the early British inhabitants and may well be thousands of years old. Its modern use is as a shelter. Nearby, on the grass, is a modern erection: S. 5762 — an Ordnance Survey column. The top of the fell is otherwise featureless. A landslip on the north side has left a fringe of crags and arêtes, providing a natural quarry from which the stones of the tumulus were probably obtained.

DESCENTS: Routes of ascent may be reversed, but, *in mist,* Buckbarrow is better left severely alone.

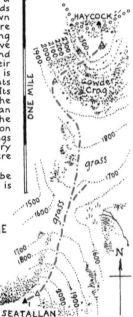

RIDGE ROUTE

To HAYCOCK, 2618′ : 2 miles : NNE
Depression at 1610′
1050 feet of ascent

A lengthy cross-country trek.

Easy grass leads down to and across a broad grassy depression known as Pots of Ashness. A doubt arises as Cowder Crag is approached, but it is not formidable and a scramble over steep scree may be made frontally, or a grassy rake around to the left, marked by a cairn, may be preferred.

For details of the route to **MIDDLE FELL**, see *Middle Fell 5.*

THE VIEW

As a viewpoint Seatallan does not rank highly. From Haycock round to Scafell a mountain barrier hides most of the district, only the Coniston fells being well seen at a distance. West and south, however, there is a full and uninterrupted panorama of the coastline and the Black Combe hinterland.

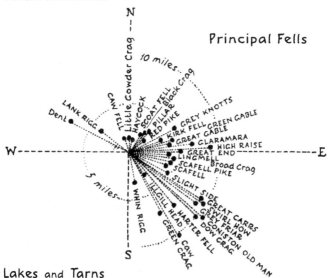

Principal Fells

Lakes and Tarns

None from the cairn, but a short walk north-east brings *Low Tarn* and *Scoat Tarn* into view directly ahead and a section of *Wast Water* can be seen to the right.

The Scafell range from Seatallan

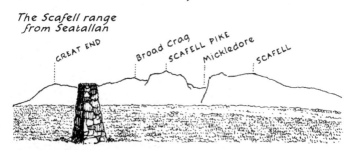

A special feature is the symmetrical appearance of Scafell Pike, the shape of which is better emphasised from this viewpoint than from any other. The summit is seen midway above the steep twin flanking profiles of Dropping Crag, left, and Pikes Crag, right.

Starling Dodd

2077'

OS grid ref: NY142157

GREAT
BORNE ▲
Buttermere ●

STARLING ▲
DODD
▲ RED PIKE

Gillerthwaite ●
MILES
0 1 2 3 4

from Ennerdale

NATURAL FEATURES

Starling Dodd, between Buttermere and Ennerdale, is one of those unobtrusive and unassuming fells that are rarely mentioned in literature or in conversation, that never really make an impact on mind or memory, that most visitors to the district know vaguely, from a study of maps, without ever wanting to know well. Its neat rounded summit surveys exciting landscapes but remains shyly aloof as though aware of its own limited contribution to the scenery.

The fell closely overlooks Ennerdale, having on this side a steep but featureless slope, the lower part being densely planted by the Forestry Commission. Its best aspect is to the north, where the extensive plateau of Gale Fell, just below the summit, breaks suddenly into a rough drop to the desolate headwaters and marshes of Mosedale Beck. Gale Fell is bounded by Scale Beck, a place of popular resort in its lower course where Scale Force, Lakeland's highest waterfall, makes its thrilling leap in a deeply enclosed ravine.

Starling Dodd is a point on a loosely defined ridge, which runs west to Great Borne before dropping sharply to Ennerdale Water and east to Red Pike and the superb traverse of High Stile. It is seldom conspicuously seen in views from the valleys, being prominent only on the walk into Mosedale from Loweswater, directly in front.

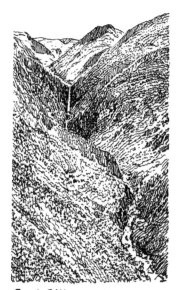

Red Gill,
Mosedale

Starling Dodd,
from High Beck, Ennerdale

MAP

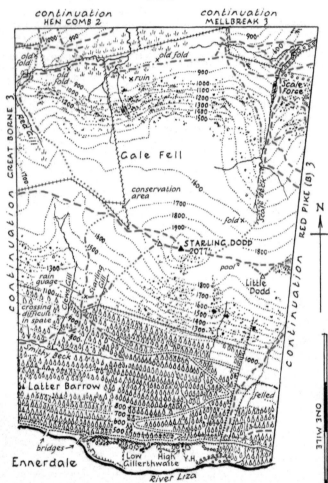

continuation
HEN COMB 2

continuation
MELLBREAK 3

continuation GREAT BORNE 3

continuation RED PIKE (B) 3

Gale Fell

conservation
area

STARLING DODD
2077'

Little
Dodd

rain
guage

crossing
difficult
in spate

Smithy Beck

Latter Barrow

felled

Scale
Force

pool

fold ×

old fold

old
fold

ruin

N

ONE MILE

bridges

Ennerdale

Low
Gillerthwaite

High
Y.H.

River Liza

Starling Dodd has three subsidiary summits, which may
surprise people who would only consider Little Dodd (1935')
warranted such a title. Gale Fell (1699') is recognised as the
second; its summit being a barely perceptable rise at a
point on the fence shown in the map above about 200
yards north of the conservation area. The third is Latter
Barrow (895'), which is a parallel lower ridge among the
forests of Ennerdale which diverts Smithy Beck westwards.

ASCENT FROM BOWNESS CAR PARK
via SMITHY BECK
1800 feet of ascent : 3 miles

An interesting round trip can be made by ascending Starling Dodd 'from the back' via the path from High Gillerthwaite to Red Pike, turning off left towards Little Dodd; see Red Pike (B) 9. Be warned, however, when descending through the forest check there is no work in progress that puts the route out of bounds; otherwise there will be a long detour.

STARLING DODD

Little Dodd

GREAT BORNE

2000
1900
1800 grass
1700
1600 heather
1500
1400
Starling Gill
1300
rain gauge
1200 bracken
gate
Clews Gill
Smithy Beck

All the fell routes in Ennerdale that begin from the Bowness car park entail some walking 'on the flat', but this is one of the shortest of those — the forest path that turns off the valley floor road is reached after barely ten minutes of marching. The 'road' is, of course, not open to public traffic beyond the car park, only for those with business along the valley.

From the gate a clear path heads straight up the fells between the two gills (Clews and Starling) and is easy to follow through a band of bracken. It peters out higher up and swathes of heather need to be negotiated. The alternative way up starts with a sketchy path beside the fence; after the crossing of Starling Gill ribbons of grass can be traced through bracken before this path, like that further to the west, also fades away.

This crossing is not at all easy when the beck is in spate, but stepping stones make it fairly simple at other times

Dr... Gill

GILLERTHWAITE 1
River Liza

BOWNESS car park ½
SP

Ennerdale Water

looking north-east

From the tree-clad floor of Ennerdale there is no sign of Starling Dodd far above, but footpaths and a forestry track enable access to the open fell where there is a choice of routes above the final fence.

ASCENT FROM BUTTERMERE
VIA SCALE FORCE
2000 feet of ascent : 3½ miles

This is an ascent of Starling Dodd, the only direct way from Buttermere, but let it be said that the vast majority of the terrain which is crossed belongs to the fell's higher and far more popular neighbour Red Pike. However, Starling Dodd clearly has a 50% share in Scale Beck, the course of which marks a distinct boundary between the two fells, so it follows that Starling Dodd is an equal partner in Scale Force, which would be a feather in any fell's cap. The waterfall has a single drop of about 170 feet and two others of about 20 feet each. More details about this secluded gem of Lakeland can be found in the *Red Pike (B)* chapter.

A : *Red Pike (direct)*
B : *Red Pike (via Ling Comb Edge)*
C : *path from Mosedale*
　　see facing page
D : *Mosedale, and Ennerdale*
　　via Floutern Pass
E : *Mosedale, and Ennerdale*
　　via Floutern Pass (alternative)
F : *Scale Knott and Mellbreak*
G : *Crummock Water lakeshore path*
H : *Scale Bridge and Buttermere*

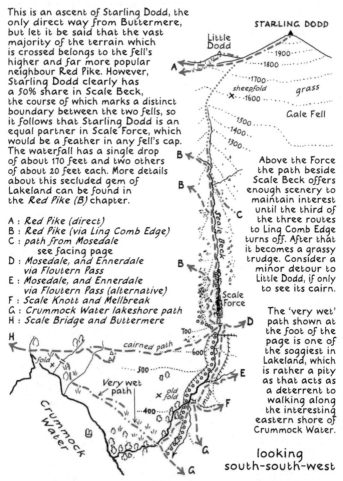

Above the Force the path beside Scale Beck offers enough scenery to maintain interest until the third of the three routes to Ling Comb Edge turns off. After that it becomes a grassy trudge. Consider a minor detour to Little Dodd, if only to see its cairn.

The 'very wet' path shown at the foot of the page is one of the soggiest in Lakeland, which is rather a pity as that acts as a deterrent to walking along the interesting eastern shore of Crummock Water.

looking
south-south-west

A roundabout route, the highlight of which is a visit to Lakeland's highest waterfall, Scale Force. As can be seen by the number of paths heading for Red Pike, this can easily be combined with an ascent of Starling Dodd's higher neighbour. For details, see *Red Pike (B) 8*.

ASCENT FROM LOWESWATER
1700 feet of ascent : 4½ miles

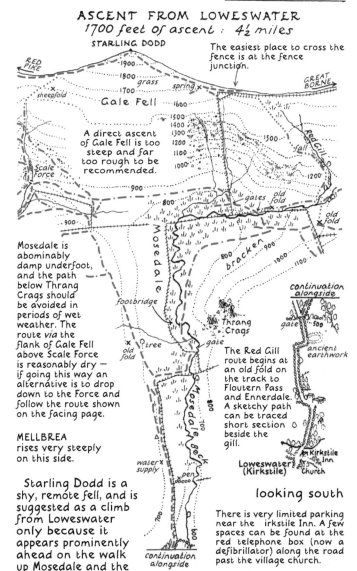

STARLING DODD

RED PIKE

1900
1800
1700
grass
spring ×

GREAT BORNE

The easiest place to cross the fence is at the fence junction.

× sheepfold

Gale Fell

1600
1500
1400
1300
1200
1100
1000

A direct ascent of Gale Fell is too steep and far too rough to be recommended.

Scale Force

900

900

800

Moorsdale

gates
old fold

1500

Red Gill

fall

1200

old × fold

800
bracken
900
1000
1100

Mosedale is abominably damp underfoot, and the path below Thrang Crags should be avoided in periods of wet weather. The route via the flank of Gale Fell above Scale Force is reasonably dry — if going this way an alternative is to drop down to the Force and follow the route shown on the facing page.

footbridge

Thrang Crags

× old fold

tree

gate

Mosedale Beck

800
700

continuation alongside

gate

500

ancient earthwork

The Red Gill route begins at an old fold on the track to Floutern Pass and Ennerdale. A sketchy path can be traced short section beside the gill.

MELLBREA rises very steeply on this side.

water × supply

pen

700

800

Starling Dodd is a shy, remote fell, and is suggested as a climb from Loweswater only because it appears prominently ahead on the walk up Mosedale and the possibility of ascent from this direction must occur to anyone doing that journey. Two routes are shown.

continuation alongside

Kirkstile Inn

Loweswater (Kirkstile)

Church

looking south

There is very limited parking near the Kirkstile Inn. A few spaces can be found at the red telephone box (now a defibrillator) along the road past the village church.

THE SUMMIT

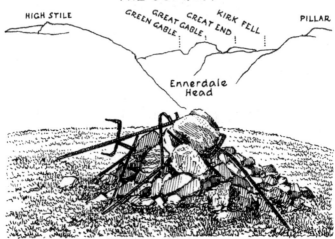

On the way to the top there are slight traces of a former fence, and one wonders what has happened to the iron posts which usually survive long after the wires have gone. Upon arrival at the summit the question is partly answered, for many of them have been used to construct a modern sculpture which sits beside the old stone cairn. The top is smooth and grassy, with a little gravel, and except for the cairns, is quite featureless.

DESCENTS: *For Buttermere*, descend north-east, joining the path from Red Pike alongside Scale Beck. *For Loweswater*, reverse the route of ascent *via* Red Gill (see previous page). *For Ennerdale Bridge*, in clear weather traverse Great Borne or descend to the forest route *via* Smithy Beck, but in mist go down by Red Gill to join the Floutern Tarn route. *For Ennerdale Youth Hostel* or *Black Sail Youth Hostel*, contour Little Dodd on a track to join the public footpath through the forest from Red Pike.

RIDGE ROUTE

To RED PIKE, 2479': 1¼ miles : E, then ESE
    Depressions at 1850' and 1880': 650 feet of ascent

Easy walking on grass, steepening towards the finish.

In the depression before Little Dodd is a curious hollow with a pool in it, like a bomb crater, and just beyond the rise is a strange field of boulders, these being the only features of note. The cairn on Little Dodd, like that of its higher neighbour, is festooned with fence posts.

ONE MILE

THE VIEW

The best feature of a moderate view is Ennerdale Water, strikingly seen in its entirety except for a small part hidden behind the intervening Bowness nott. Of the mountain array, Pillar and Company are the most impressive and, if not in too deep shadow, this is an excellent place to study the topography of the group. A sunny early evening is a good time.

Principal Fells

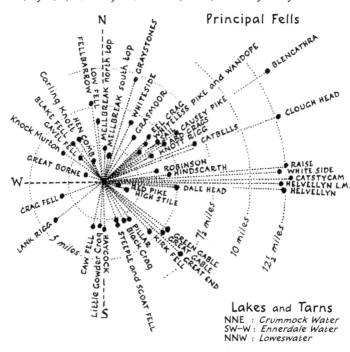

Lakes and Tarns
NNE : *Crummock Water*
SW–W : *Ennerdale Water*
NNW : *Loweswater*

RIDGE ROUTE

An easy stroll on a decent path, but not recommended *in mist* on a first visit because the summit layout of Great Borne would therefore be confusing.

TO GREAT BORNE, 2019': 1½ miles WNW, W and WNW
Depression at 1625'
420 feet of ascent

ONE MILE

Steeple

2687'

OS grid ref: NY158117

from Windgap Cove

• Gillerthwaite

STEEPLE ▲   ▲ PILLAR
         ▲ SCOAT FELL
         ▲ RED PIKE
HAYCOCK ▲

Wasdale
● Head

Netherbeck Bridge
●

MILES
0   1   2   3   4

NATURAL FEATURES

The unknown man who first named this fell was blessed both with inspiration and imagination. Few mountains given descriptive names have fared better. Steeple is a magnificent choice. Seen on a map, it commands the eye and quickens the pulse; seen in reality, it does the same. The climbing of Steeple is a feat to announce with pride in a letter to the old folks at home, who can safely be relied upon to invest the writer with undeserved heroism. Fancy our Fred having climbed a steeple!

This fell, however, is no slender spire. A cross-section of the summit ridge is not like this ∧ but this ⟋. It is a fine pointed peak nevertheless, one of the best. If the west face was as steep as the east and the south ridge as long as the north, Steeple would provide a great climb. What spoils it is its close attachment to the bulkier Scoat Fell, to which it is linked by a short arête and which is not only higher but completely dominant.

Steeple in fact is no more than an excrescence on the side of Scoat Fell, and only its remarkable proportions have earned it a separate identity. The east crags in particular, forming a half-mile escarpment above Windgap Cove, give a fine airiness to the summit and to the rocky spine of the ridge climbing out of Ennerdale to reach it. This is first-rate mountain country. The short drop west to Mirklin Cove is less fearsome, but rough. Boundary streams Low Beck and High Beck both flow into the Liza, so that Steeple is wholly a fell of Ennerdale.

The north ridge

Steeple 3

*The upper part of
the north ridge*

*Steeple, as seen
from Scoat Fell
across Mirk Cove*

MAP

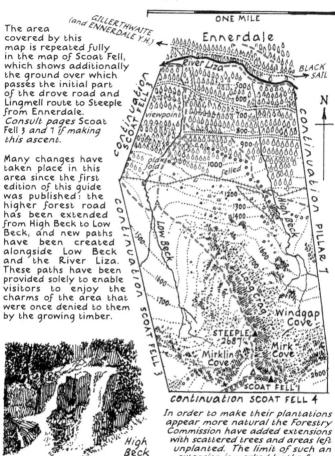

ONE MILE

The area covered by this map is repeated fully in the map of Scoat Fell, which shows additionally the ground over which passes the initial part of the drove road and Lingmell route to Steeple from Ennerdale. *Consult pages Scoat Fell 3 and 1 if making this ascent.*

Many changes have taken place in this area since the first edition of this guide was published: the higher forest road has been extended from High Beck to Low Beck, and new paths have been created alongside Low Beck and the River Liza. These paths have been provided solely to enable visitors to enjoy the charms of the area that were once denied to them by the growing timber.

GILLERTHWAITE
(and ENNERDALE Y.H.)

Ennerdale

River Liza

BLACK SAIL

continuation SCOAT FELL 3

viewpoint

500.

600

700

800

900

1000

felled

1200

1300

1400

1500

1600

1700

continuation SCOAT FELL 3

Low Beck

glacial fold.

1600

1700

Long Crag

1600

1700

continuation PILLAR 1

High Beck

Windgap Cove

STEEPLE 2687.

Mirklin Cove

Mirk Cove

2600

continuation SCOAT FELL 4

In order to make their plantations appear more natural the Forestry Commission have added extensions with scattered trees and areas left unplanted. The limit of such an extension is marked by the fence.

High Beck

Low Beck and High Beck are joyful streams on the last half-mile of their descent to join the River Liza, leaping and tumbling in lovely cascades down the fern-clad ravines they have carved out of the fellside. Not so very long ago, growing plantations hid them from the sight of travellers in the valley and muted their merry music. Except where the forest roads crossed their courses (on concrete bridges that have not the beauty bridges should have) they could neither be properly seen nor easily reached. Things are not what they used to be in Ennerdale, and they never will be, but in recent years improvements have been made. Nowadays it is possible to follow the banks of Low Beck by a public footpath, and the viewpoint shown on the map has great merit and deserves to be better known.

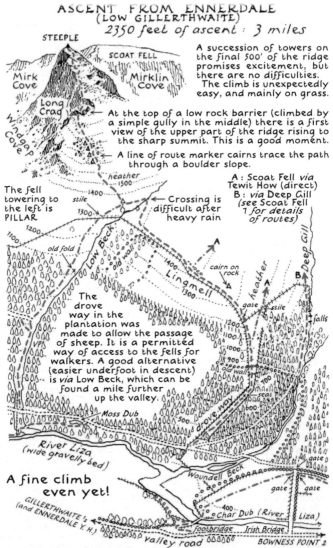

ASCENT FROM ENNERDALE
(LOW GILLERTHWAITE)
2350 feet of ascent : 3 miles

STEEPLE

SCOAT FELL

Mirk Cove

Mirklin Cove

Long Crag

Wind Gap Cove

A succession of towers on the final 500' of the ridge promises excitement, but there are no difficulties. The climb is unexpectedly easy, and mainly on grass.

— At the top of a low rock barrier (climbed by a simple gully in the middle) there is a first view of the upper part of the ridge rising to the sharp summit. This is a good moment.

— A line of route marker cairns trace the path through a boulder slope.

heather 1500

The fell towering to the left is PILLAR

stile 1400

1300

— Crossing is difficult after heavy rain

A : Scoat Fell via Tewit How (direct)
B : via Deep Gill (see Scoat Fell 7 for details of routes)

1100 1200

old fold

Low Beck

old wall

Lingmell 1300

cairn on rock

A

A B

heather

Deep Gill

gate stile

falls

The drove way in the plantation was made to allow the passage of sheep. It is a permitted way of access to the fells for walkers. A good alternative (easier underfoot in descent) is via Low Beck, which can be found a mile further up the valley.

1200 1100 1000 900 old wall 800

gate

seat

drove way

Moss Dub

600 500

River Liza (wide gravelly bed)

A fine climb even yet!

Woundell Beck

gate gate

GILLERTHWAITE (and ENNERDALE Y.H.)

400 Char Dub (River Liza)

gate gate

footbridge   Irish Bridge

valley road

BOWNESS POINT 2

Walkers who park their cars at Bowness Knott should bear in mind that the total length of this walk via the drove way is approaching five miles, and longer if the Low Beck alternative is chosen.

looking south-east

THE SUMMIT

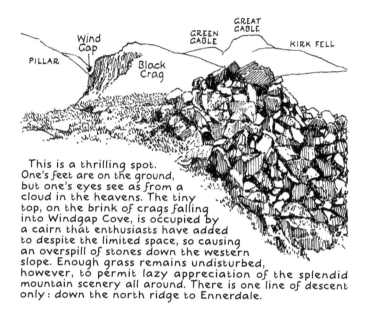

This is a thrilling spot. One's feet are on the ground, but one's eyes see as from a cloud in the heavens. The tiny top, on the brink of crags falling into Windgap Cove, is occupied by a cairn that enthusiasts have added to despite the limited space, so causing an overspill of stones down the western slope. Enough grass remains undisturbed, however, to permit lazy appreciation of the splendid mountain scenery all around. There is one line of descent only: down the north ridge to Ennerdale.

Looking towards Scoat Fell

RIDGE ROUTE

To SCOAT FELL, 2760': ¼ mile
S, but start W
Depression at 2620'
140 feet of ascent

Every step is a joy.

The arête leading on to Scoat Fell is in clear view, with a path winding up it, from the summit of Steeple, but the *col* below it cannot be reached by a beeline; instead, first go a few paces to the west and pick up a distinct track that swings round to the col.

The arête is easy, safe in mist, finely situated, and ends on the flat top, the cairn being directly ahead (100 yards).

QUARTER·MILE

THE VIEW

Although the view is greatly circumscribed by the loftier and impending masses of Scoat Fell and Pillar, there is to be seen more than Steeple's subservient position on the north side of the watershed would lead one to expect. West and north the scene is uninterrupted and there is a good sweep of mountainous country to be seen eastwards. The view of Ennerdale, where the lake is displayed almost entirely, is excellent, but visitors are likely to be impressed most of all by the craggy hollows of Mirk and Mirklin Coves nearby.

Principal Fells

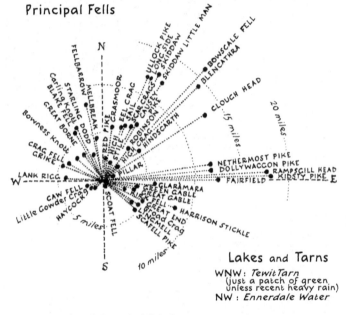

Lakes and Tarns

WNW : *Tewit Tarn*
(just a patch of green
unless recent heavy rain)
NW : *Ennerdale Water*

*Scoat Fell, with Steeple (right)
from the top of Black Crag*

Steeple, east face,
from Black Crag

Yewbarrow

2058′

OS grid ref: NY173085

RED PIKE ▲

YEWBARROW ▲   ● Wasdale
                    Head

▲ MIDDLE FELL
     ● Bowderdale

MILES
0   1   2   3   4

from Netherbeck Bridge

NATURAL FEATURES

Many mountains have been described as having the shape of the inverted hull of a boat, but none of them more fittingly than Yewbarrow, which extends along the west side of Wasdale for two miles as a high and narrow ridge, the prow and the stern coming sharply down to valley level with many barnacled incrustations. These latter roughnesses make the long summit rather difficult of attainment from either end, while the steep sides also deter ascent, so that Yewbarrow is not often climbed although it is a centre-piece of magnificent fell country and commands thrilling views. Nor is the ridge itself without incident, one feature in particular, Great Door, being a remarkable cleft where the crest narrows at the top of the craggy declivity above Wast Water.

Yewbarrow's western side is well defined by Over Beck, which comes down from Dore Head, the *col* linking the fell with Red Pike and the Pillar group. At one time, Dore Head had the reputation of providing the best scree run in the district on its northern side, descending to Mosedale, but generations of booted scree runners have scraped the passage clean in places and left it dangerously slippery.

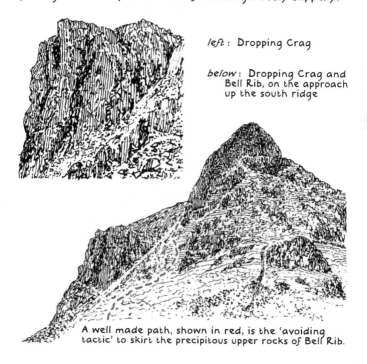

left : Dropping Crag

below : Dropping Crag and Bell Rib, on the approach up the south ridge

A well made path, shown in red, is the 'avoiding tactic' to skirt the precipitous upper rocks of Bell Rib.

Yewbarrow 3

Top of Great Door   Top of Bell Rib

The South Ridge

looking down

rocky groove

above:

   Great Door as it is seen on the descent of the south ridge. The path shown links Great Door itself to the 'false' Great Door (see below). The line of escape from the *impasse* is a rocky groove (→)

right:

   Just before reaching Great Door on the descent, a similar cleft is met which might well be mistaken for it. The terrain is confusing at this point:

   Route A is a clear path that leads to the bottom of the rocky groove shown in the diagram above, *way below* Great Door;

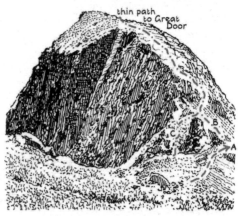

thin path to Great Door

B

C

A

   Routes B and C give access to a thin path leading to the top of Great Door. Route B is easier; Route C involves rock scrambling.

MAP

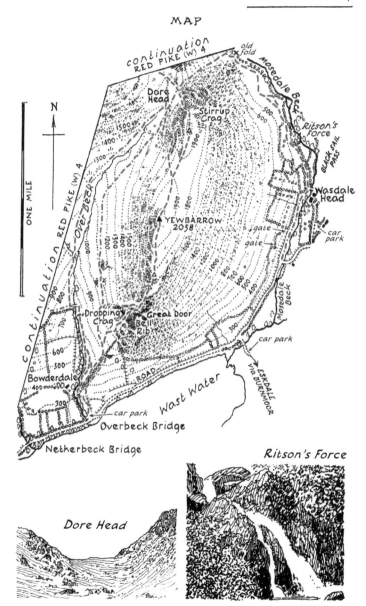

continuation
RED PIKE (W) 4

old fold

Mosedale Beck

Dore Head

Stirrup Crag

Ritson's Force

BLACK SAIL PASS

N

ONE MILE

continuation RED PIKE (W) 4

Over Beck

1500
1400
1300

1900
1800
1700
1600

Wasdale Head

YEWBARROW 2058

gate
gate

car park

1200
1300
500
400

Mosedale Beck

Dropping Crag

Great Door

700

600
500
400

Bell Rib

car park

ROAD

ESKDALE via BURNMOOR

Bowderdale

300

Wast Water

car park

Overbeck Bridge

Netherbeck Bridge

Dore Head

Ritson's Force

ASCENT FROM WASDALE
(OVERBECK BRIDGE)
1900 feet of ascent · 1½ miles

Very prominent in the early stages of the ascent is the towering pinnacle of Bell Rib, directly astride the ridge. Bell Rib cannot be climbed by a non-expert, and maps that show a path straight up it are telling fibs.

From the stile take the slanting track towards Dropping Crag and then turn off on a pitched path that finds an ingenious route up the steep slope to the right of it. Near the cross wall there are two choices:

a) Enter a constricted gully full of loose stones where progress is better on the simple rocks to the left. At the top of the gully, climb half-right up a narrow rocky groove to reach the ridge exactly, suddenly and dramatically at Great Door: a thrilling moment. The top of Bell Rib is here only a few rocky yards away on the right. Turn left, on a thin path, following the ridge leading to the 'false' Great Door where the main path to the summit can then be joined.

b) From the wall, take a thin path half-left to a low rock band (easily climbed) followed by a grassy bank which leads to the foot of the narrow groove described on page 3. Note, at this point, the main path avoids Great Door heading left towards the summit.

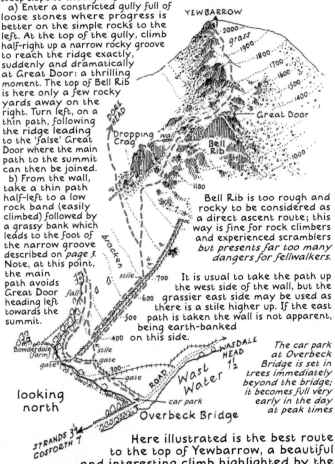

Bell Rib is too rough and rocky to be considered as a direct ascent route; this way is fine for rock climbers and experienced scramblers but presents far too many dangers for fellwalkers.

It is usual to take the path up the west side of the wall, but the grassier east side may be used as there is a stile higher up. If the east path is taken the wall is not apparent, being earth-banked on this side.

The car park at Overbeck Bridge is set in trees immediately beyond the bridge; it becomes full very early in the day at peak times

looking north

Here illustrated is the best route to the top of Yewbarrow, a beautiful and interesting climb highlighted by the moment of arrival at the huge cleft of Great Door.

ASCENT FROM WASDALE HEAD
1900 feet of ascent : 2½ miles

Start the climb to Dore Head from the path at the foot of the slope below it; short cuts across the boulders are not rewarding. eep to what is left of the grass on the right of the scree run.

From Dore Head, Stirrup Crag looks very formidable, and the upper band of rock unassailable, but getting up it is nothing more than a strenuous exercise in elementary gymnastics and unusual postures. The way lies within the confines of rocky cracks and chimneys, and there is no sense of danger or indecent exposure.

Those of faint heart may avoid Stirrup Crag entirely by proceeding from Dore Head towards Over Beck, taking a path that zig-zags stonily up to just below a line of cliffs then climbs to the depression. For such, the author bled in vain.

Follow the trail of blood left by the author, or, if the elements have removed this evidence of his sufferings, the debris of dentures, bootsoles, etc., left by other pilgrims, and step happily onto the pleasant top. Between this point and the summit of the fell is a wide depression crossed by a good path.

'From Dore Head the upper band of rock looks unassailable'

YEWBARROW

2000

depression

1800

1700

Stirrup Crag

Dore Head

pinnacle

1500
1400
1300
1200
1100
1000
900
800

grass

scree

1000
900
800

700

600

500

grass

old fold

bracken

gap

pinnacle in view

Mosedale Beck

300

gate

waterfall (Ritson's Force) — reached through the wood from a gap in the wall.

Inn

Wasdale Head

BLACK SAIL

Here illustrated is the most strenuous route to the top of Yewbarrow, a tiring plod up to Dore Head being followed by an energetic scramble up a rocky rampart.

looking south-west

THE SUMMIT

KIRK FELL

GREAT GABLE

HELVELLYN

GLARAMARA

After the agonies and perils of the ascent it is an anticlimax to find the summit a peaceful and placid sheep pasture, an elevated field, with the cairn crowning a rocky outcrop.

DESCENTS: The usual descents by way of the ridge, north or south, encounter rock and need care. The south ridge, at first easy, narrows to the width of the path at Great Door in exciting surroundings. The natural continuation of the ridge lies up the facing rocks onto the top of Bell Rib, but do NOT venture into this bad trap; instead, at this point, turn down the slope ON THE RIGHT into a short rocky gully where loose stones are a menace and skirt the lower buttresses of Bell Rib to regain the ridge at a wall, whence an easy slope leads down to Overbeck Bridge. Or, as outlined on *page 3*, an easier route can be followed from the 'false' Great Door. The north ridge route crosses a depression, rises to the cairned top of Stirrup Crag, and then drops steeply and sharply down a series of rocky cracks in the crag for a few desperate minutes: a bad passage, but neither dangerous nor difficult if care is taken. Those who do not fancy steep rocks can avoid Stirrup Crag entirely by slanting down left from the depression; in bad conditions, this is the best way off the fell.

A descent may be made direct to Wasdale Head from the summit cairn, but note that the only gate in the intake wall is that shown on *page 4*.

RED PIKE

2600
2500
2629'
The Chair
2300
2200
2100
2000

WASDALE HEAD

Dore Head
1600
1500
Stirrup Crag
1900

OVERBECK BRIDGE
1500
1600
1700
1800
1900

YEWBARROW ▲

N

The use of the Bottom in Mountaineering

A fellwalker's best asset is a pair of strong legs; next best is a tough and rubbery bottom. In ascent this appendage is, of course, useless, but when descending steep grass or rocks such as are met on the ridge of Yewbarrow the posterior is a valuable agent of friction, a sheet anchor with superb resistance to the pull of gravity.

RIDGE ROUTE TO RED PIKE, 2707'

1¼ miles: NNE, NW and N
Depression at 1520'
1350 feet of ascent

Reach Dore Head over Stirrup Crag or by the variation, as described above; then follow the good track up the opposite slope. *An excellent journey.*

HALF A MILE

THE VIEW

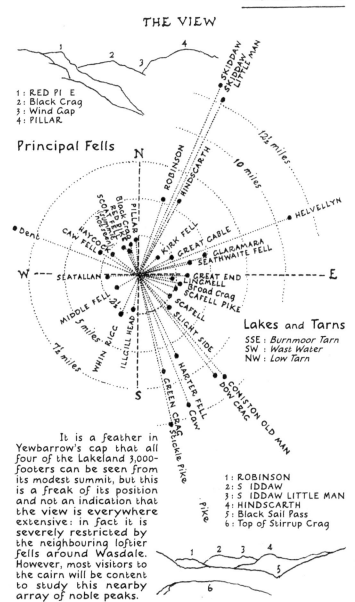

1 : RED PI E
2 : Black Crag
3 : Wind Gap
4 : PILLAR

Principal Fells

Lakes and Tarns

SSE : *Burnmoor Tarn*
SW : *Wast Water*
NW : *Low Tarn*

It is a feather in Yewbarrow's cap that all four of the Lakeland 3,000-footers can be seen from its modest summit, but this is a freak of its position and not an indication that the view is everywhere extensive: in fact it is severely restricted by the neighbouring loftier fells around Wasdale. However, most visitors to the cairn will be content to study this nearby array of noble peaks.

1 : ROBINSON
2 : S IDDAW
3 : S IDDAW LITTLE MAN
4 : HINDSCARTH
5 : Black Sail Pass
6 : Top of Stirrup Crag

THE WESTERN FELLS

Some Personal notes
in conclusion

When I came down from Starling Dodd on the 10th of September 1965 I had just succeeded in obtaining a complete view from the summit before the mist descended, after laying patient siege to it through several wet weekends, and in so doing I had concluded the field-work for my last book with only one week left before the end of the summer bus service put the fell out of reach. Thus a 13-year plan was finished one week ahead of schedule. Happy? Yes, I was happy, as anyone must be who comes to the end of a long road ahead of the clock. Sorry? Yes, I was sorry, as anyone must be who comes to the end of a long road he has enjoyed travelling. Relieved? Yes, I was relieved, because a broken leg during these years would have meant a broken heart, too.

I think I must concede that the scenery of the western half of Lakeland (dropping a vertical through High Raise in the Central Fells) is, on the whole, better than the eastern, although it has nothing more beautiful than the head of Ullswater. This is not to say that the fellwalking is better: it is more exciting and exacting but the Helvellyn and High Street ranges in the east are supreme for the man who likes to stride out over the tops all day. Those who prefer to follow narrow ridges from summit to summit are best catered for in the west. The southern half, too, is generally finer than the northern, so that the highlights of the district are to be found mainly in the southwestern sector, from the Duddon to Whinlatter. But it is all delectable country ..... One advantage I found in roaming around the Western Fells is that they are still free from the type of visitor who has spoiled Langdale and Keswick and other places easier of access. Wasdale Head and Buttermere are beginning to suffer from tourist invasion, but on the tops one can still wander in solitude and enjoy the freedom characteristic of the whole district before somebody invented the motor car.

I promised to give my opinion of the six best fells. I should not have used the word 'best', which suggests that some are not as good as others. I think they are all good. The finest, however, must have the attributes of mountains, i.e., height, a commanding appearance, a good view, steepness and ruggedness: qualities that are most pronounced in the volcanic area of the south-western sector. I now give, after much biting of finger-nails, what I consider to be the finest half-dozen:

Be quick, turn over

SCAFELL PIKE
BOWFELL
PILLAR
GREAT GABLE
BLENCATHRA
CRINKLE CRAGS

These are not necessarily the six fells I like best. It grieves me to have to omit Haystacks (most of all), Langdale Pikes, Place Fell, Carrock Fell and some others simply because they do not measure up in altitude to the grander mountains. There will be surprise at the omission of Scafell, the crags of which provide the finest sight in Lakeland, but too much of this fell is lacking in interest. It would be seventh if there were seven in the list. Contrary to general opinion (which would favour Great Gable), the grandest of the lot is Scafell Pike. Of the six, all are of volcanic rock with the exception of Blencathra.

The six best summits (attributes: a small neat peak of naked rock with a good view) I consider to be

DOW CRAG, Coniston
HARTER FELL, Eskdale
HELM CRAG, Grasmere
EAGLE CRAG, Langstrath
SLIGHT SIDE, Scafell
STEEPLE, Ennerdale

All these, except Steeple, are accessible only by scrambling on rock. The top inches of Helm Crag are hardest to reach.

The six best places for a fellwalker to be (other than summits) because of their exciting situations, and which can be reached without danger, are

STRIDING EDGE, Helvellyn
First col, LORD'S RAKE, Scafell
MICKLEDORE, Scafell
SHARP EDGE, Blencathra
SOUTH TRAVERSE, Great Gable
SHAMROCK TRAVERSE, Pillar

Of course I haven't forgotten Jack's Rake on Pavey Ark. I never could. But this is a place only for men with hair on their chests. I am sorry to omit Great Slab and Climbers Traverse on Bowfell.

The finest ridge-walks are, I think,

THE FAIRFIELD HORSESHOE (Ambleside)
THE HIGH STREET RANGE (Garburn-Moor Divock)
THE MOSEDALE HORSESHOE (Wasdale Head)
CAUSEY PIKE – WHITELESS PIKE
GRISEDALE PIKE – WHITESIDE
ESK HAUSE – WRYNOSE PASS, via Bowfell
THE ESKDALE HORSESHOE (Slight Side-Bowfell)
THE HELVELLYN RANGE (Grisedale Pass-Threlkeld)
THE HIGH STILE RIDGE, with Haystacks
CATBELLS – DALE HEAD – HINDSCARTH – SCOPE END
THE CONISTON ROUND (Old Man-Wetherlam)
(not in order of merit)

In my introductory remarks to Book One I described my task in compiling these books as a labour of love. So it has been. These have been the best years for me, the golden years. I have had a full reward in a thousand happy days on the fells. But, unexpectedly, it has been a profitable venture for me in terms of money, bringing me a small fortune, simply through the continued support of the many kind readers who have both bought and recommended the books. It is money I have not spent and do not want. One surely does not wish to be paid in cash for writing a love-letter! There is, or soon will be, enough to build and equip an Animal Welfare Centre in Kendal, and the Westmorland Branch of the R.S.P.C.A. have accepted for this purpose a gift which is really donated by the readers of these books. Every true fellwalker develops a liking and compassion for birds and animals, the solitary walker especially for they are his only companions, and it seems to me appropriate that this windfall should be used to provide a refuge in Lakeland where ailing and distressed creatures can be brought for care and attention. I thought you would like to know this. You have provided the bricks.

If Starling Dodd had been the last walk of all for me, and this the last book, I should now be desolate indeed, like a lover who has lost his loved one, and the future would have the bleakness of death. I have long known this and anticipated it, and sought desperately in my mind for some new avenue along which I could continue to express my devotion to Lakeland within the talents available to me. I am in better case than the lover who has lost his loved one, for my beloved is still there and faithful, and if there were to be a separation the defection would be mine. But why need this be the last book? Within a year I shall be retired from work (on account of old age!), but I can still walk, still draw, still write; and love itself is never pensioned off ..... so there must be other books ..... In this series I have crowded details of the fells into some 2000 pages, but as much as I have included has been omitted through lack of space. I would like now, in a more leisurely fashion, to continue acquaintance with the fells, and, out of consideration for my white hair, explore the valleys and daleheads more. What I have in mind is A LAKELAND SKETCHBOOK, which, all being well, could be the start of a new series that would aim to show the best of Lakeland in pictures and, by indicating the changes taking place in the district, in valley and on fell, serve to supplement the present series of guidebooks. I also have a good title for another book: FELL WANDERER, and might do this first if I can think of something to write about — personal experiences on the fells perhaps — not, definitely not, an autobiography (as if I dare! Let me keep my friends!). In between times I am pledged to do A PICTORIAL GUIDE TO THE PENNINE WAY, and have had four collaborators, four good men and true, sweating their guts out during the past year to provide a mass of detail and resolve certain doubts and generally smooth my own journey subsequently. This will be a unique book the way I plan it: you will start it at the bottom of the last page and you will read upwards and forwards to the top of the first, which is something that even the Chinese never thought of doing. It will seem logical, however, when you see it, and there is no question of your having to stand on your head.

Regretfully, I reject suggestions of a Book Eight: 'The Outlying Fells.'

.... So this is farewell to the present series of books.

The fleeting hours of life of those who love the hills is quickly spent, but the hills are eternal. Always there will be the lonely ridge, the dancing beck, the silent forest; always there will be the exhilaration of the summits. These are for the seeking, and those who seek and find while there is yet time will be blessed both in mind and body.

I wish you all many happy days on the fells in the years ahead.

There will be fair winds and foul, days of sun and days of rain. But enjoy them all.

Good walking! And don't forget — watch where you are putting your feet.

A.W.

Christmas, 1965.

STARTING POINTS

BLENGDALE LODGE
Caw Fell 8

BUTTERMERE
Great Borne 5
High Crag 6
High Stile 7
Mellbreak 7
Starling Dodd 5
Red Pike (B) 5, 6, 7, 8
Pillar 14

CALDER BRIDGE
Lank Rigg 6

COLDFELL GATE
Lank Rigg 6

COLDFELL ROAD
Lank Rigg 6

CRUMMOC WATER
Mellbreak 6

ENNERDALE
BLAC SAIL Y.H.A.
Brandreth 6
Great Gable 19
Green Gable 7
Haystacks 8
High Crag 4
Kirk Fell 5
Pillar 10
BOWNESS CAR PAR
Great Borne 4, 5
Starling Dodd 4
HIGH GILLERTHWAITE
High Stile 9
Red Pike (B) 9
IRISH BRIDGE
Pillar 12
LOW GILLERTHWAITE
Caw Fell 10
Haycock 7
Scoat Fell 7
Steeple 5
MEMORIAL FOOTBRIDGE
Pillar 13

ENNERDALE BRIDGE
Great Borne 4
Grike 5
Crag Fell 4

FANGS BROW
Burnbank Fell 4

GATESGARTH
Brandreth 5
Fleetwith Pike 6
Great Gable 18
Haystacks 5, 6
High Crag 5
High Stile 8

GOSFORTH
Caw Fell 8

HONISTER PASS
Brandreth 4
Fleetwith Pike 5

HONISTER PASS (continued)
Great Gable 17
Green Gable 4
Grey Knotts 7
Haystacks 7

INNISIDE STONE CIRCLE
Caw Fell 9
Grike 4

LAMPLUGH
Blake Fell 5

LOWESWATER
Blake Fell 5
Gavel Fell 5
Great Borne 5
Hen Comb 3
Low Fell 3, 4
Mellbreak 5
Starling Dodd 6

SEATHWAITE
Base Brown 6
Brandreth 7
Great Gable 15
Green Gable 5
Grey Knotts 5

SEATOLLER
Grey Knotts 6

STY HEAD
Great Gable 16

STY HEAD GILL
Green Gable 6

THAC THWAITE
Fellbarrow 5
Low Fell 5

WASDALE
GREENDALE
Haycock 5
Middle Fell 4
Seatallan 6
HARROW HEAD
Buckbarrow 2
NETHERBEC BRIDGE
Haycock 6
Seatallan 6
Scoat Fell 5
NETHER WASDALE
Seatallan 5
OVERBEC BRIDGE
Red Pike (W) 5
Yewbarrow 5

WASDALE HEAD
Great Gable 16, 20
Kirk Fell 4
Pillar 9
Red Pike (W) 6
Scoat Fell 6
Yewbarrow 6

WATEREND
Burnbank Fell 3
Fellbarrow 6